THE
COURTROOM
IS MY THEATER

MY LIFELONG REPRESENTATION
OF FAMOUS POLITICIANS,
INDUSTRIALISTS, ENTERTAINERS,
"MEN OF HONOR," AND MORE

JAY GOLDBERG
WITH ALEX S. HUOT

A POST HILL PRESS BOOK
ISBN: 978-1-64293-071-9
ISBN (eBook): 978-1-64293-072-6

The Courtroom Is My Theater:
My Lifelong Representation of Famous Politicians, Industrialists,
Entertainers, "Men of Honor," and More
© 2018 by Jay Goldberg
All Rights Reserved

Cover art by Cody Corcoran

Post Hill Press
New York • Nashville
posthillpress.com

Published in the United States of America

DEDICATION

FROM THE BRIGHT LIGHTS OF New York and Las Vegas, to the beer halls of Milwaukee, to the hustle and bustle of Chicago, to the beauty of St. Joseph, Michigan, to the steel mills of Gary, Indiana, to the mining towns of Pennsylvania, to the snow of Buffalo, to the pristine California shores, to the cherry blossoms of Washington D.C., and back to New York again...I dedicate this book to my lifelong partner in justice and the rock of our family, my wife Rema, whose love and guidance have made all things possible.

This book would not have been possible without the extraordinary and capable scholarly efforts of Alex S. Huot.

TABLE OF CONTENTS

POLITICIANS AND BUSINESSMEN

THE ENTERTAINERS

THE MAFIA

INTRODUCTION

I WAS DEFENDING THE INFAMOUS Matty "The Horse" Ianniello in federal court. Matty, a mobster with the ruthless Genovese crime family, had been charged with extortion. He was considered by the U.S. government to be a major force in organized crime in New York City. The alleged victim in this case was Andrew "The Hulk" Giordano. The government appeared to be pinning its prosecution of Matty on telephone conversations between the two men, specifically on Giordano's reactions to threats Matty had allegedly made toward him. The government claimed those reactions demonstrated that their client feared for his personal safety.

I was betting they would be unwilling to produce Giordano in court to testify that he was afraid of Matty, given Giordano's description as "The Hulk." It would have been a gift for me if they had. Giordano was six-feet five-inches tall and weighed three hundred fifty pounds. Matty, like most humans, was dwarfed by this behemoth. And a jury was expected to believe *Giordano* was afraid of *Matty*? I wasn't going to let that happen, whether Giordano was there or not.

Early in the trial, I showed an FBI agent, who was testifying for the prosecution, a Polaroid photo of the absent Giordano. I asked him if it was a true representation of that man's physique. He agreed that it was. With that fact on the record, when planning my summation (closing argument) at my office later in the trial, I had a local company manufacture a life-size cardboard placard of Giordano. It was in full color and came complete with the face, height, and girth pictured in the Polaroid. Why did I do this? Because a good defense lawyer always should be equipped with every possible weapon to successfully protect his client—including humor.

When we returned to court and it was time for me to deliver my summation, I confidently stood from my chair, cleared my throat, and made a declaration that astounded the masses in attendance.

1

"I now call Andrew 'The Hulk' Giordano to the witness stand," I bellowed, deliberately injecting extra oomph into his evocative nickname. The judge stared at me, speechless, like I'd lost my mind. The assistant U.S. attorneys for the prosecution were equally perplexed. Witnesses had already been called, cross-examinations had been conducted, and all evidence had been presented. What the hell was I doing calling someone to the stand, and someone who everybody knew damn well wasn't even there? Nobody understood my strategy—except my assistant, who right on cue burst through the courtroom doors hauling the giant cardboard placard.

"Mr. Giordano," I said in a serious tone, "please take the witness stand."

My assistant, trying to keep a straight face, maneuvered his way to the stand and placed "Giordano" there to the sweet sounds of nervous laughter and murmurs throughout the courtroom. It was a moment I relished. I had always viewed the courtroom as my theater, each case as my next performance. Actors will tell you that sometimes they have to take risks on stage in order to produce their best work, and the same can be said for a lawyer in court. On this day, I was planning to put on one hell of a show.

After my assistant had "Giordano" securely in place so he wouldn't tip over, I proceeded to ask questions that I would have asked the real Giordano were he to have testified himself.

"Mr. Giordano," I said with a stern glare into his two-dimensional eyes, "isn't it true that you were involved with Mr. Ianniello in a number of transactions?"

I stood perfectly still and silent, as if I was honestly awaiting a response. Everyone was on the edge of their seats, hushed and befuddled, anxious to see what was going to happen next. I honestly thought some of them expected that this inanimate object might respond. I may not be the best actor, but I would venture that I had executed a dramatic pause almost worthy of a Tony award nomination.

After a few seconds, laughter—a little more relaxed this time— finally emanated from the gallery, just as I had expected. Who wouldn't recognize the humor in something so absurd? They were watching a well-respected defense attorney during an intense mob trial attempt to interact with a piece of cardboard.

After Faux Giordano refused to answer me—and thank goodness he didn't, for it would have thrown me off my entire script—I continued my questioning.

"Mr. Giordano, can you honestly say that you were fearful of anything Mr. Ianniello said to you in the telephone conversations?"

A few more chuckles from the crowd. Continued silence from the "witness."

"Mr. Giordano, did the government give you any reason for not calling you to testify, other than it would have enabled the jury to assess for itself whether someone of your physical stature could really be threatened by Mr. Ianniello? The truth is you weren't afraid of him at all, were you?"

I was aware that with each question asked, I came across more and more as a crazed lunatic to many observers in the room—but not to the jury, which was all that mattered. Though they too had initially laughed at my antics, their looks became more stoic as my interrogation progressed. They were, in essence, doing exactly as I had hoped: processing my questions in their minds and answering them in the way they felt Giordano would, or should, have answered them himself had he testified.

My plan worked to perfection.

After a few more questions and a relatively short deliberation, Matty was acquitted.

I'm not always that eccentric in court, and I don't win every case, but more often than not I am, and I do. I have dedicated my life to the law and would describe myself as an "idiot savant," a depiction with which my wife Rema would concur. There is a lot I don't know about a lot of things, but challenge my knowledge and understanding of the law and you will likely lose. Still today I read and study the U.S. Constitution in what little spare time I have. When I was an undergraduate student at Brooklyn College, my political science professor, who taught concurrently at Brooklyn Law School, often asked me to help him grade his law students' papers.

I say none of this with vanity, but with self-confidence that stems from a saying my sister used to have about the two of us:

"Nobody can hurt us and no event can harm us because of what we lived through as children."

My childhood was severely dysfunctional, primarily because of my father's reckless behavior. He was a man I deeply loved, resented, and loved some more, sometimes all within the same day. My studies were my outlet. So was boxing. Thankfully, when a potential boxing career didn't pan out, my saint of a mother helped me stay on a course that ran through Harvard Law School, the New York County District Attorney's Office, President John F. Kennedy's White House, U.S. Attorney General Robert F. Kennedy's Department of Justice, and eventually into my private practice where I have defended the likes of Willie Nelson, Donald Trump, Waylon Jennings, Miles Davis, Dr. Armand Hammer, U.S. Rep. Charlie Rangel, Lynyrd Skynyrd, The Rolling Stones, Sean "Puffy" Combs, Riddick Bowe, Bess Myerson, members of Hell's Angels and the New York City mafia, the New York Daily News, and many others.

I've had a fascinating life, and I still do today. This is probably the place where I'm supposed to say that I never could have imagined it being like this—but I could, sort of. I may not have ever envisioned being in the position to have to choose between my morals and what the president of the United States wanted me to do, or relaxing on Willie Nelson's back porch in the Colorado mountains as he strummed "Georgia on My Mind" on his guitar the morning after a night of partying with him. But I knew I could make something of myself with the proper commitment to my craft, the mental fortitude to withstand adversity, and unwavering professionalism.

I wrote this book primarily to entertain you. Each chapter contains a story that stands on its own, generally about my work relations with a well-known local, national, or international celebrity, politician, or businessperson. But I also hope it serves as a reminder that you can succeed at anything with legitimate hard work and fearlessness, and by following your moral compass. As you will read, each client I have ever represented has received every ounce of energy I could possibly give. No matter the case and no matter whether I won or lost, nearly every person in the courtroom—including the judge, the jury, my client, and our opponent—walked out with respect for me and the effort I put forth.

When country music legend Waylon Jennings once asked me to defend him against drug charges, he wrote and sang about our case in a song titled, "Don't You Think This Outlaw Bit's Done Got Out of Hand." Yes, that's the actual title. I guess it's true that country music singers always wear their hearts on their sleeves. Anyway, one of the lines in the ballad goes: "And New York sent a posse down like I ain't ever seen."

I was that posse.

Like many New Yorkers, I felt like Frank Sinatra was speaking to me when he sang in "New York, New York": "If I can make it there I'll make it anywhere." But it was when Waylon forever immortalized me in the annals of country music that I knew I had made it. And it has been something like I ain't ever seen.

THE
FORMATIVE YEARS

CHAPTER 1

AGAINST THE ROPES

MY FATHER WAS A DEGENERATE gambler. When not stricken with this terrible disease, which would recur at the start of every baseball season, he was a devoted and loving husband and father.

Several of his "friends" said to me that he had a penchant for losing bets. They thought it was funny, but I did not. He was so committed to gambling, he would bet on which raindrop would hit the base of the window first during a rainstorm. And he was usually wrong. A losing gambler needs a continual source of money, and for that reason, he borrowed money from loan sharks, members of the mafia, and virtually every tenant in the sixty-unit building where we lived. Or he just took it from my mother, if he could find where she hid it.

When I was six years old, my mother was in the hospital giving birth. Her fingers swelled so much that she took off her rings, including her diamond wedding band. When she left the hospital, she asked for the rings to be returned, but we learned from the nurses that my father had taken them, and no doubt my mother knew why. The World Series had just gotten under way.

Only days removed from the hospital, my mother dragged me and my newborn sister to the local pawn shop to recover the jewelry. They still had it, but of course she had to buy it back for more than my father had sold it. I remember it like it was yesterday, my baby sister swaddled in a blanket in my mother's arms and me in my dress shirt and shorts, holding tightly to my mother's leg. What woman has to buy back her wedding band from a stranger because her husband pawned it so that he could bet on a game while she was giving life to his child? It was the worst treachery, what my father put her and us through.

Numerous times gangsters had tried to break into our home to collect my father's debts. "Joey! Joey! We're gonna get you, Joey!" they would threaten, while pounding their fists on the door. I could see their angry faces through the peephole. We were terrified. Mother would yank me back and shield my sister and me, one arm over each of our bodies, in case they were able to break through. They never could. We stayed completely silent until they went away.

To avoid being killed, my father often had to pack up, run to a different city, and use an alias for weeks at a time until he thought it was safe to come home. When I was thirteen, I would stand by the mailbox to make sure there was no one around who could sneak a peek at the return address of any letter my father sent us, lest they identify where he was. My parents verbally and physically fought a great deal over my father's gambling debts, forcing neighbors to frequently call the police. Trying to stay out of the fracas, I often found myself studying on a bridge table while the police cautioned my parents to behave and quit fighting. After the police left, the fighting resumed. When I got older, I served as a referee when my father would push my mother around. In the end, he would promise her that he would stay clean, but it wasn't long before he was in trouble again.

My sister and I were not invited to birthday parties in our apartment building because my father had failed to pay back so many tenants. We could only gaze out the window and into the backyard to see the other kids enjoying themselves. I never took the elevator in our building, but instead walked up and down the six flights of stairs, to avoid seeing the many neighbors from whom my father had "borrowed" money. If I brought a friend home, it was only a matter of time before my father would find out who that friend's parents were to try to finagle money from them. He was such a salesman. I finally had to stop bringing friends home.

I lived a lonely existence.

I waited anxiously each and every Friday night at the window to see if my father turned the corner to come home, for this would mean he had cash from his weekly paycheck. I remember sitting at the window waiting for him while I listened to the radio broadcast of the Joe Louis and Billy Conn fight at the Polo Grounds in June of

1941. Louis defeated Conn by knockout in the thirteenth round in what some have dubbed the greatest fight ever. My father never did turn the corner that night. He obviously had bet on Conn.

When he did come back, he would normally call first from a phone booth at a gas station across the street, asking Mother if he could return. On one occasion, when he had been gone for some time, and knowing that Mother's patience was wearing thin, he called and asked my sister and me to escort him home. I was fourteen, she was eight. We took the subway by ourselves to the entrance of Prospect Park in Brooklyn, met him there, and happily brought him back. Mother would forgive him yet again, but in no time he was ransacking the drawers and cupboards searching for money, desperate like a drunkard looking for liquor.

That same year, in total despair, I took the train to Coney Island one day following a heavy snowfall to escape the chaos. The boardwalk was deserted. I wiped a bench clean with my gloves and sat in solitude, gazing at the ocean, shivering. I felt lost.

How can I continue to endure this? I asked myself, as images of my parents arguing with each other played over and over in my young, impressionable mind. *When is all of this going to end?* Knowing that it likely wouldn't be anytime soon, I tried to find something to keep myself occupied outside of home. One distraction was boxing.

Practically since I was old enough to read, I had a subscription to *The Ring* magazine, the premier boxing publication of the day. I read it religiously. And, for some time, my father had the gloves of the immortal Benny Leonard from when he defeated Freddie Welsh on May 28, 1917, winning the World Lightweight title. The gloves were an heirloom that influenced my interest in boxing. Benny Leonard was Jewish, ranked No. 8 in *The Ring*'s "The 80 Best Fighters of the Last 80 Years," and No. 7 on ESPN's greatest 50 boxers of all time. In 2005, he was named the No. 1 lightweight boxer of all time by the International Boxing Research Organization. Not surprisingly, Leonard is a member of the World Boxing Hall of Fame. My father had a personal relationship with Leonard, and one day he introduced me to him. I considered Leonard to be god-like. My father, of course, eventually sold the gloves to Nat Fleischer, the legendary publisher of *The Ring*, in order to pay off some gangsters.

This was considered the "Golden Age" of boxing.

In February of 1947, there was a major prizefight at Madison Square Garden between Tony Janiro and Beau Jack. Jack was the two-time Lightweight Champion of the World. My father took me to the fight, and he bet, of course, on the eventual loser, Jack. During the fight, Jack broke his kneecap when his foot got caught on the canvas, but he continued to fight with one arm while supporting himself by holding the ropes with his other hand. The doctor at the ring finally interceded in the fourth round, and Janiro was declared the winner by technical knockout.

Despite Janiro's win, it was Jack who won me as a devoted fan. I followed his career faithfully. I attended every fight he had at Madison Square Garden, unaccompanied by my father or anyone else. The last time I saw Jack was when he was approaching seventy-five years of age. The fight game had taken its toll. He was shining shoes at the Fontainebleau Hotel in Miami Beach. I gave him a crisp 100 dollar bill for a one dollar shine. Rema couldn't understand how I could pay that much. My thinking was to the contrary. I wondered if it was enough, given what he meant to me.

My father had a monetary interest with Louis Ingber (he later changed his name to Lou Stillman) in the operation of the legendary Stillman's Gym. It was located on Eighth Avenue between 54th and 55th streets. It was the preeminent gym from the 1920s to the 1950s and was viewed as the center where professional fighters trained. Stillman's was the "University of Eighth Avenue," according to writer A. J. Liebling of *Sports Illustrated*. It was the training place for prizefighters of note. My father used his influence with Ingber to allow me, in my teens, to train there on several occasions. All of the champions trained there, as did the well-regarded challengers. This was at a time when there was only one boxing ranking organization.

When I was eighteen, I stood out at the gym. I was six-feet two-inches and weighed just one hundred and forty pounds. I had the opportunity at rare times to spar at Stillman's with real professionals, like Rocky Graziano. Graziano, portrayed by Paul Newman in the Oscar-winning film *Somebody Up There Likes Me*, was considered one of the greatest knockout artists in boxing history. He was ranked No. 23 in *The Ring*'s "The 100 Greatest Punchers of

All-Time!" and I developed a close relationship with him. Of course, when he "sparred" with me, he dramatically pulled his punches. He had a musculature that defied description. His body was so hard and his muscles bulged.

There were others I sparred with, but none was equal to Graziano, whose every blow was the equivalent of being hit by a baseball bat. Even though he tried to go "light" on me, it was very difficult for him. I maintained contact with Graziano until he died in 1990. I treasured the simple note he wrote to me when we were working out at Stillman's: "Keep punching kid—Rocky." I did as he said, and I compiled a record of 10-0. I earned a trophy for my skills, which still sits today on my desk in my office.

My mother became concerned about my future intentions given my steadfast interest in boxing. She even accused me, because of the times I worked out at Stillman's, of bringing home the pneumonia bug that had hit my family. My mother asked whether I intended to go to college and beyond, or continue boxing. I told her I would consider my academic studies, but first I had an upcoming fight of great importance with Lou Greenberg. Greenberg was much shorter than I was, and before the fight he asked me to go easy on him. I scoffed at his request.

"I'm going to flatten you!" I exclaimed in true Jack Dempsey style.

But, unlike Dempsey, I didn't keep my word. I broke my left wrist during the fight, and Greenberg knocked me out in the third round, using his lack of height to his advantage. To the layman, when someone is hit on the chin, the thought is that the chin alone suffers the pain. In reality, it is only a somewhat minor effect of being hit. When one is hit on any part of the face, electrical impulses are directed to the brain causing it to swell, but the area is contained with no place for the brain to expand. I lay in agony on the dressing room table.

After the fight, and with considerable thought, I decided to quit boxing. I credit Greenberg and his right uppercut for my decision. I finished my "career" with a record of 10-1.

Boxing was not the only sport I engaged in during my teen years. I was a member of the high school basketball team, but I broke my knee in one game, ending my involvement with that sport. The knee break was one year to the day after I broke my wrist against Greenberg. I also played baseball at Marine Park for hours at a time at the east end of Brooklyn. I would be there so late my mother would scold me for missing dinner.

I went on to attend Brooklyn College, where one catch in physical education class nearly landed me on the football team. We were engaged in a game of touch football on the school field. I was a wide receiver. I ran down the sideline, cut to the center, and caught the forty-yard pass with my fingertips. Our teacher, who was also the head football coach, was so impressed by the catch that he asked me after class to play for him. I said I would speak to my parents, but they nixed the offer.

"Are you kidding?" my mother said. "Those football players could kill you!"

I was an obedient son and didn't argue. She gave the orders and I listened. As much as I wanted to say, "So I am allowed to box and get blasted with punches to the head, but I can't play football?" there was no discussion. But I will never forget that catch, right on the fingertips and in stride. I could have been good.

Another interest I had in college was comedy. My aunt had a relationship with an owner of the Copacabana night club who, during a lull on a given evening, would allow me to open for the well-known true performers. This opportunity, of course, as you read in my defense of Matty against The Hulk, would serve my interests later in life when I felt it was appropriate as a lawyer to bring humor into the courtroom. I've learned that humor is one of those things you either have or you don't. I've seen attorneys fall flat on their faces trying to use it. Fortunately, I had it. I inherited it from my father, who was such a talker, but I used it for a better purpose.

There I was on a Saturday night, on the same stage where the likes of Dean Martin, Tony Bennett, and Frank Sinatra had performed. My comedy was well received, and I was even asked to return one night to open for Freddie Roman, a well-recognized comedian who has performed in venues from Atlantic City to Las Vegas.

As enjoyable as comedy was, it was not my calling. In fact, while still in college, I would venture to a place where there was no room for comedy whatsoever—the U.S. Army. The Army called for such adherence to rules and regulations that it captivated me. I remember a judge saying to me years later that there were no grays in life, only black or white. That is the same perspective that drew me to the Army. As I look back, it is obvious that I gravitated to areas where rules and regulations were foremost: boxing, the Army, the law. That also probably explains why I tried to step in the middle of my parents' fights rather than run away from them—to create some order in my environment.

I joined the ROTC in my first year at Brooklyn and humbly was—according to the expressed opinion of professional Army officers—the most outstanding cadet of the lot. Upon graduation I received a commission as a second lieutenant with active duty requirements. I completed my active duty with the rank of captain and returned to New York where I continued my military service, eventually retiring with the rank of lieutenant colonel.

As I will describe in detail in the next section, my first job out of Harvard Law School would be as an assistant district attorney in New York County. District Attorney Frank S. Hogan allowed the reserve officers on his staff to take a hiatus from their professional duties to continue serving in the Army. We were gone for three weeks at a time. I was assigned to Fort Drum in Watertown, New York, in the Judge Advocate General Unit. While in that unit, I worked on cases in which soldiers were charged with violations of Army regulations. Some I prosecuted, others I defended, and a few I investigated. I got a taste of it all.

One of my most successful prosecutions was a high-profile murder case. An officer had been riding in the back seat of a Jeep when the driver crashed the vehicle, killing the officer. The driver was accused of speeding and causing the crash. I was the lead attorney, and my work resulted in him being court-martialed. My effort in that case and others was considered so exceptional by my commanding general that I was granted "time in grade" waivers. In seven years I had reached the grade of lieutenant colonel, a rank that would have normally taken ten to twelve years to achieve.

Army cases were different from those I would eventually work on in the district attorney's office because there were no jury trials in the Army. Every case was decided by one judge or a three-judge panel. But the Army work certainly provided me with solid practice in several aspects of trial law, and it confirmed for me my love for trial work.

After graduating from Brooklyn College, I knew the only law school I wanted to attend was Harvard, given the enormous contributions it had made to the law. The list of Harvard alumni, which included Supreme Court Justices Joseph Story, Felix Frankfurter, Oliver Wendell Holmes, and William Brennan, also played a role in my decision. To me, it was not merely a school; it was a place to be worshiped. My grades at Brooklyn had to be extremely high to get in, which they fortunately were, especially considering my last name. Harvard had only three or four Jews in a class of about five hundred, and I wasn't coming from Princeton or some other fancy school.

In fact, early in the first term of my first year at Harvard, I was in class asking typical questions of my professor, just like anyone else. When class was finished, six guys, all big, probably current or past football players, surrounded me outside of class.

"We don't need you asking anymore questions for the rest of this term, you got it?" the biggest one of the bunch said, as he poked his finger into my chest and stared me down. I got it. It wasn't stated, but I knew my last name was what triggered their anger. It was the first time I would be subjected to anti-Semitism there, but also the last. I kept my mouth shut for the rest of the term, and I never had another confrontation with them or anyone else again. Someone once asked me if that greeting at my new school ever made me consider leaving. It did not. Attending Harvard was my dream, and nothing was going to derail that dream. I ended up being one of the top students in my class, and I was a regular in the Harvard Voluntary Defenders program, in which I worked as an intern under various local defense attorneys.

I would graduate in 1957, though I didn't attend the ceremony. Several of us from New York didn't. You see, Harvard was steeped in Massachusetts law. Graduates from New York had to rush home after classes ended to enroll in a six-week program to learn the ins and outs of New York law before the bar exam was administered.

When I walked in the house after my train ride home, my mother told me how proud she was of me. My father had just packed his bags and run away again to avoid the men hunting him for their money. Nothing at home had changed.

Despite everything I have said about my father, there is something I want you to know: when he wasn't gambling, he was truly the greatest father in the world. He was warm and loving and gracious and generous. He was a successful and sought-after dress salesman, the best in the business. It was only when the "bug" hit and the addiction of compulsive gambling took hold of him that he made the lives of everyone associated with him miserable. For six months each year, from the final out of the World Series in the fall until opening day the following spring, I was able to live a relatively normal life.

I remember one year arriving at Harvard a month late because of an illness. My father took the train with me to Cambridge. He unpacked my luggage and lined each drawer with a piece of newspaper. Only when he saw that I was fully ready to undertake the battle on my own did he return to New York. I even remember that when I was at camp in the Adirondacks, he would make the eight-hour trip by train just to spend a day and a half with me. Of course, we also attended many sporting events. Sure, he had bets on many of them, but some were father and son outings with no strings attached. Either way, we enjoyed our time together.

My father died at the young age of fifty-seven, the year after Rema and I were married. He was a diabetic and had been sick for nearly a decade. My mother died fifteen years later. I owe so much of what I have today to her. I had received only half of a scholarship to Harvard, yet my mother was still able to afford to send me there because she had hidden from my father a lot of the money he had earned, so that she could use it one day for my schooling. She even let me take a summer off from work when I was seventeen so that I could study my passion—the history of the U.S. Supreme Court. She was strict in many ways; if I came home with a 97 percent on a paper, she wanted to know where the missing three points were. But she was that way because she knew my potential, and she was going to do everything in her power to help me reach it.

In retrospect, my difficult childhood prepared me for my life as an attorney. Born with my father's gift for gab and my mother's discipline, I figured out at a young age how to use those qualities to fight through adversity and stand up for what is right, which are at the core of every case I handle—and why I believe I rose so swiftly and successfully within the legal profession.

The New York County DA's Office

CHAPTER 2

MY FIRST DREAM JOB

I WANTED TO BE AN assistant district attorney in New York County right out of college—a lofty goal, to say the least. Frank S. Hogan was the district attorney, and his office was recognized as the premier prosecutorial office in the country.

One day, while at Harvard, I attended a lecture given by a hero of mine, New York State Supreme Court Justice Samuel S. Leibowitz. He spoke of his experiences as a criminal defense lawyer, representing clients such as Al Capone and "The Scottsboro Boys," nine black men accused of raping two white women in Alabama in 1931. If one were to ask virtually all students of law today, "Who was Samuel S. Leibowitz?" they would respond, "We have no idea." So fleeting is fame.

As one of three hundred hungry future lawyers in attendance at Leibowitz's lecture, I raised my hand.

"How is it possible to get into the district attorney's office and serve as an assistant district attorney?" I asked.

"Only through political connections," he responded succinctly.

Not what I wanted to hear.

Despite his answer, however, with no connections to any politicians, I applied to the district attorney's office in New York County upon graduation to see what would happen. About a week later, I received a phone call to come in for an interview with District Attorney Hogan himself. It went well enough that I was called in for a second interview, and eventually a third. It was then, during the course of our conversation, that I told Hogan what Justice Leibowitz had said about getting hired. Hogan leaned in.

"Leibowitz said *what*?"

"He said the only way to get a job here was through political connections."

Hogan sat still for a moment, digesting what I had said. I wasn't sure if I'd just helped my chances of working for him or completely destroyed them. Then, with an acerbic look and pipe in mouth, he slowly leaned back and said, "Justice Leibowitz was incorrect when it comes to the New York County District Attorney's Office, and you can tell him that if and when you see him again."

I was hired on the spot.

Perhaps it was partially a spite appointment, but I didn't care. I was in.

Hogan was known to many simply as "Mr. District Attorney" but also as "Mr. Integrity" due to his honesty and incorruptibility. He had a mythical hold on New York law enforcement and was, in all respects, a legend in his own time. He had served as the chief deputy to District Attorney Thomas E. Dewey, who had exposed corruption, crime, and the nefarious activities of many well-known mobsters, including Lucky Luciano.

Once being accepted as an assistant district attorney, one would seldom see Mr. Hogan, who was a workaholic. He would often fail to greet the run-of-the-mill prosecutors like me. I remember circulating a story that there really was no Mr. Hogan. I had said that I inspected his Cadillac early in the morning and the odometer registered the same mileage that it did at night. I was kidding of course, but the point was made.

I was given my own large office, probably fifteen feet by twenty feet, and with a phone. I was issued a badge and had a police visor on my car that gave me power I'd never before experienced. One time I was driving through the heart of Manhattan in heavy traffic and needed to turn left, even though the sign clearly said no left turn. I was in a hurry to get to court. A cop was directing cars.

"Excuse me, officer," I yelled out my window as I flashed him my badge. I didn't have to say anything more. He stopped traffic in all directions long enough to allow me to make the illegal turn. I may have brandished the badge for similar purposes a couple more times when Rema was with me just to impress her during our courtship, but that was it. I was raised too virtuous to continue using it for reasons other than its intended purpose, even to make unlawful left-hand turns.

There was a time, however, when I realized nobody in our office had a monopoly on virtue. Even Hogan on a very rare occasion could be influenced to do a favor for an enormously important person. In one case, that important person was Charles E. Wilson, former CEO of the General Electric Company. Wilson's son-in-law, Hugh Pierce, was indicted with Alfred Sutter for misappropriating funds intended for the Civil Air Patrol. Both were former colonels. Pierce was running a scheme wherein he persuaded wealthy individuals to donate a number of yachts to the Civil Air Patrol for use in sea rescue missions. Of the eight yachts that were donated, Pierce turned around and sold five of them, keeping the profits for himself. Sutter was the investigator assigned by the Civil Air Patrol to look into Pierce's actions, but he had Pierce pay him some of the money as restitution. Instead of giving it to the Civil Air Patrol, Sutter kept it for himself.

With Pierce being the son-in-law of Wilson, pressure was put on the district attorney's office to give him favorable treatment over Sutter. It was clear to me that the fix was in to pin a majority of the wrongdoing on an undeserving man. We were instructed to favor Pierce over Sutter when writing up the pre-sentencing memorandum. Elmer Bobst, a pharmaceutical giant and close friend of President Nixon, even reached out to me in what was clearly an attempt to intimidate, telling me that Sutter was to blame. Bobst had sold his yacht for 135,000 dollars and had given 20,000 dollars to Pierce for the Civil Air Patrol, which Pierce had kept for himself.

To me, it was clear that both defendants were at least equally culpable, and Pierce probably more so than Sutter. One did not convince the other; the decisions they made were their own. The case was before Justice Irwin Davidson in the Court of General Sessions. He was a judge known for his intelligence and integrity, and I could not, in good conscience, go along with what was planned at the time of the sentence.

I climbed the back stairs from my office on the seventh floor to Judge Davidson's chambers on the sixteenth floor.

"Judge," I said firmly, "there is something you need to know."

I told him what was planned, and that it would be entirely unfair to treat the defendants differently at sentencing.

"I appreciate you sharing this information with me," he said.

Not only did he appreciate it, but he agreed with it, and he later ruled as such. There was no doubt in my mind that, had Hogan found out what I had done, it would have been the end of my short career, but I couldn't see a person being punished more severely when the other person was likely more guilty. In retrospect, was it a smart thing for me to do? From a professional standpoint, no. Who in the field of law would have trusted me ever again? But I did what was right based on my deep sense of justice and fairness. And, for that reason, I am proud I did it. That case was also a stepping stone to a much larger one that would change the course of my legal career.

CHAPTER 3

THE QUIZ SHOW SCANDALS

DURING THE MID- TO LATE-1950S, the nation was captivated by television quiz shows such as *Twenty-One* and *The $64,000 Question*. In every episode, two prominent contestants were pitted against one another to see which of the two would correctly answer questions from various categories, with each question worth a specific number of points or dollar value. The shows were based in New York City, and people were captivated by them. If a quiz show started at 8:00 p.m., businesses let employees out of work early enough so that they could get home, have supper, and return to town in time to be part of the show's audience. Those who didn't attend the shows in person were glued to their television sets watching them.

Multiple-time winners were going home with life-changing amounts of money. The most famous was Charles van Doren, a young instructor at Columbia University who, on *Twenty-One*, "won" 129,000 dollars and was featured on the cover of *TIME* magazine. That dollar amount would be equal to more than one million dollars today.

But, as the quiz shows became the most popular shows on television, there were grumblings that they were fixed. Viewers noticed that some contestants were answering what seemed to be impossible questions, while others were missing easy ones. The suspicion was that producers had, in advance of the shows, provided selected contestants with the questions and answers and had told other contestants when to incorrectly answer questions. One reason they may have done this, it was believed, was to make sure the more charismatic contestants won so that viewers would return the following week. Why would contestants agree to fix a show? Well, money always talks. And then there was this explanation during Congressional testimony by van Doren after the scandals had been revealed:

> *"(Co-producer Albert Freedman) told me that the show was merely entertainment and that giving help to quiz contestants was a common practice and merely part of show business. This of course was not true, but perhaps I wanted to believe him. He also stressed the fact that by appearing on a nationally televised program I would be doing a great service to the intellectual life...by increasing public respect for the work of the mind through my performances."*

But proving these scandals was difficult for law enforcement as those involved with the shows, be it in front of or behind the cameras, stuck to the story that the shows were on the up and up.

There was a 1994 movie entitled *Quiz Show*, starring John Turturro and Ralph Fiennes, which supposedly recounted how federal authorities were the first to eventually uncover the frauds. The movie was incorrect in material respects. It was Assistant District Attorney Joseph Stone, a senior member of the Frauds Bureau, who was a hero for his tireless work in connection with the investigation of the quiz shows scandals and in revealing they were out and out frauds. His book *Prime Time and Misdemeanors* recounts the investigation.

So, how did I get involved in all of this? Around the time that these quiz show allegations were being investigated by our office, Hogan had decided to run for the U.S. Senate. He wanted the quiz show case cleared up so that it would, at the very least, not be a distraction to his campaign, and at best, possibly help him win the seat. I was one of three or four assistant Das he put on the case.

For about a month I had interviewed numerous contestants and people who worked for the show, but every one of them stonewalled me. I even interrogated Dr. Joyce Brothers, a psychologist who would just a few years later become a famous newspaper advice columnist and television personality. She had been a contestant on

The $64,000 Question and had won the top prize of 64,000 dollars by answering questions in the category of boxing. She had claimed that she had read every book about boxing there was in order to prepare for the show. I didn't believe her, and boxing was, of course, right in my wheelhouse. I called her into my office to test her knowledge.

"Dr. Brothers, how many times did Rocky Marciano defend his world heavyweight title?"

She firmly pressed her lips together.

"Okay, fine. Who did Jack Dempsey lose the heavyweight title to in 1926?"

Nothing.

"Tell me, who was the..."

She abruptly interrupted me mid-question.

"I knew every answer to the questions put to me on the shows, and I know the answers to what you are asking me now, but I will *not* permit myself to be questioned here!"

I wanted to offer her some advice about her rude behavior, but she had already stormed out of my office.

Every witness I interviewed was just like her, refusing to crack...until James Snodgrass came along. I wish I could say we finally got what we wanted as a result of my extensive digging and investigating, but that's not how it happened. Snodgrass was served right to me on a tennis court.

Snodgrass had appeared on *Twenty One* on NBC. He had been going against returning champion Hank Bloomgarden, who had already won more than 50,000 dollars. The two were locked in what appeared to be a battle of wits, with the men tying six times before Bloomgarden finally prevailed in the seventh match.

I knew Snodgrass's lawyer personally and had called him repeatedly, asking him to have Snodgrass come to my office to speak with me. I was snubbed over and over again, but that all changed one morning when I played tennis with that attorney. Without any prodding, he told me during our match that he would bring Snodgrass to my office on Saturday to meet. I don't know for certain why Snodgrass had finally agreed to it. Maybe his conscience had gotten the best of him. Or, maybe he felt the temperature rising, knowing that our team was not going to quit our investigation until we had proven what we thought to be true.

Snodgrass arrived at my office on schedule, and he revealed absolutely everything.

He said five days before the shows were televised, he would be given the questions and answers from the producers. He told me that to prove this was the case, he would go home, type the questions and answers, put them in sealed envelopes, and send them to his home by registered mail. The stamped dates on the envelopes, of course, preceded the television programs he later appeared on. He saved all of the envelopes, which he then gave to me, still sealed. I sent the envelopes with their contents to the police department crime laboratory. Through a laboratory process, experts were able to read enough of the contents of each envelope to convince Hogan that Snodgrass was telling the truth—the programs were fixed. Using this as leverage, I was able to convince producers to come into the office one by one to confess. Contestants fell in line, feeling the need to come clean.

The investigation did not result in criminal charges, since there was technically nothing illegal about what the game shows had done. Their job was to entertain viewers, and they had done just that. But they also ticked off those same viewers, who felt scammed. As a result, the shows were eventually canceled, producers were out of jobs, and our investigation caused Congress to conduct hearings on the scandals. When the hearings concluded, lawmakers made it a federal crime to rig a quiz show.

Snodgrass, like van Doren, would later give a fascinating testimony to Congress. The hearing was led by Chief Counsel Robert Lishman, and Snodgrass gave compelling detail about how the scam worked behind the scenes. Here is some of that testimony:

Lishman: Mr. Snodgrass, is it not a fact that on the occasions when in advance you were given the questions and answers, you would put them in a sealed envelope immediately after receiving them and address them to you at your home address in a registered mail envelope?

Snodgrass: That is right.

Lishman: What was your purpose in doing this?

Snodgrass: Well, I still haven't explained it to myself. It was just something that I knew maybe someday—that maybe I would have to prove, that I would perhaps say something and I would be called to task for it, and I would have to be able to prove it. I don't know. I just did this to protect myself.

Lishman: Now, Mr. Snodgrass, is it not a fact that when you were given these questions and answers in advance, you were instructed to memorize them and immediately destroy them.

Snodgrass: I was never given anything to destroy. The questions were always read to me.

Lishman: Did you type them up immediately?

Snodgrass: When I would go home, I would then reconstruct the session and send it to myself.

Lishman: Now, Mr. Snodgrass, I am going to hand you—

Subcommittee Chairman: Just a moment, Lishman. Let me get a little more information from him about this. Mr. Snodgrass, let me see if I understand you correctly. Where would you be when these questions and answers would be given to you?

Snodgrass: In Mr. Freedman's office at the offices of Barry & Enright.

Subcommittee Chairman: They would present you with the questions there in writing?

Snodgrass: He read them off a piece of paper. He asked me the questions.

Subcommittee Chairman: He asked you the questions?

Snodgrass: Yes.

Subcommittee Chairman: You would undertake to answer them at that time?

Snodgrass: That is right.

Subcommittee Chairman: And if you did not know the answer, he would provide the answer?

Snodgrass: He provided the answer; yes, sir.

Subcommittee Chairman: Then you would go home?

Snodgrass: I would go home. He provided the answer and maybe the sequence that they were to be answered in. Then I would go home.

Subcommittee Chairman: You would go home and reconstruct them on the typewriter?

Snodgrass: In one case longhand, twice on the typewriter, and sent them to myself by registered mail...

Lishman: Mr. Snodgrass, I am going to hand you a sealed envelope. I don't know the contents in it. I would like to have you first, before opening it, read exactly what there is on the face of this letter and indicate how it was registered and the date and so on, and ask you whether or not it is not addressed to you in your own handwriting? Is it not one of the letters that you mailed as you have just described?

(Document handed to Snodgrass)

Snodgrass: The envelope is addressed to Mr. James Snodgrass, 231 West 16th Street, New York, N.Y. The sender's name is J. Snodgrass, 231 West 16th Street, New York, N.Y. It was mailed and registered at the Old Chelsea Station, New York, N.Y., May 11, 1959.

Lishman: Is that one of the letters that you mailed to yourself?

Snodgrass: This is one of them; yes, sir.

Lishman: That letter is not opened; is it?

Snodgrass: No, sir; it has not been opened.

Lishman: Is there a stamp mark showing the date on the face side of that envelope showing it had been posted May 11, 1957?

Snodgrass: Yes. The meter thing from the post office is May 11, 1957, New York, N.Y., 43 cents worth of postage, 415674 is the registry number.

Lishman: Thank you. I will state for the committee that we have the benefit of a police laboratory report of the New York City Police Department that this letter has not been opened, and it has been delivered to us in the same condition as reported by the Police Department of the City of New York. At this time, I would like to ask that this letter be received in the record, following which I would like to have Mr. Snodgrass open that letter and read its contents into the record. I would like to have him do this publicly so all members can see that he is opening an unopened registered letter...

Snodgrass (reading his letter):

New York, New York, May 10, 1957.

To whom it may concern:

The following are some of the questions, specifically the one I will be asked for the television quiz show Twenty-One on the night of May 13 (Monday).

First category: "Movies"—I take 11 points. The question is worth 11 points.

In the story of Snow White and the Seven Dwarfs, after she is banished from the palace of her stepmother, the Queen, Snow White goes to live in the forest with seven dwarfs. In the Walt Disney version, what were the names of the seven dwarfs?

(I shall answer in this sequence—Sleepy, Sneezy, Dopey, Happy (pause) the grouchy one, Grumpy (pause) Doc (pause) Bashful.

Second category: "England"—I take 10 points.

What was the name of the ruling houses to which the following monarchs belonged—Richard II, Henry VII, Edward V, George VI?

31

(I shall answer something like this. Richard II was the last of the Plantagenets; Henry VII was a Tudor. I shall then ask to come back to Edward V. George the Sixth of course was of the House of Windsor. Then I think about Edward V and mention that he was the kid murdered in the Tower of London by Richard III; he was not a Tudor, he was of the House of York.)

That ends the first game with a score of 21. Presumably Bloomgarden and I shall be tied.

Subcommittee Chairman: Who was he?

Snodgrass: He was the champion and I was the challenger.

Subcommittee Chairman: Mr. Bloomgarden.

Snodgrass: Bloomgarden. He was the champion and I was the challenger.

Snodgrass (continuing to read):

First round game 2: "Presidents."

The first President of our country was a President...I will read it as it is—it doesn't make sense:

The first President of our country was a President as was President Eisenhower. Identify the following Presidents who also were generals. This man won fame by defeating the British at New Orleans during the War of 1812? (I answer correctly—Andrew Jackson.) This general led the American forces at the Battle of Thames in 1813? (I stress the fact that Thames is in Ontario, Canada, also during the War of 1812. William Henry Harrison.) This man enlisted in the army as a private, was appointed a brigadier general and fought with General Scott in capture of Mexico City (According to the plan of the show I am to miss this question. I am to say "Ulysses S. Grant" which is wrong. The proper answer is "Franklin Pierce." This general defeated Santa Ana at the Battle of Buena Vista? (Zachary Taylor.)

Second round—"The Twenties" (I again try for 11 points since I am at zero.)

The following authors were awarded the Pulitzer prize in the twenties. Name the work for which they received this prize.

Stephen Vincent Benet ("John Brown's Body"), Edna Ferber (for her novel "So Big"), Edith Wharton (for "The Age of Innocence"), Thornton Wilder ("The Bridge of San Luis Rey").

I must say in the dressing room prior to the program there was a change in schedule and I was told not to miss the question but to get it right. So there will be a discrepancy here between what is on this paper and what actually happened...

Despite finally cracking the quiz show scandals, Hogan would lose his bid for a seat in the Senate, but he remained the district attorney and would be forever immortalized for uncovering the truth behind the shows. He was so overjoyed by what I had accomplished on the case that it led to a true friendship between the two of us. I even rode in his Cadillac—he was, in fact, a "real person"—and he attended my wedding. My work was the talk of the office for quite some time among Hogan and my colleagues, which was a wonderful boost for my confidence and for my status within the department so early in my career.

CHAPTER 4

"WHAT IS PI?"

WITH THE SUCCESS OF THE quiz shows case, Hogan assigned me to the trial part (meaning I would try cases, one after the other) of Justice John M. Murtagh. The defense bar considered him to be an arch conservative with biased leanings favoring the prosecution. In other words, defense lawyers feared him.

Murtagh had been City Commissioner of Investigation, Chief Magistrate, Chief Justice of the Court of Special Sessions, and eventually a justice of the New York State Supreme Court. We took an instant liking to one another.

One of my earliest and most memorable cases in his court—due primarily to my buffoonery—involved Ralph Henry, who was head of a large and sophisticated numbers racket in Harlem. The numbers game is an illegal lottery played mostly in poor neighborhoods, wherein a bettor attempts to pick the last three digits in the gross take for the day at one of the racetracks, be it Aqueduct or Belmont. The payoff ranges from seven hundred to one thousand times the amount bet. The betting slips each bettor fills out are given to a comptroller, and they are then recorded in columnar form and later turned over to the immediate deputy of the head of the syndicate.

Leon Powell was a comptroller for Ralph Henry's numbers racket. The city police arrested Powell as he sat on a stoop on 135th Street. He was an elderly, wizened, unshaven black man. His clothes were haggard. To the experienced eye, he held true betting slips. Both he and Henry were tried in the state supreme court after indictment. Powell took the stand to exculpate himself and testify the slips were not betting slips, but instead nothing more than random mathematical computations he liked to scribble to keep his aging mind active. It was an absurd defense.

"Mr. Powell, these are obviously betting slips, correct?" I said to him as I began my questioning.

"If you say so," he replied.

"I do say so, as that is exactly what they are. Now, tell me, what were you doing with these betting slips?"

"I was just using them as scratch paper."

"Scratch paper?"

"Yes, I use the slips to do mathematical computations," he said matter-of-factly. "I'm a mathematician."

"A mathematician?"

"Yes, sir," he replied.

"You expect us to believe that?"

"It's the truth, sir."

"Have you ever used those slips for betting purposes?"

"No sir."

"Where did you get the slips?

"I don't know, they were just lying around."

"Just lying around..."

"Yes, sir."

"So, let me get this straight: you found some pieces of paper lying around, which just happened to be betting slips, and you decided to use them to add random numbers together for the fun of it?"

I turned my back to him as he began to state his answer, an answer that didn't matter to me in the least. I had asked the question to give myself time to mentally prepare and physically position myself for my big dramatic moment on the courtroom stage. The lights were bright. If there had been an orchestra on site, they would have timed their crescendo with the one-line, three-word zinger I was about to chuck at him that was going to tip the scales of justice in our favor.

"Yes, sir," he insisted. "I do the computations to keep my mind sharp."

On the word "sharp," I wheeled around as fast I could and pointed my finger directly at him.

"What is 'pi?'" I snapped loudly.

Powell calmly smirked at me. He didn't hesitate.

"Pi is 3.141592..."

Holy shit! I thought to myself as he continued rattling off digit after digit. I don't know how far he extended it past the decimal, but he completely lost me on the number three.

"Okay!" I snapped, abruptly interrupting him. "Thank you."

Powell had stolen my moment. The gallery laughed at me. The judge rolled his eyes. Remember when I called myself an "idiot savant?" My question wasn't necessarily a bad one—every mathematician should know the value of pi. The problem was that *I* didn't know the value of pi. Powell could have said 10.48594 and I wouldn't have had a clue.

Henry and his group were convicted. Powell, however, was acquitted. How much my pi question aided his acquittal, I'm not sure, but I have a pretty good idea.

Years later, Murtagh gave lectures to the bar association about the fact that a lawyer is at his absolute lowest when he asks a witness questions to which he doesn't know the answers himself.

"For example," he would say to his audiences, "let me tell you the story of one attorney, Jay Goldberg, and the case of the Harlem betting slips..."

CHAPTER 5

THE POWER OF LOVE

IN ANOTHER CASE I TRIED for Hogan, Robert Beaman, a notorious defendant also involved in the numbers racket, stood before Judge Murtagh to receive his sentence following his conviction. The judge's sentences relied to a great extent on the police department's "yellow sheet" records, which were supposed to reveal the defendant's criminal record. The longer your record, the longer your sentence would likely be, because it meant that you had been given numerous chances and yet continued to break the law. Fortunately for Beaman, his yellow sheet showed that he had no priors. As a result, Murtagh gave him a slap on the wrist with probation.

Several days later, a court reporter informed the judge that he had recognized Beaman, not from out on the streets, but in the courtroom. He believed Beaman had had a number of convictions over the years, and he suggested that the yellow sheet was perhaps bogus. A check with the police department reflected that the court reporter was absolutely correct. Beaman's record was extensive. So how did the forms fall into the hands of unauthorized persons who were able to report that there were no convictions for a defendant awaiting sentencing?

The investigation into the matter would normally be conducted by the chief of the special sessions bureau in the district attorney's office, but Murtagh insisted to Hogan that I head the investigation. As I stated, Murtagh and I had a mutual respect for one another, and he knew that I would get to the bottom of this deception.

Detectives assigned to the case fastened on Major Grant—not an Army officer, but simply a man with the first name "Major." It was believed that Grant would likely know who was responsible for the phony yellow sheets. Why? When the court reporter recalled seeing Beaman in court previously, I did some digging and found an officer who remembered arresting Beaman eight years earlier. I looked up that case and found that Grant was a co-defendant with Beaman. Since criminals who once worked together will often stay in touch with one another, or at least know what each other is up to, I had a hunch that Grant would know who was responsible for obtaining blank yellow sheets and falsifying them for Beaman.

Through our research, we believed that Grant was staying at the home of his parents in southern Virginia. I accompanied two New York detectives and two Virginia state troopers there. Most assistant Das would have sent detectives and troopers and waited for them to report back. I wasn't that type of attorney. I let them do their jobs, but I also liked to be part of the mission from start to finish, immersing myself in every aspect of the case to be sure that once it got to trial, I knew everything that I needed to know inside and out through firsthand experience.

When we got to the home, a small log cabin, we waited covertly in the grass out front behind some shrubbery. It was a miserable night for conducting a stakeout. It rained and rained and rained some more. After several hours soaking in it and with no sign of Grant, I finally sloshed my way through the lawn and knocked on the front door. His parents answered. As I would learn, they were sharecroppers who were responsible each season for collecting tobacco leaves. They were probably in their late 70s or early 80s. They didn't have much, and they seemed as innocent and harmless as the rain that had been falling all night. They were very cooperative and provided me with some useful information about the location of their son.

But, even better than that, I was a witness to their indelible love for one another.

I know—what does that have to do with this case? Well, nothing at all. But when you're hiding for hours in the dark in a waterlogged field in Virginia waiting for someone to show up who never does, you have a lot of time to think. I thought a lot that evening about my newlywed wife who was back home by herself in New York, and when I saw this elderly couple interacting with one another and so concerned about their son and about doing the right thing, I realized just how much I missed Rema. Grant's parents had been married for more than fifty years. *How glorious that they have not only stayed together this long through thick and thin, but their love for one another is still so evident, even to a stranger like me,* I thought to myself. I knew that was the kind of relationship I wanted with Rema.

Rema and I were in our twenties then. Today, still together and madly in love after all these years, I am so very grateful for that rainy evening in Virginia. Yes, I got information I needed for my case, but Grant's parents also made me recognize how much I missed my wife, and that what we had could be just the start of something very special together.

It is often said that young people need to witness or experience something to know that it is really possible. That is what that night was for me and my marriage. It would also be one of the last times I would ever handle a case without Rema literally at my side. Wherever I would go, for whatever case I was on, she would go with me, whether it was to stake out someone or to try a case in court. We've been a true team in every sense of the word, and I would not have achieved what I have achieved without her.

Okay, back to the case...

The detectives and I returned to New York, and the state troopers returned to their Virginia barracks. With the help of Grant's parents and some other local people, we were able to track down Grant in Harlem. We brought him back to my office to interrogate him, and he couldn't have been more cooperative. He gave us the names of the wrongdoers: a prominent criminal defense lawyer and a sergeant in the police department. Why did they falsify the yellow sheets? Money. Nearly every explanation in any criminal wrongdoing is tied to money. Beaman was a major numbers player, and he had money to dole out to these men to protect himself.

The lawyer and sergeant were indicted, tried, convicted, and sent to prison. The lawyer was disbarred and the officer lost his job.

Grant, I am happy to say, was given simple probation for his cooperation, which I hope brought some semblance of peace to his parents, who certainly deserved it.

CHAPTER 6

ESPIONAGE

SOON AFTER THE GRANT CASE, Judge Murtagh called me one day and asked me to meet him at a place of my choosing so that he could introduce me to a friend of his. I didn't know what it was about or who the friend was, but I respected and trusted the judge, so I agreed. I chose the Harvard Club.

Murtagh entered the club with a short, blondish man whom he introduced as James Donovan. He told me that Donovan, an insurance lawyer, had been recommended by the Brooklyn Bar Association, with the concurrence of the U.S. district judge to whom the case was assigned, to represent Russian spy Rudolf Abel.

Abel was arrested in mid-1957 and indicted for conspiracy to transmit defense information to the Soviet Union, conspiracy to obtain defense information, and conspiracy to act in the U.S. as an agent of a foreign government without notification to the secretary of state. His case was the model of a speedy trial, not otherwise seen in criminal cases. He was convicted in October of that year after only about three hours of deliberation. Donovan convinced the district judge to spare the life of Abel. He argued that one day the Russians could take custody of an American "spy" and there might be a need to arrange a transfer. The judge agreed, and on November 15, 1957, Abel was sentenced to thirty years in prison. The story is recounted in the movie *Bridge of Spies*, starring Tom Hanks. I was so close to the story, though I was physically absent for its dramatic conclusion...and for good reason, as you will see.

By March 28, 1960, legal remedies for Abel were at an end when the U.S. Supreme Court affirmed Abel's conviction in a 5-4 decision. The holding of the court was of great importance; Abel had no standing to object to a warrantless search of his hotel room by Immigration Naturalization Service officers, who then shared the fruit of the warrantless search with the FBI. For the government, the decision was a hard-fought win, in which only four of the nine justices believed that Abel should have been granted a new trial due to an illegal search (*Abel v. United States*, 362 U.S. 217 (1960)). The bench, bar, and public at large were in agreement that Donovan's trial and appellate work were masterful.

On May 1, 1960, CIA pilot Francis Gary Powers, who was in a U.S. spy plane thought to be flying so high that it was impregnable to missile fire, was shot down over East Germany. Powers, like Abel, received a speedy trial in East Germany and was convicted on August 19, 1960, of espionage. He was sentenced to ten years confinement, three to be spent in prison and the rest in a labor camp.

The idea for an exchange of Abel for Powers was first suggested in a letter that Powers's father wrote to East German officials. But, to bear fruition, there had to be negotiations between East German officials and U.S. officials, including the U.S. Department of Justice and others, to determine whether a transfer could be arranged. The U.S. believed that, aside from Powers, two others, including a college student, were also being held on what the government believed were trumped-up charges of espionage. Our government would give back Abel, but we were interested in regaining custody of Powers and the two others. The negotiation seemed to be endless. The paperwork enormous. The meetings too numerous to count. Red tape was truly evident.

Donovan and Murtagh wanted to meet with me to see if I would consider joining Donovan's firm, Watters & Donovan, to serve as Donovan's legal assistant. To me, it was a no-brainer; working on the Abel and Powers case was too good of an opportunity to pass up. But Hogan wasn't pleased when I told him. He was very upset, in fact.

"Jay, the standard time for someone to serve as an assistant DA is three years minimum," he said. I had been there for about two-and-a-half years.

"But this is an incredible opportunity for me," I replied, standing my ground. What would look better on a resume and give me the best possible experience? Additional years as an assistant DA or front-line work on an international espionage case? The answer, to me, was easy.

We went back and forth for a while, but I never wavered. In the end, I decided to leave. Though Hogan still wasn't happy, he said he respected my decision and wished me luck.

The job change was the right move at the right time for me. At Donovan's office, I spent more than a year carrying out such tasks as arranging meetings, attending meetings, and advising Donovan on what I believed to be appropriate strategies. It wasn't work that would have necessarily been considered very exciting to anyone else. It wasn't as sexy as coming face to face with hardened criminals in court or staking out their parents' home in a rain-soaked Virginia field, but it was exhilarating to a young, twenty-something, up-and-coming attorney. I did everything Donovan asked of me and then some, and all my work paid off.

On February 10, 1962, the transfer of Abel for Powers and another was effected. It was an historic day. A glorious day. A proud day.

And I missed it.

All of that hard work, all of that drama, and I wasn't there to witness the exchange. It was like being handed the football play after play and taking your team all the way down to the goal line, only to be pulled so that someone else could run it in for the score. Except, in this case, I removed myself from the game.

Just as the transfer was about to take place, I received a phone call from, of all people, Frank Hogan.

"Jay, how's it going?" he asked.

"Fine, Mr. Hogan. What can I do for you?"

"I need you to come to my office tomorrow to meet with someone."

"Really? Tomorrow?"

"Yes."

"Who is the meeting with?" I asked.

"I can't tell you."

"You can't tell me?"

"No, I can't tell you. What I *can* tell you is that it's about a position I have recommended you for."

"What's the position?"

"I can't tell you that either."

I laughed. "Are you serious?"

"Totally. Just trust me on this, Jay," he said. "You will want to be here. Come in at 3:30. I'll see you then."

Without giving me a chance to reply, he hung up.

I hadn't been with Donovan for very long, and my work for him had been so important to our country. I wasn't sure that I really wanted to consider yet another job in such a short time span. And I certainly didn't want to miss the transfer, which meeting with Hogan would have required. On the other hand, Hogan, the man who was not happy with me when I had left his firm for Donovan's, was the one recommending me to this unknown person for this unknown position. It had to be something big, in my opinion, so I decided I needed to go.

The next day, I walked into the waiting area of Hogan's office right on time.

"You can go in," his secretary said to me.

I opened Hogan's door. He was sitting behind his desk. Sitting across from him was the man he wanted me to meet:

Robert F. Kennedy.

Yeah, this was going to be something big.

THE KENNEDYS

CHAPTER 7

"I WANT YOU TO WORK FOR ME"

I RECOGNIZED ROBERT F. KENNEDY immediately, which was obviously a glaring sign that I had been summoned for a significant purpose. It was rare for me to be star struck, but like many people when standing before a Kennedy, I was strongly taken by his presence. He was wiry, well-tanned, and as my wife would later opine, he had a certain appeal to women. He had just been appointed U.S. Attorney General by his brother, President John F. Kennedy, and he was recently confirmed by the Senate. He was now in his late thirties and had lived a life of public service. He served in the U.S. Naval Reserve, ran his brother's successful U.S. Senate campaign in 1952, and served as chief counsel on the U.S. Senate Select Committee on Improper Activities in Labor and Management in the late '50s.

He was speaking to Hogan when I walked in. Hogan nodded at me to sit in the chair next to Kennedy. Kennedy didn't look at me, not to be rude, but because he was focused on what he was saying to Hogan. When he finished, he turned to me and didn't waste any time getting into what he wanted. He didn't introduce himself or ask me who I was. I think it was a given to all in the room that he knew me because I was the one he was expecting, and I knew him because, well, he was Robert F. Kennedy. He spoke as if we were old friends.

"Jay, have you ever been to the Chicago area?" he asked.

"No, sir, I have not."

"Have you ever been to Gary, Indiana?"

"Mr. Kennedy, I have never been further west than Lakewood, N.J."

He chuckled. "Well, let me tell you about Gary," he said.

In his book, *The Enemy Within*, Kennedy said that his work as chief counsel on the U.S. Senate Select Committee led him to conclude that Lake County, Indiana, which was in the Northwest District of Indiana and the home of Gary, had the most corruption and the highest murder rate of any county in the country.

Gary lay some thirty-five miles southeast of Cicero, Illinois, the home base of deceased gangster Al Capone. Remnants of his mob were thought by some FBI agents to still be active in the Lake County area. The weight of authority, however, was that control of the county was in the hands of the Chicago mob, led by Sam Giancana. The county abutted Calumet City, Illinois, which was an open city, with prostitution and a disreputably high murder rate. All of this combined to make Lake County and the city of Gary in particular a hotbed of crime, corruption, weapons traffic, and everything else evil, where the citizens were truly captives of the criminal element. Judges were bought off. Prosecutors were controlled. Police chiefs did not function as they should have. What were the citizens to do?

Forces of good government had joined together to form the Northwest Indiana Crime Commission, begging Attorney General Kennedy that if there could be vigorous federal prosecutorial action, this would have a profound effect on crime, not only in Lake County, but in its environs.

"I have a position that Mr. Hogan believes you are highly suited for," Kennedy said to me. "I want you to work for me. I want you to go to Gary to rid the area of the crime and corruption."

I probably should have taken a moment to ponder what he had asked given that it was a life-changing request, but I didn't. Kennedy was asking me for help, and I wasn't about to hesitate giving him the answer he expected. There would be time later for me to process what I had gotten myself into.

"I have the capacity to do that, sir," I said with conviction. "Would I have the backing of not only you, but of the FBI?"

"You would," he said.

I think he liked my aggressiveness. He was aggressive in stating why he was there and what he wanted me to do, so I felt I had to at least match his character. Also, Hogan had obviously highly recommended me to Kennedy, so I didn't want to let down my former boss. In retrospect, I was glad Hogan didn't tell me in advance who I was going to meet that day. I am big on preparation, but how do you prepare at such a young age to meet such a person? It was best for me to be put on the spot as I was.

Kennedy dove into the details of what my role would be. He said he wanted me to serve, for the time being, as a special attorney in the Northwest District of Indiana, attached to the Organized Crime and Racketeering Section in the Criminal Division at the Department of Justice in Washington, D.C. He stated that if the person he intended to nominate as U.S. Attorney, John Masters, were confirmed, I could stay on as Masters's special assistant in Indiana. However, if for any reason Masters were not confirmed or his nomination were withdrawn, I would be sworn in by U.S. District Judge Luther Swygert as acting U.S. Attorney for the Northwest District of Indiana, even though I was not a member of the Indiana Bar. Judge Swygert was later appointed to the U.S. Court of Appeals for the Sixth Circuit. Safe to say, my future role, if I accepted the offer, would depend on what lay ahead for Mr. Masters.

"Mr. Kennedy, I appreciate the offer," I said. While I knew I was going to take the job, and while I'm certain he knew that too, I asked him if I could run it by my wife.

"Of course," he said.

The meeting with Kennedy and Hogan lasted about twenty minutes. I kept cool in their presence, but, admittedly, I did a little dance after I walked out and closed the door behind me. The secretary smiled. At my happiness—not at my dance moves—I'm sure.

When I got home and told Rema what had transpired, she was ecstatic.

"You met Robert Kennedy?" she said with stars in her eyes. I think she was excited about the job offer, too.

There was no real discussion about whether or not I would take it. We both knew we were relocating to Gary, assuming we could find it on a map. I wanted to go, and she was very committed to seeing me do what I wanted to do. We also knew how important this mission was to the citizens of Gary.

A couple weeks after informing Kennedy that I would accept his offer, he flew me to Washington, D.C., to meet with Deputy Attorney General Byron White to get his approval of my hiring. I recall being in Kennedy's office with all of his men. It was below zero outside, and a steward came into the office to ask us what we'd like to drink. One person asked for coffee. Another for hot chocolate.

"I'll have an iced tea," White said sternly.

Damn, I thought to myself. *Zero degrees outside and he wants iced tea?* I liked that. So trivial, yet so symbolic. It gave me a sense that I was dealing with a hard-nosed guy. He pledged his full support for me during the meeting, which gave me a huge boost of confidence going forward.

Three months after Kennedy made his offer to me, Rema and I left New York for Gary. The play *The Music Man* was popular then, but I didn't expect to find myself welcomed by a big brass band. The reception, however, was somewhat close. The *Gary Tribune* reported, "A federal prosecutor was on his way, but we don't know where he will be staying or when he will arrive." I was just an attorney, but the headline made me feel like a star.

Now, to be honest, RFK was not the unbiased, no-holds-barred, law enforcement officer the press heralded. One of his first acts was to indict New York Supreme Court Justice J. Vincent Keogh; Elliott Kahaner, chief assistant U.S. Attorney for the federal court in Brooklyn; and Anthony "Tony Ducks" Corallo, a notorious racketeer. They were charged in a conspiracy to obstruct justice by attempting to influence federal Judge Leo Rayfiel in a case before him. I happened to be in New York for a few days and stopped in to observe the trial. "Tony Ducks" was represented by a friend of mine, the late James M. LaRossa. He told me some of the alleged facts of the case, and he was pessimistic as to the likely verdict. His feeling was accurate. The three were convicted and jail sentences followed.

However, rumors in the Department of Justice were that Congressman Eugene Keogh, a confidant of President Kennedy and brother of Justice Keogh, was involved in the conspiracy as well, but he was not indicted as he should have been.

I would witness further slippage of RFK and JFK from their pledge to engage in a struggle against organized crime and political corruption, which ultimately allowed it to grow. Whether it be the "syndicate," the "mob," or the "outfit," those involved in organized crime and political corruption had gotten away with numerous multi-billion-dollar gambling and industrial rackets, tax evasion, and even murder. These crime syndicates were already well organized when the Kennedys came into office, but the Kennedys didn't do all they could have to derail them.

There was no FBI organized crime section when RFK came to the Justice Department. The government's understanding of the extent of the danger posed by the mafia was so limited, that the names of suspected members of the mafia were noted on index cards and stored in shoe boxes in the offices of the Assistant Attorney General in charge of the Criminal Division.

Under RFK's direction, law enforcement agencies were brought together by new legislation and instructed to combat organized crime and political corruption. However, the talk of the office was that when it came to making a decision, RFK had three criteria: First, "Is it good for my brother?" Second, "Is it good for the Democratic Party?" Third, "Is it good for the country?"

What often compromised RFK were the actions of JFK by reason of his relationship with Sam Giancana—leader of the Chicago "outfit" that controlled the majority of rackets within the states of Illinois and Indiana. To be sure, JFK, as I will soon reveal, took steps to abort my investigation into activities in Lake County, Indiana. I had reason to believe this was an intended "favor" to Giancana for his help on the campaign.

The manner of RFK's appointment to attorney general offended FBI Director J. Edgar Hoover, for JFK was quite flippant about it by stating his brother needed experience in the law. Hoover was in his mid-sixties when the thirty-five-year-old attorney general technically became Hoover's "superior" in the Department of Justice. This was particularly galling to Hoover, for he had headed the FBI (first called the Bureau of Investigation) since 1924, before RFK was even born. Hoover's hostility to RFK was to be expected. Hoover considered RFK abrasive in not extending him the courtesy and respect he felt he was entitled to. RFK even acted in a way that offended the strict and formal way the FBI director conducted his affairs, which included the stringent dress code imposed upon his special agents and the way in which his office was run.

RFK's office had a dartboard and crayon drawings made by his children pasted to the walls. He generally sat behind his desk with rolled up sleeves and his feet planted firmly on the edge of the desk. But, to me, he still had a halo around him.

The behavior of President Kennedy, including his relationship with Marilyn Monroe, was well-known to all of us. I was told by Secret Service agents that when JFK visited various cities, he would ask them to find women for him. His behavior was so reckless. But I was shocked to find out that his brother was no different.

I could not believe it when rumors were floating about his supposed liaisons with younger women, including Marilyn Monroe. To someone who was not and never has been a womanizer, I couldn't understand this. I felt his out-of-office behavior was beyond the pale. He had eleven children, but he still had an abundance of energy. I thought he went home to eat, play with his kids, watch some television, and go to sleep. But he had a dark side. His wife, Ethel, suffered in silence. When Rema and others visited her at her home, she was warm and gracious despite what her husband was putting her through.

The historic faceoff between RFK and J. Edgar Hoover led to a number of instances in which RFK had to pull back on his quest to bring to justice leading mobsters and those engaged in political corruption. RFK was not what Hoover had expected as the attorney general. My efforts, and the roles Hoover, JFK, and RFK played in really hoping I would fail, are dealt with in the books *Bobby and J. Edgar: The Historic Face-Off Between the Kennedys and J. Edgar Hoover that Transformed America* by Burton Hersh, *Kennedy Justice* by Victor S. Navasky, *Perfect Villains, Imperfect Heroes: Robert F. Kennedy's War Against Organized Crime* by Ronald Goldfarb, and *My Indiana* by Irving Leibowitz.

Hoosiers believed Lake County should not be considered part of Indiana, as it resembled Chicago at its worst. It belched pollution that mixed with the gas and industrial fumes of East Chicago. It was a dense, grimy string of factory smoke stacks, oil refinery tanks, coal piles, and steel mills. It was said if you lived in Gary, you either worked in the terrible heat generated by a steel furnace, or you did not work at all. Author Irving Leibowitz states in *My Indiana*:

> "What's wrong with Gary? Why do Hoosiers instinctively distrust Lake County? Why can't a politician from Lake County ever be elected Governor or Senator? Lake County is corrupt. The underworld wants it that way. So long as gambling, prostitution, and robberies are confined to certain notorious districts of the community, decent citizens shrug and go blissfully about making a living, mowing the lawn and cooking supper."

I had my work cut out for me, and then some.

CHAPTER 8

ON MY OWN

THE FIRST TIME REMA AND I went to Gary following my appointment, we stayed at the Holiday Inn. I was supposed to meet with the Assistant Special Agent in Charge (ASAC) of the FBI's Northern District of Indiana office. However, there was more than a hint of a problem when the ASAC failed to appear, without any explanation, for a dinner I had arranged. I soon learned the ridiculous reason he left me out to dry.

A copy of a report was given to me in which the FBI had noted that I left "classified documents—302s—unsecured on my hotel room desk," rather than having kept them out of sight in a briefcase during the time I was to be out of the room. I realized I was new to the job and had a lot to learn about protocol. Interesting, though, how there was no time to meet me, but time enough for agents to either enter or look into my room, most likely while it was being cleaned. The ASAC eventually forgave me long enough to meet with me a couple days later.

"I'm investigating the Hobbes Act and loansharking violations," I said to him.

"I've never heard of the Hops Act," he replied.

I paused, giving him a moment to correct himself. He didn't.

"I'm not investigating the Whiskey Rebellion," I said facetiously.

He didn't find that funny. I'm not even sure he understood it. Anyway, as I expected after his "Hops" comment, he didn't provide me with a whole lot of help.

As I got to work, I determined there were victims of repeated extortion carried out by hoodlums with threats of violence. And what I found was that almost all of these extortionists were represented by none other than John Masters, RFK's pick for U.S. Attorney. That led me to open an investigation into Masters, where

I learned that on some occasions he had taken the collections on behalf of the hoodlums. He was clearly a person who aided and abetted criminal conspiracies. I invited him to my office to provide an explanation for what I had discovered but, not surprisingly, he refused to come. How could the FBI give him a clean bill? I told RFK all that I had learned. He was stunned...and very appreciative. He agreed that Masters was not fit for the job.

This was my first accomplishment toward the much larger goal RFK had tasked me with in cleaning up Gary. I've often been asked if I feared for my life considering the type of people I was dealing with. I never did. One may find that difficult to believe, but my childhood prepared me for such work. I've always been physically tough, which I had to be to box as a teen against some of the best. But I've always been even more mentally tough because of what I went through and witnessed with regard to my father. I had one focus in Gary, and that was to accomplish what RFK had asked me to do. I was not going to compromise under any circumstances. There was no room within me for fear.

As a consequence of Masters being out, by reason of the promise Robert Kennedy had made to me, U.S. District Judge Luther Swygert (later elevated to the Seventh Circuit) swore me in as Acting U.S. Attorney for the Northwest District of Indiana.

At the time there was only one assistant U.S. Attorney in the Northern District of Indiana, but he was assigned to South Bend, not Gary. He still signed all of the indictments since he was a member of the Indiana Bar and I was not. There was only one federal judge sitting in the area covering Lake County, and there was another federal judge sitting in South Bend. Times sure do change, for today there are thirteen sitting federal judges in the Northwest District of Indiana.

My investigation of Masters was confirmed by later events. He moved across the state line to Chicago and set up a practice following his admission to the Illinois Bar. Sometime thereafter, he became a judge in Cook County. Soon after that, he and others were indicted in Illinois by federal authorities for violations of the RICO statute arising from a pattern of corruption. Can you imagine such a person as the chief law enforcement officer supposedly enforcing justice in a crime-ridden county such as Lake County, Indiana, which cried out for good government? And to think he was *that* close to becoming U.S. Attorney.

Despite my elevated status, my job would become even more difficult, and I felt Rema was my only ally. The deeper I delved into Gary's corruption, the less support I had from the government—because so many in the government were the problem. My investigations had revealed widespread corruption that involved city council members and even the mayor. I contacted Allan Gillies, the special agent in charge of the FBI office for Indiana, to tell him what I had found. Remember, I was assured by RFK when I took the job that the FBI would fully support me.

Gillies said he would fly up to meet me. He suggested, for security purposes, that we meet at an abandoned airstrip at the Gary airport. Planes didn't take off or land from that airstrip... perhaps because the airlines were afraid somebody would steal the tires from the planes? When I say the crime there was off the charts, such thievery likely wasn't out of the realm of possibilities. It was an odd place to meet, but I trusted that, for our safety, Special Agent Gillies knew best.

Rema and I arrived at the airport about 11:00 p.m. I wasn't kidding when I said that ever since that stakeout in the rain in Virginia, she has been by my side. If I have a case, she's there in the courtroom. If I need to strategize for a case, she is there to offer her input. If I need to meet a stranger in the dead of night on an abandoned runway in a dangerous city in sub-freezing temperatures, she's there. When I stated in the dedication that she has been my lifelong partner in justice, I meant that literally.

As we waited for Special Agent Gillies to arrive, the whole scenario seemed straight out of a Hollywood movie. The night sky was starry and clear. There was a light dusting of snow on the cold concrete. The temperature was in the teens. Fortunately, for being just east of the Windy City, the air was calm—that was about all we had going for us. No commercial planes arrived or departed that late. We stood there bundled up with our hands in our pockets, alone and anxious. We didn't think we had been followed, but we couldn't know for certain. This was the murder and corruption capital of the world, and everyone knew we were in town to change that. I may have never feared for my life, but it didn't mean I didn't look over my shoulder every now and then.

When a two-engine plane finally landed and taxied to us, out stepped Gillies, who was truly from Hollywood's central casting: muscular, handsome, and with a beautiful mane of white hair. We greeted each other with a handshake, and I introduced him to Rema. We felt as if our great hope had arrived—but we couldn't have been more wrong. Our encounter lasted just a moment. The pilot didn't even shut down the plane's engines.

"I know you have a case that you think might warrant FBI participation, but you know that matters of this sort are made by the director," Gillies said. "I can't give you the director's reasons, but he does not want to get involved."

"What do you mean?" I asked.

"I'm sorry," he said. "No agents will assist you in this case."

I was floored.

"What about the protection I was promised?" I asked.

"We cannot provide that. There are two agents assigned to Gary and they have a lot of work to do."

"So...we're on our own?"

"Good luck," he said as he shook my hand, boarded the plane, and took off into the night sky. There Rema and I stood, just as we had before the plane had arrived: alone, in the dead of night, in the frigid air...but this time with no hope.

"This is bullshit! Absolute bullshit!" I exclaimed as I watched him take off. Why, one might ask, would they not help? As I would quickly figure out, it was a tangled web that had nothing to do with cleaning up Gary.

Hoover wasn't going to help me because he didn't like RFK and wanted nothing more than to see him fail. So, if I failed, RFK failed. And I would find out later that the mayor of Gary, whom I suspected was at the heart of the corruption, was said to be the one JFK would soon nominate as ambassador to Greece. So if I couldn't bring down the mayor, the president would get to blindly keep his man. And if the president was happy, his brother would be happy.

Do you see the problem here, along with its absurdity?

It appeared I was doing my job *too* well, certainly far better than Hoover or either of the Kennedys had expected. So, instead of encouraging me to keep going, they were trying to hinder my efforts by not providing me with the support I needed, so that I didn't get in the way of what they wanted for themselves and their cronies. If I failed, they could publicly make the claim that they tried to help Gary, put the blame on me for the lack of success, and move on.

None of that, however, was going to stop me. I was driven by my sense of justice. I'd come too far to not do everything within my power to take away the fear of the citizens of Gary. How could a city and county function with organized corruption and nobody to help them? I realized this was all on my back, and I was willing to carry it as far as I could, help or no help.

Just weeks after that meeting with Gillies, when our residence became known to some of the hoodlums in town, someone placed a cardboard outline of a black hand under the windshield wiper of our car. The black hand was a symbol of the mafia's interests. I called Byron White, and he communicated with FBI liaison officer Courtney Evans. The best the bureau was able to come up with was that this was simply a case of "Hoosier humor."

I took it upon myself to enlist the assistance of Francis Lynch, a former FBI agent who was the current investigative chief of the Northwest Indiana Crime Commission, and IRS Special Agent Oral Cole, to protect Rema and me and help with my investigations.

And onward we went.

CHAPTER 9

STANDING UP TO RFK AND JFK

WE INVESTIGATED THE UNION BUILDING Construction Company in Passaic, NJ, which had been awarded the contract to build the Indiana toll road. Construction of the toll road afforded corrupt politicians a golden opportunity. The level of extortion was so great that the company had to pay every councilman through whose district its trucks passed, both to and from the toll road. Can you imagine?

The president of Union Building told me that in the forty years the company had performed work in municipalities nationwide, in each and every case, they were required by local officials to submit to extortionate demands.

How did the extortion in Lake County work? It was pretty simple, actually.

Key members of the Gary and Hammond municipal governments created dummy corporations with phony names that were listed as principals. This allowed more than fifteen million dollars (that would be well over 100 million dollars today) to be funneled to the sheriff of the county, police chiefs throughout the county, the district attorney, a county judge, every member of the city council in Gary, as well as the then "kingpin" mayor of Gary, George Chacharis, who headed the crime ring and had known ties to Sam Giancana. All of these individuals used criminal means to control the county. Chacharis, aided by Mayor Richard Daley of Chicago, played a key role in the 1960 convention supporting JFK. This was the guy about to be nominated by our president as ambassador to Greece.

People brought to my office for questioning admitted their thievery with little persuasion necessary because of the stage I had set. When they walked in, the first things they saw were two large pictures I'd hung on my wall of RFK and JFK. Even if the Kennedys weren't supporting me as they should have, those I interrogated didn't know that, which made the pictures very powerful images. When they sat down in the chair across from my desk, they were facing the back of the high-backed judge's chair I was sitting in that I'd borrowed from the one sitting judge. I was dealing with dangerous associates of the "political mob" and did not want them to see my face, so I conducted all of my questioning with my back to them. Sure, they may have seen me in the papers, but maybe not.

"There is a ten ton truck barreling down the road marked 'Federal Government!'" was my stern opening line to each of them. "You can stand in the roadway and try to stop the truck, or you can stand on the sidewalk and cooperate." The members of the ring were so scared that, one by one, they chose the sidewalk and admitted their involvement. One person was so terrified of me that he complained to the FBI, which reported his complaint to the Department of Justice, that I had threatened to literally run over him with a ten ton truck. My methods may have been a bit unconventional, but they got me many of the answers I had sought.

As reports of my efforts and success in bringing malefactors to justice hit the papers, I had become a town celebrity. Almost nightly Rema and I were invited into the home of a different local CEO. They fed us. They entertained us. If we went to a restaurant, citizens hounded me for autographs...really. This wasn't what I had come to Gary for, but it was certainly nice to be recognized for what I was trying to do. Corporations couldn't have been more supportive, even purchasing advertising on a billboard on Broadway in the heart of town, imploring any person with information as to corruption to call my office. Here, too, the FBI falsely reported this was an effort by me at self-promotion. I had nothing whatsoever to do with the sign. The FBI, which should have had my back from the beginning, was getting desperate to stop me—and they were failing miserably.

My biggest break occurred when I was lying awake one morning in bed at about 3:00 a.m. and I was finally able to figure out how to nab the mayor. Despite all of those guys coming into my office and spilling their guts during my interrogations, none of them would incriminate the mayor. My team and I had to figure that one out on our own. One piece of the puzzle that helped me nail him was a book on the Greek language that Oral Cole, the IRS special agent I had hired, had given to me. I don't recall why he gave it to me, other than that the mayor was Greek and maybe he thought it could come in handy in some way. As I paged through it, my brain was stuck on the mayor's name: George Chacharis. With the help of the book, I was able to determine that "Chacharis" was a derivation of the name "Combs." That was the name used in many of the dummy accounts set up to extort money. George Combs was George Chacharis!

When I finally put it together at that very early morning hour, I awakened Rema.

"Honey, we have to go down to the courthouse now! I figured out what I need on Chacharis!"

"What? Now?"

"Yes, now! Security will let us in. Let's go!"

We threw some clothes over our pajamas and raced through the blustery winter winds to our car. It was easily below zero with the wind chill, just a wretched night. I unlocked the passenger side door and opened it for Rema. She shivered her way in before I slammed it shut behind her. I then walked around back and opened the trunk to throw in my briefcase.

That's when...the explosion...

"Oh my God!" I cried.

No, the car didn't blow up.

A bunch of Coca-Cola bottles did.

We'd left a carton of them in the trunk overnight. They'd gotten so cold that they shattered. There was glass and a syrupy mess everywhere. I slammed the trunk shut, threw my briefcase into the back seat, and got in behind the wheel.

"The Coke bottles exploded," I said, through my chattering teeth.

"Oh my gosh, I totally forgot they were in there," Rema replied.

I put the key in the ignition, but I didn't turn it. I sat there for a moment staring straight ahead.

"What's wrong?" Rema asked.

"You know, the exploded bottles in the trunk have me thinking..."

"What?"

"Well, I'm pretty important to most of the people here, but there are a few in this town who would probably like to rub me out. I'm thinking maybe you should start the car just to make sure nobody has rigged a bomb to it."

The look she gave me could have killed me faster and easier than any bomb explosion. I was kidding of course. But it was 3:00 a.m. and bitterly cold, and I felt like I needed to lighten the mood. She disagreed.

With this discovery about Chacharis and with the aid of the now-cooperating individuals whom I had questioned in my office, I assembled a case against Chacharis and other Lake County political figures to be presented to the grand jury. Obviously, Chacharis's chances for appointment and Senate confirmation as our ambassador to Greece would be crushed with an indictment. But I had yet another obstacle to overcome. An enormous one that I had not expected.

On the eve of the scheduled presentation before the grand jury, I received a call from my boss...not to congratulate me but, believe it or not, to try to stop me. Robert Kennedy demonstrated during that call that he was not at all above putting politics over fighting crime.

"Jay, I understand you are presenting a case to the grand jury tomorrow," he said.

"Yes, sir." I said proudly. "I have assembled some thirty-five witnesses to testify to the mayor's involvement, as well as those co-conspirators with him in a widespread web of corruption, who controlled every aspect of the crime and corruption within the county. I expect there will be indictments."

"Jay, I think in fairness you should let the mayor come to your office so you can show him a list of the witnesses, for one or more may have an ulterior motive to testify against him," Kennedy said.

"Wha...What?" I couldn't speak. How could he make such a request?

"Just give him a chance to review the evidence," Kennedy said.

In all of my years as an attorney and as a student of the law, I'd never heard of such a thing.

"With all due respect, sir, I can't allow the mayor this kind of inspection," I said. "It would jeopardize the case and the life and safety of the witnesses. I just can't do it."

"I am not *asking* you to do it," he replied. "I am *directing* you to do it."

I was stunned, but not shaken. I gathered my thoughts and stood up for myself.

"I am very sorry, sir. It may be insubordinate, but it would be contrary to the way I believe a prosecutor should act," I said. "Again, I am sorry."

He was growing irritated with me, and I with him. We appeared to be at an impasse. And at an impasse, it's the boss who normally wins.

"Then you will have to put off the grand jury and come back to Washington this evening," he ordered.

But I haven't yet shared the most jaw-dropping piece of this conversation.

Remarkably, as we were talking, I was able to hear RFK say— despite the fact that he had apparently put his hand over the phone's mouthpiece—"George, he won't let you see the papers or tell you about the witnesses." Yes, the very target of the investigation was right there in the attorney general's office! This astounded me. Where was the commitment to the "no-holds-barred" effort to root out crime and corruption? It wasn't with Kennedy.

Cole drove me to Chicago so I could immediately fly to Washington. At 10:15 p.m., a teletype message was sent from the IRS office in Gary to headquarters in Washington. Cole had told the IRS what was happening, and the IRS expressed concern in a message to RFK about whether his actions would abort the investigation. Additionally, an IRS internal memorandum accused the Department of Justice of leaking evidence to Chacharis without my knowledge. When I arrived, sometime after 11:00 p.m., RFK not only had Chacharis in his office, but also present was Alexander Campbell, the Democratic National Committeeman from Indiana. Both Chacharis and Campbell maintained a close relationship with RFK and JFK.

I glared at the two men when I arrived at RFK's office. None of us said a word to each other. Sensing the tension, RFK told Chacharis and Campbell to leave the room so that the two of us could talk privately.

"Jay," Kennedy said, "why are you going after the mayor? Can't you just zero in on the mobsters involved?"

"I cannot do that, sir," I said. "The center of corruption is the politicians, not the mobsters."

It was obvious to me that my boss was trying to obstruct justice.

"Mr. Kennedy, I cannot let the politicians get away with this, and you are not going to want me to tell the mayor who is testifying against him," I continued. "This is most crime-ridden killing operation in the country. If the mayor finds out the names, you can't be sure they won't be assassinated, and you will suffer great harm because I will have to tell the truth about your order."

I outlined for Kennedy what the proof would show and what the witnesses would testify to. He never said I was right. He just nodded after I made each point. I knew that I had run a huge risk threatening to disobey his order—my career was potentially on the line—but no matter what his initial intentions were for sending me to Gary, *my* intentions from day one were clear: to clean it up. And I was a grand jury away from finishing the job.

We talked for about fifteen minutes. When I was finished, with no sense of what he was thinking, Kennedy called Chacharis and Campbell into the office to join us.

"Gentlemen," Kennedy said, getting directly to the matter at hand, "I am letting Mr. Goldberg present his case to the grand jury."

Whoa!

We were all shocked. I was also thrilled, of course. Chacharis? He bawled. I mean he literally broke down and cried and cried and cried like a little baby. Campbell showed little reaction. He probably would have cried too, if he hadn't gotten to see firsthand from his buddy how ridiculous he would have looked, especially in front of RFK.

It was now approaching midnight. Robert Kennedy directed the FBI to fly me back to Gary immediately.

As I left his office, I encountered in the hallway Henry Petersen, a career deputy at the Department of Justice who had risen to a high position in the criminal division. He knew, of course, what was going on. I told him it did not seem to me that RFK appreciated what I had accomplished.

"Of course not," he said. "How would you feel if somebody locked up your friends?"

He went on to say I made a mistake not following RFK's order. Ironically, Petersen, who would in the coming years be in charge of the Watergate probe during President Richard Nixon's tenure, "came under criticism for his contacts with the White House during the early period of the (Watergate) inquiry and for what was regarded as his sympathy for the White House view that the investigation could be 'dangerous to the presidency' if it reached too far," according to the Washington Post.

Not that I needed it, but that criticism Petersen received was more validation years later that his take on my actions toward RFK was wrong. I had done the right thing.

CHAPTER 10

COCONUTS TO THE RESCUE

WEEKS LATER, WHEN I WAS in Washington for medical treatment, and with my rescheduled presentation to the grand jury in Lake County just days away, a letter on White House stationery signed by Kenneth O'Donnell, a special assistant to JFK, was delivered to me. The letter stated that my work was finished and there should be no further proceedings in Lake County. I had just battled my boss; now I was getting pushback from my boss's boss. And it couldn't go any higher than the president.

What prompted this latest interference, as President Kennedy would later tell me himself, was that Congressman Ray Madden from Gary, a powerful member of Congress since 1943 who was on the House Rules Committee, had called the White House and spoken to the president. He told him that if Chacharis were to be indicted, he would see to it that the president's proposed amendments to the Farm Bill would not reach the floor of Congress for a vote. The natural conclusion, President Kennedy would tell me, was that it was more important to get the Farm Bill amendments through than to end the widespread corruption in Lake County, Indiana.

Maybe in hindsight the amendments were worth so much more in providing aid to farmers across the country. But how ridiculous that indictments against corrupt individuals were tied to it at all. How angry I was that the president had given in to the pressure to recall me and cease investigative activities in Lake County instead of doing what was morally right.

But I was not going down without a fight.

I called officials at Indiana corporations Standard Oil and U.S. Steel, and I told them of the latest developments. Both companies consistently had been loud voices in the call to clean up Lake County. I knew they appreciated what I had accomplished so far and that they wanted me to continue with my mission. And it was their effort, in reaction to my call to them, that I believe saved the day.

That effort, though unusual, tugged at the heartstrings of the president. They arranged with a Chicago company to send fifty coconuts to the White House, engraved with the message "Help!" The coconuts were sent along with a letter urging the president to instruct the attorney general to send me back to Gary to finish the job I had started.

The companies drew on the coconut analogy based on the president's efforts during World War II to have him and his crew rescued after serious damage to the PT109 he was commanding. According to the John F. Kennedy Presidential Library and Museum:

"While Kennedy was serving in World War II as commander of the PT109, his boat was hit by a Japanese destroyer and his crew was stranded in the Solomon Islands. Lieutenant John F. Kennedy carved a coconut shell and gave it to two natives to deliver to the PT base at Rendova so he and his crew would be rescued. He later had the coconut shell encased in wood and plastic and used it as a paperweight on his desk in the Oval Office. Message carved on coconut shell reads, "NAURO ISL...COMMANDER...NATIVE KNOWS POS'IT...HE CAN PILOT...11 ALIVE...NEED SMALL BOAT... KENNEDY."

Mr. O'Donnell called my home in Washington soon after the shipment of coconuts—which I did not know the companies had sent—had been received by the president.

"Jay, the president would like to speak with you," Mr. O'Donnell said.

"That's fine," I replied, and he put me on hold. I didn't know why the president wanted to speak with me and, quite frankly, it *wasn't* fine. I thought he was trying to obstruct my work, the very work that he and his brother had sent me to Gary to do. But it was the president. Of course I was going to listen to what he had to say, at the very least out of respect for his office.

After several minutes, he finally picked up the phone.

"Jay?"

"Hello, Mr. President."

"You've seen my memo from Mr. O'Donnell?"

"Yes."

"Do you know that I received a shipment of coconuts from some corporations in Gary?"

Coconuts? Ha! I was cracking up inside. I knew his coconut story. What a novel idea to get his attention. And to think that he probably had the original coconut, which he had turned into a paperweight, on his desk when the shipment of coconuts from Gary arrived.

"No, sir, I am not aware of any coconuts."

"Jay, I have never seen such an outpouring of public support for such an investigation," he said. "You need to go back to Gary and do the best job you can consistent with your responsibilities."

What? Really?

I wanted to ask, "So, all it took were some damn coconuts?" But I restrained myself. He had just given me the green light to finish what I had started. The reason for him changing his mind was irrelevant.

"Yes, Mr. President," I said. "Thank you."

I'd done it. *We'd* done it. Francis Lynch, Oral Cole, Rema, the citizens and corporations of Gary. It truly would have been tragic to abort the case for political reasons, and the president now realized that. He said he would hold up the nomination of Mayor Chacharis until the legal process had played out. Clearly, he was concerned that shutting down a case of this magnitude would lead the giant corporations to publicly report his misbehavior.

Who would have thought that the mark I would leave on the U.S. Department of Justice and all of Lake County, Indiana, would come down to a box of coconuts?

When I flew back to Chicago, upon stepping off the plane, I waived to the massive crowd that had traveled from all over Lake County to greet me. They could taste victory. A columnist for the *Gary Low-down*, the largest black newspaper in the country wrote: "Weeks ago, while others were saying nay, the *Low-down* predicted the return of Jay Goldberg to the grand jury firing line, and like MacArthur, he has returned."

Robert Kennedy was later asked by a reporter from the *Chicago Tribune* about the Chacharis matter, and he responded that he had been in touch with me every day during my investigation. That was hardly true. The investigation went forward *despite* his efforts, not with his support. In fact, after my second return to Indiana, I took deliberate steps to dodge his calls to avoid any more potential pitfalls.

In late 1962, after the grand jury was convened and heard testimony, an indictment was returned charging Mayor Chacharis, the sheriff, and more than twenty others with racketeering, obstruction of interstate commerce, and tax violations. Against my wishes, Mayor Chacharis was allowed to plead guilty to violations of the Internal Revenue Code, despite being the ringleader of a vast criminal enterprise. This directive came from headquarters in Washington, and I could do nothing about it. RFK had appeased Chacharis by allowing him to plead guilty to a violation of law. He resigned as mayor and served less than two years in prison. The others were not treated so lightly, for while some were given the option to plead guilty to tax violations, a majority had to plead guilty to racketeering or obstruction of interstate commerce.

Following the pleas of guilty and the handing down of prison sentences, I flew to Washington for a roundtable meeting between RFK and his attorneys from across the U.S. We each reported the work we had done thus far.

"We secured the indictment of Mayor Chacharis and many others in Lake County, Indiana," I said.

"Yeah, thanks a lot for that," Kennedy replied. "My brother was about to make him ambassador to Greece." Everyone in the room laughed.

"Just doing what you asked me to do, sir," I said with a smile.

"You keep this up, Goldberg," he said facetiously, "and my brother is going to put me on the Supreme Court."

His sense of humor validated for me that were good with one another. It was rough getting to where we were, much rougher than it had to be, but in the end, justice prevailed.

On February 2, 1963, the citizens of the Northwest District of Indiana, as well as the corporations responsible for my return, held a testimonial dinner in my honor. They presented me with a plaque that read:

"This special merit award is given to Jay Goldberg, acting U.S. Attorney for the Northwest District of Indiana, for his courage, dedication, and skill in rooting out crime and corruption in Northwest Indiana, making the area a safe and enjoyable place to raise children and bring it back to the high traditions for which Indiana is known."

They also presented me with a telegram they had received from District Attorney Hogan:

"It comes as no surprise that your honoree Jay Goldberg while serving as acting United States Attorney for the Northwest District of Indiana had performed extraordinarily well in exposing crime and corruption in Lake County, Indiana. I am so pleased that I recommended him to Attorney General Robert F. Kennedy, for he has fulfilled all that I expected."

It was mid-October 1963 when RFK and I met, now that my work was completed in Lake County, to decide if he needed my services any longer. Henry Petersen said it would be too risky to send me to Las Vegas to try to clean up the corruption there, for I could run into trouble from Frank Sinatra. And he was dead serious. Isn't that shocking, the power Frank Sinatra wielded? Shocking *and* disgusting, if you ask me.

So they turned their focus to Pittsburgh. It so happened that there was also a need for a "clean up" there, very similar to Gary. Rema and I moved to New Kensington, Pennsylvania, about twenty miles northeast of Pittsburgh, where we stayed for about a month. Through my investigation, which included talks with a much more cooperative FBI, we realized that the corruption likely, as in Gary, went through the mayor. That was when I'd decided the case wasn't for me; it was time to move on. Not only was I worried about the Kennedy brothers subjecting me to the same pressures that they had subjected me to in Gary, but I was growing weary of politics in general.

RFK said he understood, and he offered to send me to Buffalo instead where it was believed New York's biggest mobster, Stefano "The Undertaker" Magaddino, was living. Going after a mobster sounded intriguing, but Rema and I opened the newspaper, took one look at the weather in Buffalo, and immediately said no. Weather in New York City and Gary was rough, but Buffalo appeared to be of a different dimension. I told Kennedy that I felt it was time for me to head back to New York to start my own private practice, and he granted my request.

In late 1967, a Democratic contributor from New York hosted a celebration at a penthouse apartment in New York City in honor of Richard Hatcher, the new mayor of Gary, Indiana, who had been elected as the second black mayor of a major city. While RFK, then a senator from New York, was receiving plaudits from Hatcher for all he had accomplished for Lake County, RFK told the guests what he had failed to say to me in the intervening years: "The credit goes not to me, but to my then-assistant, Jay Goldberg."

I tipped my glass, a martini, to him. Kennedy was not only gracious that evening, but he showed a degree of warmth that had been missing in the early days of his tenure as attorney general. He was now on his way to be nominated for the presidency. Sadly, a year later, on June 6, 1968, everything ended in Los Angeles at the Ambassador Hotel when he was assassinated.

To say Kennedy was a complex man is an understatement. By 1966, three years after his brother's death, he'd undergone a personal transformation. His speeches contained stirring messages, appealing to the countries of the world for equality among men and women. The nation lost someone who had championed universal well-being and equality as he crisscrossed the country in support of his candidacy. He did not limit the power of his speech, for what is regarded as one of his most eloquent addresses was given in 1966 in Africa:

> "Hand in hand with freedom of speech goes the power to be heard, to share in the decisions of government which shape men's lives. Everything that makes man's life worthwhile—family, work, education, a place to rear one's children and a place to rest one's head—all this depends on the decisions of government; all can be swept away by a government which does not heed the demands

of its people, and I mean *all* of its people. Therefore, the essential humanity of man can be protected and persevered only where government must answer—not just to the wealthy, not just to those of a particular religion, not just to those of a particular race, but to all of the people."

His role as the nation's chief law enforcement officer, along with his commitment to politics and his brother, left him with numerous conflicts which he often found difficult to resolve. On the one hand, he helped advance the federal government's long-neglected fight against the threat from organized crime at a time when J. Edgar Hoover was still pre-occupied with communist threats, both real and imagined. On the other hand, his commitment to fighting organized crime and political corruption was sometimes seriously compromised by his political and familial loyalties.

I am grateful to the Kennedys for trusting Hogan, who trusted me to fill the role the Kennedys needed. Working for them may have been the most difficult job I've ever had, and I've defended some of the toughest criminals around. But the results were satisfying, and the opportunity propelled my career.

Before I left the Kennedys after turning down Buffalo, I had one piece of unfinished business. It wasn't something I had to do, but something I wanted to do.

I stopped into the FBI offices to say goodbye to J. Edgar Hoover.

I'd never met the man, but we of course knew who each other was. He was the guy who wouldn't help me in my effort to clean up Gary, and I was the unknown lawyer from New York hired by his nemesis. I don't know why I visited him—just to extend an olive branch, I guess. It was an easy call for me to make considering I felt I had an edge on him—I'd done my job successfully despite his wish to see me fail.

As I expected, he was gruff, and our meeting didn't last but a minute. There was no chitchat.

"I just wanted to stop in to wish you well," I said, as he stood and reluctantly shook my hand. He didn't care that I was there. No smile. Very little eye contact. Nothing. He was emotionless.

"Good luck to you," he said in a monotone voice.

He paused for a moment. Then he uttered five words that nearly knocked me to the floor in the same way a Rocky Graziano punch did many a time.

"You did a nice job."

It was lovely to hear. I don't know if he truly meant it, but he said it, so I accepted the praise.

"Thank you," I said. "And good luck to you."

There was an awkward moment of silence. I realized our extremely brief meeting was over, so I began to make my way toward the door.

"Hey Jay...here," he said. I turned around like the kid in the Coke commercial that was aired during the Super Bowl years later, when Mean Joe Greene calls to the young boy walking away and tosses the kid his jersey. Except Hoover wasn't my hero, and he wasn't holding a famous jersey. He was holding instead...

An autographed photo of himself?

He had pulled it from a stockpile he had in his desk drawer. This was evidently his thing to give to people who came to his office, which didn't seem big enough to hold his ego.

"Thank you," I said with a forced smile. "Well...have a good day."

The photo meant as much to me as I meant to him. I left his office with it, but I have no idea what I did with it after that. I'm not even sure it made it with me to my car. I've never seen it since.

RETURN TO
NEW YORK CITY

CHAPTER 11

CORRUPTION IN THE CITY

WHEN I RETURNED TO NEW York City, I opened my own practice, putting my skills to work in criminal defense law. I felt it was time to try to cash in on the legal skills I thought I had perfected in the military, the DA's office, Donovan's office, and while working for the Kennedys. None of those jobs paid much, certainly not commensurate with the work I had done. Plain and simple, now in my early thirties, it was time to make some money for my family.

While I did get a steady stream of everyday clients who needed my services, whether it was for a simple charge of writing a bad check or a more complex one like dealing drugs, my main focus was on a new uniform I had donned: that of "Masked Ostensible Law Enforcement Crusader." After returning Gary to a respectable civilized society, I found New York City, my hometown, was also a hub of corruption. This was before the Knapp Commission hearings, a panel formed in 1970 to investigate corruption within the New York City Police Department. Crime fighting and protecting the public weren't nearly as important as making money to certain members of the police force. If I had a narcotics case, the police officer would always, and I mean *always*, approach me to tell me how much money the client had to pay to beat the case. This was done with such a degree of frequency that it sickened me.

Eventually, the blatant corruption became too much for me to ignore. I took it upon myself, with nobody else's knowledge, to carry a briefcase wired for sound. I caught a number of detectives in the Special Narcotics Unit making bribe requests. The recording device I carried exposed me to a great deal of danger, but I could not accept such corruption.

Many people who hear me tell this story wonder what details I'm leaving out. Certainly the DA's office was aware of this. Or maybe a judge asked me to do it? I must have had a team of attorneys helping me. No, no, and no. I did this completely on my own. This was truly a one-man mission on my time and dime. I paid for the electronic equipment I needed to record them, and I knew what a risk it was to my personal safety and career, but I couldn't allow the corruption to continue. Would I have done this if I hadn't served in Gary? Probably not. But I now had the experience and, I guess one would say today, the swagger, to do it. I did it for an entire year and with no fear. My actions may have been illogical and irrational to some, but, from my view, absolutely necessary.

I didn't even tell Rema about it, probably the only thing in my life I have ever kept from her. While she supported me every which way, I worried that she might try to dissuade me because of the potential danger, and I didn't want anybody telling me what to do in this matter. How could I continue to seek justice for clients when there was no justice in the way the system they were going through was operating?

The closest call I had was when I was in the men's room one day and my hidden recording equipment was on. I had a beeper in my pocket, which at that time was a bulky instrument that was normally worn on the waist and could be mistaken for a gun...or tape recorder. As I was standing at the urinal, two cops walked in behind me. They happened to be two of the toughest cops in the department in terms of the number of arrests they had made over the years, and two of the biggest in physical stature. They feared no one, including attorneys.

When I finished my business, I walked over to the sink. That's when they made their move.

"You got a recording device on you?" one of them said as he shoved me forward, grabbed me around the waist, and frisked me. The other cop stood nearby, keeping one eye on me and one on the door.

"No," I said firmly.

"I don't believe you," he said.

"I've got nothing," I insisted.

The frisker pulled out the beeper.

"You better not be lying to me," he said.

"I'm not," I replied.

But I was.

The recorder was on and captured everything. It wasn't on me, though. It was in my briefcase, which was next to me on the tile floor. They never thought to look in there—I said they were big and tough, not smart. Had they found it, they would have taken my head, smashed it into the wall, destroyed my face with their fists, probably knocked out several teeth and broken a few bones, and nobody would have come to my aid. The cops would have claimed I slipped and there would have been no attempt to prosecute them. But I was too angry about all the wrongdoing to care.

"We're watching you," the frisker said. "One wrong move and you'll pay."

"I understand," I said, playing along with them.

After they left, I rushed the tapes of that incident straight to the district attorney's office. The detectives caught on the tapes were forced to resign, and they never laid another hand on me again.

From there, I turned my attention to the public morals squad. Yes, that was a real organization—a group of plainclothes officers who were responsible for arresting "alleged" homosexuals, bookmakers, and numbers runners. New York City is quite different now than it was in the '70s, isn't it? I recall police officers would hide behind the urinals at Grand Central Station to see whether a person was pleasuring himself while looking in the direction of others using the facilities, and then they would arrest him. They would also wait under areas of New York City bridges to try to entice persons they thought to be homosexuals.

Gambling was another moral they went after. They thought it to be so immoral that a special gambler's court was established. The values we now take for granted were completely at odds with those back then.

The "worst" of them all was law enforcement's campaign against materials thought to be obscene. Just to show what New York was like, in 1950, it was absolutely prohibited for a newspaper to show a picture of a woman with her navel exposed. I remember actress

Jane Greer appeared with her navel showing in an issue of the *Daily News,* and it was declared scandalous.

I was once approached for help by criminal Willie "The Ox" Cohen, who said that unless he paid protection money each week, officers were going to plant numbers and gambling records on him and then arrest him. Willie was brought to my office by the chief of staff for Congressman Leonard Farbstein, who Willie had gone to in an effort to put an end to the extortion he was suffering at the hands of the police. There was a great deal of tension in this investigation, for Hogan's chief assistant, Richard Kuh, and the chief inspector, Sydney Cooper, doubted the truth of the allegations. However, I was supported by assistant district attorney Joseph Stone, whom I knew well from our time cracking the quiz show case. He acknowledged the realities of corruption in the NYPD.

I convinced Hogan to have a plan where Willie would be given a sum of marked money, meet with the police officers whom he had accused, and then, after surveillance showed that the meeting concluded, the officers would be stopped and searched. The group waited in Hogan's office to see whether my view and Stone's view was correct. It was, for following the officers' meetings with Willie, they were stopped one by one, searched, and Willie's marked bills were found in their pockets.

Another problem was that police officers would often invariably pocket a piece of the money they found when executing search warrants. For example, if they seized 5,000 dollars, they would inventory only 1,000 dollars as seized. It was a well-known practice, but I saw the need to bring an action on behalf of defendant William Sawyer. He had been arrested and saw that only 1,000 of the 5,000 dollars he had on his person at the time of his arrest was reported in the inventory. This was big news in New York, for now I was striking at the moral fiber of members of the police department's narcotics squad. I was getting dangerously close to some pretty bad men. I remember one night leaving the courthouse on Centre Street in Manhattan.

"The only person who is going to get hurt in all of this is you!" shouted an NYPD lieutenant while leaning halfway out the window of a passing car.

I wasn't worried. My attitude was that if I could clean up Gary without getting hurt, I could do the same in New York City. So many cops woke up each day trying to figure out how they were going to make a score. That was what motivated them, and it is what motivated me to stop them.

During my investigations, which I was never afraid to talk about publicly due to the nature of what several of the men who were supposed to be protecting our citizens were doing, I received a notice from the New York City Bar Association Disciplinary Committee that I would be charged with a violation for commenting to the press on a pending case. The letter said my actions could prejudice a defendant's right to a fair trial. I had two weeks to respond or face disciplinary action, which could lead to a warning, suspension, or worse. I feared nothing and wrote back to the committee: "I will not answer your outrageous notice. I am doing a public service by exposing corruption, and the committee should be ashamed of itself for trying to thwart my efforts."

Lawyers are usually extra respectful to the committee, but I felt that I had a higher duty than the canon commanded. I never heard from them after sending them my response, but I did learn that several years later a federal judge had ruled this restriction on speaking to the press about a case was a restraint on freedom of speech, so broadly was it written.

Within a couple years I hadn't put an end to the public morals squad, but I had decimated it significantly. I did the same with the narcotics squad. Roughly fifty people had been indicted in all as a result of my labor. It was well worth the time and risk.

The fact that I wasn't killed is remarkable to many who hear my stories, but I wasn't surprised that I lived to tell about it. I don't know for sure why I wasn't physically harmed, but my guess is that it was because I was too much in the limelight. I went public with my discoveries of corruption, sending out press releases on a regular basis. Many people also knew that I wasn't far removed from successfully serving the U.S. Attorney General and his boss, the president of the United States. Anyone who harmed me probably figured they would have a very difficult time getting away with it because of the love people had for me and because of the connections I had to those in high places. I think that is why whoever filed the complaint against me with the Bar Association Disciplinary Committee went that route. They figured it could be an easy and discreet way to ruin my life without physically touching me. But they failed.

When I felt I'd gone as far as I could with it, I removed my "Masked Ostensible Law Enforcement Crusader" uniform and focused solely on defending clients. I had garnered so much press from my efforts to end corruption that my name was becoming well-known within the city, which led to numerous potential clients knocking on my office door. Some were everyday people. Others were well-known for their work in politics, the entertainment industry, athletics, or even the New York City mob. I had built a reputation for being tough, fearless, and often victorious in whatever or whomever I was representing, and word spread. This would become my life.

CHAPTER 12

THE CASE THAT STILL HAUNTS ME

I RECEIVED A CALL ONE day from the cable network program *Investigation Discovery*. They had reviewed the case described below and decided to give it a one-hour treatment. They felt the case had so many operatic themes that it would appeal to the viewing public. The crew had to travel from abroad, but they made it clear that they felt their efforts were justified. And so, we tell the story.

New Castle is a village in the northern-most part of Westchester, New York. It has a Main Street and is well populated. There is one prominent hill in the village. At the top of that hill is a house that is rumored by the local children to be haunted. Living there were the Nikcs, an Albanian family whose members always dressed in black. The family was made up of a father, mother, son, the son's wife Rigaletta, and their two young children. The Nikcs adhered to the principles of the *Kanun*, a strict set of traditional old-world Albanian laws which few of their countrymen still follow. It is filled with notions of revenge, retaliation, and violence. To modern Albanians, it is an unpleasant reminder of the past, but not so in the Nikc home.

Antonio Nikc (the son) and Rigaletta, came together in an arranged marriage. They had a daughter from their union, and another daughter thought by Antonio to be the result of an adulterous relationship that Rigaletta had had with Joseph Rukaj. Joe, who had an automobile dealership and also worked in construction, was a cousin of the Nikcs. He longed for Rigaletta when he saw her at family affairs, but he did not have the courage to speak to her. After all, she had no idea who he was and she was with her husband. The Nikcs were an established and wealthy family within the Albanian community. Joe's side of the family wasn't so fortunate, and he always felt terribly inadequate at the difference in their financial situations.

However, that all changed one day in an extraordinary way.

Joe had bought a New York State lottery ticket and he won—17.1 million dollars. The next time he saw Rigaletta at a family gathering, he confidently walked over, introduced himself, and told her of his good fortune. They spent a good deal of time talking. Joe was as handsome as any movie star, and gradually, he and Rigaletta talked so long that they arranged to meet at a restaurant in Manhattan. Their meetings became somewhat frequent. It was not long before Rigaletta became pregnant. Everybody knew the child was Joe's.

When the child was born (she was named Magdalena), Antonio treated her with scorn. Rigaletta repeatedly told Joe of the mistreatment his daughter had been receiving. Against Rigaletta's wishes, Joe brought an action in family court in Westchester County to establish paternity. It was expected that if it were shown that the child was his, he would seek custody. Rigaletta begged him not to go forward with the suit, for she expected that Antonio would take his vengeance out on her and the child. The commencement of the lawsuit was explosive news within the orthodox Albanian community. This was a community that was tightly knit and secretive.

A rift developed between Joe and Rigaletta after he filed suit. One day he called her sixteen times, threatening to come over to her home to take his daughter...and he apparently tried to follow through. Joe went to the Nikc home that same evening and took a gun with him. After driving up the long driveway to the top of the hill, he got out of his car and knocked on the door, but no one answered. He got back in his car and had just begun proceeding down the driveway when he saw Rigaletta emerge from a side entrance. Unbeknownst to Joe, Rigaletta had been convinced by the Nikcs that she had to follow one of the guiding principles of the *Kanun*, which in this case was that if one is in an adulterous relationship, to vindicate the honor of the family, she is required to kill her lover.

Joe stopped the car, stepped out, and walked towards Rigaletta. With her were Antonio and Antonio's father. Rigaletta, following the teachings of *Kanun*, shot Joe in the chest. Her father-in-law also approached Joe, but turned away when Joe fired his weapon. Joe fatally shot Rigaletta in the head and her father-in-law twice in the back. The whole episode lasted less than five seconds.

Conscious of his innocence and near death, Joe drove to the police station and told the officers what had happened, but nonetheless he was arrested and charged with the murder of Rigaletta and her father-in-law, along with attempted kidnapping.

The case was assigned to the chief county judge, who with others in law enforcement, was unsympathetic to Joe even though he was the first to be shot. A guy I knew who was a neighbor of Joe's called me to tell me about this "good man" who had been charged, and he asked me if I would represent him. Rema and I were literally on our way out the door of our home to go on vacation when he called. We canceled the vacation, and I headed up to Westchester. Such can be the life of an attorney.

Our defense plan was to argue that Joe acted in self-defense, and that for filing suit claiming he was Magdalena's father (which a DNA test later proved to be true), the Nikc family had plotted to kill him.

The trial began six months after the shooting. The prosecution was allowed—and I found it so unnecessary and prejudicial—to place in evidence a picture of Rigaletta, pretty as she was, lying on the autopsy table, unclothed, and with a small bulge in her stomach indicating that she had been pregnant when she was killed. The picture showed where the bullets had entered her body, which the medical examiner later said destroyed multiple organs. I know judges routinely allow such photographs to go into evidence, but I cannot see that it serves any purpose other than to prejudice the jury. After all, it was conceded that she was killed while pregnant. The photograph served to only inflame the jurors' emotions.

The case was of great importance to the Albanian community. Each day more than one hundred people came to the courtroom dressed in all black and sat behind the prosecutor. I asked that they be scattered throughout the well-attended courtroom so as to not prejudice the jury any further. The judge denied my request, and they all sat behind the prosecutor. The atmosphere in the courthouse was one of impending violence. On the bathroom door there were threats to defense counsel, which I ignored, but which caused other members of my team to ask for escorts in and out of the courthouse.

Joe wanted to testify on his own behalf. I counseled him not to because I really thought we had the case won, and I did not want the prosecution to have a chance to cross-examine him. Joe accepted my advice and decided not to testify.

Joe was acquitted of the kidnapping charge, and he was acquitted of the murder charge in the shooting of Rigaletta because she had fired at him first. However, he was convicted of murder in the second degree for shooting her father-in-law in the back. His punishment was twenty years to life in prison.

I have two regrets, one that I could have controlled and one that I could not.

The one I could have controlled was allowing Joe to testify, but I didn't even consider it because I didn't want the prosecutor to have a chance to question him. It is the route most defense attorneys will take in any case. It is one I took numerous times, especially with my mafia clients, because of their checkered pasts. But if a defendant stands the risk of a conviction with a serious penalty and is ultimately convicted without being allowed to testify, he will do his sentence always believing that the lawyers ruined his chances of him convincing the jurors of his innocence. I don't know that allowing Joe to testify would have changed the outcome, but we'll never know. I have no doubt he spent twenty years wondering what might have been.

The regret I could not control, and something I believe should be changed within our legal system, is that jurors are not told before a trial what the punishment could be. I am convinced that the jury thought they were doing Joe a favor by acquitting him of the murder of Rigaletta and only convicting him of killing the father-in-law. Yes, he could have received forty years to life instead of the sentence of twenty years to life he was dealt. But had they known how long he could possibly be incarcerated for a conviction of killing just one of the two people, would they have convicted him? Don't we want our jurors to be fully versed when dealing with someone's life?

Regarding what I could have controlled, I urge all attorneys that if a defendant is accused of a crime in which he could get a stiff penalty and he believes he can tell a story supporting innocence, consider letting him tell it. Don't necessarily follow the standard unwritten rule among lawyers that he shouldn't. If he feels so strongly about his innocence, especially if he has no criminal past, taking the stand could be the best action.

There were so many victims in this case, but none more than Magdalena. I have often wondered what her life was like after the verdict. She was left with a dead mother, an imprisoned father, Antonio who had treated her harshly, and the rest of the Nikc family who considered her an outsider.

I could see how upset Joe was with me after the verdict, and I couldn't blame him. What if I had let him testify?

What if. What if. What if.

It was a heartbreaking case, one that continues to haunt me.

CHAPTER 13

MISS AMERICA, HER CONSORT, AND A SUPREME COURT JUSTICE ON CRIMINAL TRIAL

NORMAN LISS, A WELL-REGARDED PERSONAL injury lawyer and a close friend of mine—the one who witnessed my door-kicking episode when I was campaigning for state senate—attended a ceremony at the U.S. District Court for the Southern District in Manhattan in late 2014, marking the 225th anniversary of what is known as the "Mother Court." Liss told me each member of the panel was asked to share the most interesting case they covered. Irene Cornell, who has covered the courts as a reporter for more than forty years, said that the most interesting case she covered was the Bess Myerson case, specifically noting my humor-laced closing argument.

The criminal cases in which I have been the defense attorney are numerous, many of them notable, but if I had to pick one case that best held the attention of the public, it would have to be my defense of Bess Myerson, the first Jewish Miss America, who won the crown in 1945.

Jennifer Preston wrote a wonderful book on Bess Myerson and what made her tick, entitled *Queen Bess*. Preston wrote that Bess was determined not to disappear into obscurity following her reign. But, behind her glittering public image was a different, darker Bess who led anything but a storybook life. She was a woman wrecked by insecurities, who divorced three times, whose destructive love affairs were marred by an obsessive jealousy, with one husband beating her. She was twice arrested for petty shoplifting despite her personal fortune estimated to be in the millions. She came to be involved with a millionaire sewer contractor named Carl Andrew (Andy) Capasso. He was twenty years her junior. Despite her public persona, her life was one of loneliness. She was desperate and searching for love and acceptance, driven by the will to satisfy Andy in any way she knew possible. The story of Bess, Andy, and Justice Gabel is best recited, covered, and analyzed by Jennifer.

Bess was a close friend of New York City Mayor Ed Koch, who appointed her commissioner of the Department of Cultural Affairs. At one point, she had been considered as the Democratic candidate for the U.S. Senate, but ill health and her hospitalization ended that effort. Bess was not new to the public eye, however. After becoming the first Jewish Miss America, she faced discrimination because of her religion from sponsors who usually hired the reigning Ms. America to endorse their products. Bess was strong-willed and stood up for what she believed was right. Following her victory she embarked on a six-month lecture tour for the Anti-Defamation League.

Bess met Andy when he came to the hospital with Mayor Koch to visit her. It was thought that Bess had had a stroke, but she ended up being fine. Bess found Andy enormously attractive, and hoped that upon her release from the hospital she would be able to start a relationship with him. Andy was a wealthy sewer contractor in New York City and, to me, a double for Sylvester Stallone. Frankly, I could not understand how this man, years younger, could be so attractive to Bess when he was often given to using four-letter words. I thought Bess would find that offensive, as she always acted with grace and class. But, Bess nevertheless started a relationship with Andy.

The problem was that Andy was married.

When Mrs. Capasso learned of the affair, she filed for divorce and asked for temporary maintenance and child support. The case was assigned to the well-respected New York Supreme Court Justice, Hortense Gabel. Justice Gabel had been a foremost leader and advocate of women's rights, and she was highly regarded by all members of the bar. If one had to compile a list of the most influential, honorable, and intelligent justices, she would have been at the very top.

Notable in the judge's personal life was her troubled daughter, who adopted the name Sukhreet because she heard it used while on a trip in India, and who would become a focal point in the Bess Myerson case. Many considered Sukhreet to be mentally ill. She could often be seen walking down the street with a parrot on her shoulder. Despite all efforts by Justice Gabel, friends considered Sukhreet unemployable given her psychological state.

In Andy's case, Justice Gabel awarded his ex-wife 1,850 dollars a week in temporary maintenance and child support. Andy was beside himself, believing the award was clearly excessive.

After hearing Andy complain so much about the temporary award, it was alleged that Bess believed if she were to hire Justice Gabel's daughter Sukhreet as a cultural affairs assistant, Justice Gabel might, on re-argument, reduce the amount that Andy would have to pay. It was alleged there were meetings between Bess and Justice Gable, in which Bess asked Justice Gable to reduce the weekly maintenance. Justice Gabel did indeed reduce the award to an amount that satisfied Bess and Andy. Andy's wife and her lawyers believed there was something fishy about this, considering that Bess had hired Sukhreet to be her assistant. Her lawyers believed that Justice Gabel, along with Bess and Andy, had conspired to obstruct justice.

The U.S. Attorney, Rudolph Giuliani, sensing the high potential the case had for publicity (he was absolutely right, for the publicity was enormous), approved a prosecution and brought charges of bribery and obstruction of justice following the reduction of the order of temporary maintenance and child support.

Few cases match the pretrial leaks and negative allegations released either by Giuliani or the FBI. This continued for six months leading up to the trial. The case came to be known in the press as the "Bess Mess." Bess added to this in a terrible way when she was arrested for shoplifting while in Pennsylvania, an action that certainly must have prejudiced her in the eyes of the public.

To make matters even worse, retired federal Judge Harold Tyler had been commissioned by Mayor Koch to conduct an investigation into whether the parties were guilty or not. He concluded that they were guilty. This was widely publicized by the government before the trial. Have you ever heard of such a thing? The circus was well into motion.

Bess and Andy were both long-time friends of mine. I had been introduced to Bess many years earlier at a social function, and we continued to stay in touch. When they came to me for guidance, I opted to represent Andy. I could have chosen any lawyer in the city to represent Bess, as representation would have given them enormous publicity. I chose Fred Hafetz, who had served as chief of the criminal division of the U.S. Attorney's Office for the Southern District. He was known as a dogged prosecutor and defense lawyer whose cross-examinations were the talk of the town. The cross-examinations were so intense and powerful that I swear I once saw him tongue-tie a witness with a single question—and that question was "What is your name and address?" Few lawyers would work so hard on a given case as Hafetz. He worked seven days a week.

The normal way a jury is selected in a case of this kind would be for one hundred people to be called into the courtroom, and the judge would question the panel as a whole as to whether they thought they could be fair, despite whatever they had read or heard from the media. Using this method, the attorneys would then select the jury. Unlike state court practice, in which jury selection is more thorough, the standard federal practice does not afford lawyers a sound opportunity on which to make a considered judgment. Judge Keenan, however, in light of the negative publicity, decided to call each person into the jury room individually and question them as to whether they could be fair and impartial. The fairness of Judge Keenan in adopting this procedure demonstrated his strong sense of justice.

To help us select the jury, I decided to enlist the services of Rema, a career counselor and professional jury consultant. I had used her expertise many times before, and her success rate in selecting jurors was impeccable. If you are ever around my wife and think maybe you can slip something past her, don't bother. You will only make a fool of yourself. Her sixth sense about people is unlike anything I have ever witnessed.

The judge went through the potential jurors one by one, eventually getting to Person 35.

"She's the one!" Rema said in a quiet but excited voice to Andy. "She is your juror."

"Really?" he said. "Why?"

"She will fall in love with you. There's no way she will ever convict you."

The potential juror was a young Italian girl who looked impressionable.

"I disagree," Andy said. "History has shown that only Jewish women like me."

"I have to agree with Andy," one of the attorneys on our team said.

"Same here," another one stated.

But, since I was the paymaster—and henpecked as well—I had come to believe in my wife's judgment.

"We're going with 35," I said without any further discussion.

Person 35 was selected and seated as juror number 6.

The trial proceeded for two months. Immediately prior to deliberations, Judge Keenan moved juror number 6 into the position of foreperson. If Rema's intuition was correct, which I was certain it was, this could only be good for us.

The government put forth a very strong case. They portrayed Bess as an arrogant public official and a greedy mistress. They claimed that her obsession with Andy led to her abusing her position by hiring Sukhreet, all in an effort to reduce Andy's child support and maintenance payments. Judge Gabel was painted as a once proud judge who betrayed her position out of a desire to help her daughter when she reduced Andy's required payments. Andy, of course, was painted as the beneficiary of Bess's obsession with him.

The case was a real tearjerker, for Justice Gabel had sacrificed her reputation for the benefit of her unemployable child. And what was the payback? Sukhreet claimed that she fell in love with one of the government investigators working on the case. She wore a body recorder, taping her mother's conversations at dinner, and later testified against her. She said she was writing a book. On cross-examination I offered her a title: *Daughter Dearest*. It was a play on words from Joan Crawford's daughter's recently published book *Mommie Dearest*. Following the conclusion of the court day, the *New York Post* had a full page picture of Sukhreet leaving the court with the headline "Daughter Dearest."

Fred Hafetz, lending his enormous technical skills, cross-examined Sukhreet most effectively, and he gave an extraordinary summation for Bess. He looked at no notes. My faith in him was justified, for no one could have asked for a better co-counsel. We were a wonderful combination. Fred was intense. I, on the other hand, lent humor to the trial, for there were aspects of the government's case that cried out for it. The government likes to have an atmosphere comparable to a wake, but I strongly believe in a quote from Mark Twain: "A laughing jury seldom convicts."

Shirley Harrod testified for the government. She was an admirer of Andy's ex-wife, and had served as the couple's cook. She testified that she and her husband overheard incriminating statements, for they would stand by the door to the dining room and listen to the conversations between Bess and Andy while they were eating. She did this on multiple occasions. She was skillfully cross-examined by Haftez and, when I cross-examined her, she acknowledged her behavior.

"Mrs. Harrod," I said, "do you enjoy listening to people while they masticate?"

There was a gasp from the gallery. The judge leaned forward, stunned by what I had said. The jury was wrapped in attention. Exactly the reactions I had expected.

"Whoa!" I exclaimed as I raised my hands to the judge. "I said 'masticate.' It means 'to chew.'"

The jury burst into laughter, and the judge allowed the question. You must remember that those selected for jury service are generally as nervous as the defendant. The government does little to recognize this, but it is important for the defense lawyer to be aware of this. Humor can often be appealing, provided the lawyer has the talent to deliver it, and it is appropriate to the occasion. I lent a light feel to the case when appropriate, bringing out as many humorous points as I could. Some jurors seemed to be waiting for my cross-examinations, as they appeared to be sleeping until I took the podium to begin.

Of course, I dealt with the points in the case that did not call for humor as well. Neither Bess nor Andy testified. Justice Gabel, who did not testify, offered character witnesses who all testified to her pristine record, high reputation, and integrity. I also convinced Sukhreet one day to come to court and sit behind her mother. Why did she agree to do it? I don't know. Her emotional instability, maybe. Or maybe she felt guilty for what she had done to her mother. I believed a juror could take her presence as a sign of sympathy she had for her mother, even if Sukhreet were there hoping to witness a conviction. Either way, my judgment could not be assailed. Repeatedly during summation, I turned the jury's attention to Sukhreet and attacked her for her actions, also pointing out her supposed "love" for the government investigator.

Everything aspect of our case went exactly as we had hoped.

In the end, our clients were acquitted.

When we all retreated to the robing room after the verdict, the judge turned to the government lawyers and paid me one of the most beautiful compliments I'd ever received: "Goldberg just laughed the case right out of the court." See the December 15, 1988 article by Howard Kurtz published in *The Washington Post*, "At Myerson Trial, A Harvest of Scorn," regaling the ready with our humorous summation.

We walked out of the courthouse into a sea of media lights from network vehicles. It was evening, but the lights were so bright that if you did not look at your watch you would have mistakenly thought it was the middle of the afternoon. We were obviously thrilled with the outcome and happy to answer as many questions as the media had. Victory always makes the spotlight much more tolerable.

A week after the return of the verdict, Rema and I were at home when our phone rang. She answered.

"Mrs. Goldberg?" the sweet-sounding voice on the other end said.

"Yes?"

The woman gave her name. Rema couldn't quite place it.

"I'm juror 6," she said.

"Oh, hi," Rema said, obviously surprised.

"Would you mind if we got together for lunch one day soon? I would like to talk to you about something."

Rema agreed. And while most of us might expect the meeting would have something to do with the verdict of the trial or something related to it, Rema knew that wasn't it at all. When they met for lunch, the juror validated Rema's hunch from when the jurors were selected.

"Do you think you could possibly fix me up with Andy?" the juror asked.

It blew my mind when Rema came home and told me about it. I never doubted my wife's instincts; she had a track record for picking jurors that was unmatched. But to be so specific as to say that one particular juror would actually romantically fall for our client—how could anyone be *that* good at something so subjective? But she was, and there is still today nobody better at it.

For the record, Rema presented the juror's feelings to Andy, but he politely declined to get involved. He was grateful for what the juror had done for him, but that was as close to her as he cared to get.

There can be no greater compliment paid to me than that received from Fred Hafetz when he wrote on January 31, 2018, "I always say: I am greatly indebted to you for how much I learned from you about the courtroom and being a trial lawyer."

As I look back at the case, there were so many memorable moments, but it was the humor that stood out and (in my opinion and the judge's opinion) won the case, especially the summation that I will share with you in a moment. Despite what some attorneys may think, humor, sarcasm, and wit do have a place in the courtroom. We are taught that since serious matters are dealt with in court, a degree of decorum is expected and humor is the antithesis of what one should expect. But I believe otherwise.

Socrates wrote "know thyself," an aphorism that must be a guiding principle for the lawyer who intends to use humor. Many attorneys think they are funny based on the reactions they receive in social settings. But do they have the skill to be able to carry this trait of humor into the courtroom? Do they have the requisite insight? Some do, some do not. And not all cases are ripe for humor. But many are, at least at some point during the trial.

The Bess Myerson case could not be allowed to proceed with solemnity; there were so many places where humor, sarcasm, and wit could effectively be used, which is the last thing a prosecutor wants.

Though it can be difficult to see humor through the printed word, the following are excerpts of my closing argument in the Bess Myerson trial. For the sake of space, I have included the beginning and the end, where the humor is most evident. Professor Joel Seidemann, in his book *In the Interest of Justice*, named this summation one of the "ten finest summations of the past hundred years." *The New York Times* described it as "filled with sarcastic humor that ridiculed the prosecution's case."

This is the only time that the law provides me an opportunity to share with you and reason together with you. The law, in its wisdom, provides government counsel with an opportunity to speak with you two times.

If you search the record in this case, you will conclude that, despite the presence of a staff of three prosecutors and an investigation that commenced two and a half years ago, the prosecutors have failed in their obligation to present solid proof to a point beyond a reasonable doubt, and thus, it matters not one bit to me that they have two chances to speak to you, because two times zero will still turn out to be zero.

It has been said by a legal scholar that the most effective tool in the search for truth is cross-examination. It is so easy to prepare a witness during rehearsal sessions, and then put him on as a windup toy, asking questions that have been rehearsed, but it's the art of cross-examination that's designed to search out the truth.

I stand here on behalf of one person, Andy Capasso. Stripped to its essentials, the charge in this case is that a scheme supposedly existed to victimize the City of New York of money that was paid to Sukhreet Gabel for her employment at the Department of Cultural Affairs from the period of August '83 to June of '84. The second falsely claimed victim is Nancy Capasso, who through the restructured order of Justice Gabel, lost temporary maintenance.

This million-dollar federal case involves a claim when reduced to its essentials that, through the restructured order of Justice Gabel in September of 1983, this supposed victim, Nancy Capasso, lost—and properly so, you will conclude—the grand sum, considering City, State, and federal taxes, of less than 500 dollars a year.

The claim is that the city was victimized and Nancy Capasso was victimized for the reason that Justice Gabel, in rendering her decision of September 13, 1983, was corrupted because a job had been given to her daughter.

In our system we have two sets of judges. Judge Keenan is supreme on the law. No one here may question that. When he rules, that is the law of this case. But just as he is supreme, so too you, as the jury, are supreme within your sphere. You are what we call the "supreme judges of the facts."

When you think that you as a group exercise the power to decide the fate, the future of three people, that you hold that enormous power in your hands, you understand that it is no overstatement to say that for you this is an extraordinary occasion.

A doctor may operate on a patient. When you deliberate, you will be operating on the lives and future and fate of three people. That's the heavy responsibility that you have as the supreme judges of the facts.

When you analyze the thirty-four witnesses in this case, and the thirty-five trial days, you will be convinced that the government sought to divert your attention from their lack of proof. They gave you so much smoke and dust that you have to ask yourself: Why was it necessary that we hear this proof? What desperation was there on the part of these adversaries that caused them to present this kind of material to us that has no real bearing on the issues in this case?

Was it important, for example, for you to know through the testimony of Sukhreet Gabel that Bess Myerson tried on

Nancy Capasso's bathing suits? Or that Bess Myerson threw out Nancy Capasso's potted plants? That was some part of the proof in this case.

How important was it that you learned that for a time Bess Myerson didn't want people to know that she was sleeping—this is the eighties, now—she was sleeping with Andy Capasso, that she used to make it appear that she slept in Herbie's room [Herbert Rickman, a frequent visitor to Capasso's home], she ruffled his bed, and when guests came—remember that—she ran out the back door, and then came in the front door? What was the purpose that the government brought this out?

Or that Bess, over a lifetime of sixty-four years, she had accumulated enough jewelry to fill a box?

Well, aside from the proof being that Bess was a millionairess, it was the burden she carried from being selected Miss America forty years ago. The government felt that it might prejudice you, that it might divert your attention, and so they developed it for you. But wait, was it key to have Sukhreet testify that Bess Myerson fell on a tennis court? He [the prosecutor] even has it on his chart: "Bess Myerson fell on the tennis court." Sukhreet Gabel says she witnessed it; Bess bruised her knee. And the prosecutor went to the trouble of making an entry to that effect on his chart, so important was it to his case.

Was it important that Andy Capasso gave gifts to Bess as he courted her? I would suspect this proves he is a decent human being—a breath of fresh air, a witness said. He gave the same gifts to Nancy Reese Herbert [Nancy Capasso was married to Mr. Howard Herbert before marrying Andy Capasso] after she spotted him the first time in the trench outside her house digging a sewer, as she sipped her coffee after the children had gone off to school.

Was it really important to Mr. David Lawrence, [the prosecutor] that Mayor Ed Koch thought that Mr. Capasso's home was an estate? Do you remember that?

He put the question to the honorable mayor: "Now, at the estate of Mr. Capasso..." That was the question, when the mayor interrupted him and said, "No, hold it." You see, the fatal flaw committed by Mr. Lawrence, if I may be so bold as to correct him on trial strategy, is that one question earlier he had said to the mayor, "Did you know the housekeepers?"—obviously the Harrods—and the mayor, obviously—I know his head—the mayor, obviously thinking back on Andy's steady offering of hamburgers, hot dogs, macaroni salad, that he had gotten at the hands of the Harrods, said to himself, "Listen, this was no estate. This was a home. I've gotten better meals at Popeye's, Forty-fourth Street and Eighth Avenue."

Throughout, there was a steady effort to divert you. We were locked in a pursuit of trivial matters in this federal court.

Why was it necessary? Because when you don't have proof of the charges, you have to rely on this smoke and dust, these diversionary issues. But you have to spot what the government is doing and realize the purpose.

You know, ladies and gentlemen, at least in Brooklyn, where I grew up, there was an expression: "Don't make a federal case out of it." It was meant to suggest, don't take something and turn it into some big deal, a federal case. This is what you have before you.

Nancy Capasso, through the structured order [Judge Gabel's revised order]—pity poor Nancy, having lived in a state of royalty, by her own declaration, she has suffered, as I have said, for a justifiable reason, to the extent, after federal taxes, of reduction of 578 dollars [per year] and we are here.

[The prosecutor asked] Mayor Koch, "Did Bess Myerson tell you that she was going to hire Sukhreet Gabel?" Was there any showing that any commissioner ever has to clear with Edward I. Koch before they hire some assistant? All this was asked, I suggest, in bad faith.

Aside from my observation that there is this smoke and dust diversionary material thrust at you, I make also the observation that this case had an inordinate amount of biased, disgruntled, disturbed people, who the government used to try to make up for its lack of proof, witnesses who—well, in the old vaudeville days when a person performed very badly from the side of the stage, there would be a hook, and the person would be whisked right off the stage. I don't know if you people are this old, but there was Amateur Hour with Major Bowes, when a person would perform, and if the performance was utterly terrible, he would ring a bell, and off the person would go. Then, in the seventies, you remember we had The Gong Show. When a person was on center stage and was really bad, Chuck Barris—remember?—gong, and that was the end of the performance.

This is the only new addition I can make to the court structure, that jurors should have at their chair a button that could sound the gong. I'm going to give you a few as we go along. You see if I overstate it.

You see, so much of this case, I told you thirty-four witnesses, had so little to do with Andy Capasso, I examined by my own count about five or six out of the thirty-four, and, quite frankly, I don't know whether I examined those witnesses because they were really relevant to Andy Capasso or [because] I wanted my picture drawn by the artists [i.e. courtroom sketch artists].

How and why were we here, and what were we doing? What TV or daytime serial could I put this case into?

The first one that came to my mind early in the trial was the dispute [concerning] Nancy's claim that her potted plants had been wrongly discarded and her bathing suit had been used. That was a perfect case for Judge Wapner. Any question about that? That clearly was a People's Court case.

But with Shirley Harrod you had the PBS program, right? Upstairs, Downstairs. Look what Shirley Harrod told you. She was the first one for which the gong would be in order.

She would have you believe that she and her husband, Ray Harrod, were fired because they supposedly listened at the breakfast room door during Bess and Andy's meal to conversations between Bess and Andy when Mrs. Harrod swore that was not her purpose. Of course not. She just wanted to see them masticate. Wait a minute, that means chew.

You heard about Sukhreet Gabel's hospitalization, her fifteen shock treatments and her care by a psychopharmacologist. And then you had that sterling special assistant Herbert Rickman's a hypochondriac, right? His fear, according to [FBI] Agent St. Germain, that he is in the beginning stages of Alzheimer's disease. As soon as he got up to be cross-examined, he [Rickman] had to run to the toilet up back and forth several times.

I said to myself all this took on shades of General Hospital. The government didn't need a paralegal like Joan Alexander; rather, it could have used a paramedic.

And even the defendants were part of it, too. Justice Gabel had suffered a heart attack, she had been hospitalized for a stroke. Bess Myerson had endured ovarian cancer, chemotherapy, and a stroke herself.

What a tragedy that we are here because Nancy Capasso has sold the government on a bill of goods that just won't hold up.

And, finally, David Lawrence, stood up here, my learned and esteemed adversary, and he had the mayor on the witness stand, and there had to be the same showing of concern by the government to the mayor for having made the walk over from City Hall. Do you remember David Lawrence standing here and saying, "Mayor, how is your health? And state to us, how are you feeling?"

That had to be the mayor's consideration for having walked over. But I nonetheless objected, concerned as I was that, desperate as the government is to bring Andy Capasso into this case, who the heck knew whether the mayor's elevated cholesterol and his stroke might somehow be related to the hamburgers, hot dogs, and macaroni salad.

Luckily for me, the judge sustained my objection.

That's where we were in this case. I make the following observation to you. Never has so much time—thirty-four days, thirty-five, thirty-six days—so much energy, and taxpayers' money, charts, agents, and the like been spent on such trivial pursuits, such diversionary issues, while bringing to you such little proof to support the government's case.

We had no chance to confront Nancy Capasso. Of course, I could have subpoenaed her, but who wants her? Lucky Mr. Herbert [her first husband]. Unlucky Mr. Capasso. What could have set her off to cause her to orchestrate this case? This gives you some idea of it. Let me read you what she says:

"Over the years the children and I have had unlimited charges and credit-card privileges with American Express, two cards, Visa, Diners Club, Hertz, Avis, gasoline charges, Bergdorf Goodman, Bonwit Teller, Martha's, Henri Bendel, Bloomingdales, Tiffany, Saks, Altman's, Paul Stuart, Balducci—food got in there David Webb Jewelers, the Palm Restaurant. We also for the past eight years had two full-time live-in maids and part-time help once a week when we went to Westhampton or Florida. We purchased numerous works of art, just one recently at Sotheby's for 192,000 dollars. When I say that our entire family lived in a style of royalty."

This is what Capasso said about himself, and [Nancy] agrees with it:

"I took over the expenses as well as the parental responsibility of raising all three of those children through their minority and acted in the capacity of their father. So far as almost every aspect of their upbringing was concerned, I fed, I clothed, housed, educated, and loved those children in every way a father could do and then some."

I remember there was testimony that he participated and learned the Jewish prayers for the bar mitzvah of Nancy and Herbert's child, the eldest boy, but he is to be destroyed on a complaint that she falsely makes. Because of 500 dollars. This princess. Denied royalty. She didn't learn the lesson that the Revolutionary War was fought for, so there would be no royalty. What arrogance.

Nancy Capasso had lived in a style of royalty. She couldn't get along two million dollars and 358,000 dollars a year. Poor, poor Nancy. What a victim.

There was clear testimony that Justice Gabel from the outset felt that she had granted Nancy Capasso too much money based on these papers. By early- to mid-August, well before Sukhreet Gabel was hired, the judge had drafted at least four decisions, drafts of decisions, in which she had decided to restructure the award for the benefit of the children.

So it wasn't, as the government says, a quid pro quo, a job to the daughter on August 29, the reduction on September 14. The judge by mid-August had gone through four drafts in this monumental, unique case.

For Andy Capasso to be found guilty of these substantive counts, you would have to conclude that Andy Capasso counseled, advised, directed, the hiring of Sukhreet Gabel. Strong words. A very simple challenge: Don't come back with charts, Mr. Prosecutor. [The prosecutor presented various charts in his summation.] Tell these jurors, read them a page reference, where this jury can glean for itself that Andy Capasso ever knew of or, if he knew of, that he didn't say, "Bess, I think you and Rickman...I think it is a stupid thing to do."

If Mr. Abrams [the prosecutor] had to list on a chart the references on the record that he says show that Andy Capasso advised, counseled, commanded, the hiring of Sukhreet Gabel, it would be an empty chart.

There were two mistakes in judgment. There was a mistake in judgment when Bess Myerson publicly hired

Sukhreet Gabel and when she wrote her letter to the mayor when she realized there was an appearance of impropriety and she sought to cover it.

[Myerson instructed her assistant, Richard Bruno, to write a letter to Mayor Koch falsely claiming that the hiring of Sukhreet Gabel was routine and was done after all the rulings were made in the Capasso divorce.]

But we are not trying a case of appearances of impropriety, or misconduct, we are trying a case where you are going to have to decide whether the person who engaged in that conduct is one who acted with a corrupt intent.

There is no proof whatsoever with respect to Andy Capasso. There is another mistake in judgment, and it rests with this table [the prosecution table]. They made a mistake in judgment because they bought the case from Nancy Capasso, and then they brought it but they didn't inspect the ship. They would have seen the holes in it. If they had examined Nancy and Felder [Nancy's lawyer], they would have realized that the judge had reached out perhaps for a favor, as she did with Felder, but that didn't mean she was corrupt when she made her June decision. They didn't adequately do their homework.

Bess Myerson, besides putting her, as noted, on the public payroll, filed a planned action report with Joe DiVincenzo, at the Office of Management and Budget a notice containing her name, notified the Department of Personnel, and introduced her openly around. If this was a scheme, Bess could have said to herself, "Listen, this is too conspicuous. There's got to be a better way. Andy Capasso has a lot of money. Let's do it another way." But that wasn't her program, that wasn't her plan, and it certainly wasn't her doing.

If one looked at it now with the benefit of hindsight, one would say, "Don't do it, don't do it, Bess. It wouldn't look good."

But you see, Judge Gabel was not someone who was new to Bess Myerson. The proof is the opposite. Marcella

Maxwell [Director of New York City Commission on Human Rights] says that they were friends for at least twenty years.

In 1986, these gentlemen [the prosecutors], anxious to make a case—because the papers tell you this is a high-publicity case, there is a lot of gold, perhaps, emotionally at the end of the rainbow if they get a wrongful verdict, a lot of publicity—they take this disturbed girl in [Sukhreet Gabel], a girl who by 1986 has a self-confessed love-hatred relationship with her parents and Bess Myerson, a girl who has no friends, who uses the 1,800 dollars a month allowance that her parents—her eighty-year-old father and her seventy-odd-year old mother—send her all for her medication, so she is on heavy medication, they take this woman, without the benefit of counsel, knowing that Hortense Gabel is impaired by having a suffered a stroke and been hospitalized for weeks, and they put her up to taping her own parents; her mother, blind, ailing from a stroke.

There's got to be a level of decency below which even an advocate will not sink in a quest to make a case. It is ugly. And they knew what they were doing. One guy playing Mr. Good Guy, Tony Lombardi [government investigator], David Lawrence playing Mr. Tight-Ass—that's what she [Sukhreet Gabel] said. They knew they were doing the good guy/bad guy approach on this disturbed woman in 1986, without medication, without counsel, and they take her forty-four times, and they move her and manipulate her, take her to an empty courtroom and tell her how to dress, and put her on the witness stand for dry runs, and what are they doing? In effect giving her a forum for the unfair destruction of her parents.

Ladies and gentlemen of the jury, you don't have those two weeks. You are going to have to make a decision. Suppose you don't hesitate to rely on the word of Sukhreet Gabel, and two weeks from now you find that she opened on Broadway at the Belasco taking over from Jackie Mason in The World According to Sukhreet Gabel. It could happen.

And you find out that everything she told [that] bunch of suckers was not true. It is too late for you. There is nothing you can do. She tells you, "I cannot assure you that what I say today wouldn't change in two weeks." That alone destroys her.

She says she sometimes mistakes what she thinks might have happened for what really happened. "Oh, dear, am I making this up?" She says that following shock treatment, she had memory derangement and that her mind and her memory [are] like Swiss cheese, full of holes.

The question was asked: "It is correct, is it not, that from a deposition transcript of June 17, 1987, you acknowledge perjury in your grand-jury appearance?" "That is correct." Question: "No question about it?" "No question about it." So this is a woman who gave false testimony in the grand jury. Mr. Lawrence asks Sukhreet Gabel in the grand jury, "Is there anything you told us today or on prior occasions that is inaccurate or untruthful?" Now we know in this session she has lied. Look how she tells Mr. Lawrence, and the grand jury, something that we now know was a lie:

"I want to answer you with the utmost seriousness. Never, on no occasions, have I either omitted information or confused information. I am conscious of the oath I took to tell the truth, and nothing but the truth, and the meaning of those words, and to the best of my knowledge, from the bottom of my heart, I told you every bit of truth that I know. I have never told you an inaccuracy or untruth on purpose."

She doesn't touch on Andy Capasso, but, by God, if the test of reasonable doubt is whether a prudent person would hesitate to act in matters of importance in their own lives, and the government comes to you and says, "Don't hesitate, rely on her word," how can you in good conscience fail to do that?

The prosecutors, in their quest to make a case, struck blows so low that they scuffed their knuckles on pavement. They weren't below the belt; they hit the floor.

This is not a civil case. This is a criminal case in which things much more important than money are at stake, and so the law imposes this enormous responsibility on these gentlemen and lady at the bar. They must prove their case to a point beyond a reasonable doubt, and if, after looking at this case, you say to yourself, "Well, I think this happened or maybe this happened or it might have happened, but there is no proof in this record beyond a reasonable doubt," your duty becomes crystal clear.

Knowing what you now know, if you find yourself hesitating to believe that the government has presented solid proof that a scheme existed to bribe Justice Gabel or that Andy Capasso sought to reduce the awards other than through lawful efforts; if you find yourself hesitating to believe that the government has proven beyond a reasonable doubt a plan to bribe Judge Gabel or that one would be envisaged, given her standing in the community, or that she would forsake a lifetime of dedicated service; if you find yourself hesitating to believe the group—I call it the bevy, the bunch of bitter, biased, disturbed, and disgruntled people called by the prosecutor—that hesitation on your part will be the key to your finding of reasonable doubt and to the mandate of acquittal of these defendants.

Grieve not one moment for the fact that he spent a lot of money and time on their charts, or that every morning they wheel in their cart and all these exhibits. Grieve not one moment for them, because, you see, the local United States Attorney's office is part of a much bigger operation called the United States Department of Justice in Washington with its headquarters, and over the entrance to that building are the words that are at the heart of our system of justice, and those words are that "the government of the United States, the people of our country, never lose a case despite an acquittal, so long as justice is done."

Recognizing that our system is a unique contribution to the science of government, your careful scrutiny of this record, free of conjecture, surmise, prejudice, editorialized charts, will lead you to conclude that Andy Capasso and these defendants are entitled to an acquittal, a verdict of not guilty.

Bess Myerson died on December 14, 2014. She was still so well-known that her death was widely covered in two full-page articles on separate days by *The New York Times*.

THE DONALD'S QUEST
FOR A SO-CALLED
KILLER LAWYER

CHAPTER 14

DONALD TRUMP... MY FIRST MATRIMONIAL CASE

"There has never been a lawyer more important to me than you. *It is very important to me that you know that.*" [On D.J. Trump's personal stationary to me, emphasis his – January 9, 2012];

"I love you both and you, Jay, are the all-time best lawyer. Love" [Letter to Rema and to me – September 17, 2012];

"I don't have to be told by this or any other publication to know that you have always been the best." [Letter to me, November 13, 2015, following my listing in publications of *The New York Times* and *The Wall Street Journal*, of the "Best Lawyers in America" and "Best Lawyers in New York"];

"Rema and Jay, I miss you both" [Letter to Rema and to me – April 4, 2016].

WHAT COULD HAVE CAUSED THIS show of affection?

Was it because I secured for him a lead role in an episode of Sex and the City [my wife's sister Victoria Hochberg was a director], or was it when I invited him to my home to participate in a volleyball contest on a team against high rollers who thought they were athletes? He was a major athlete, in college and even elsewhere. In any event, it was fortunate for my wife and myself to have a relationship so close, so loving, with him. My wife and I have seen him at play and at work.

This show of continuing affection from 1990 to the present was born of winning every case for him. Some ten litigations. He told a colleague of mine that the cases were won, and he still doesn't know how they were won. He said he believed "no other lawyer in New York could have won this enormous string of litigations that went from New York to Las Vegas." And so, we start at the beginning of the relationship.

I had never handled a matrimonial case, but there had been a magazine story entitled "Killer Lawyers," where I was profiled as one who was admired by other lawyers. Donald had seen the article, and said when we met that he didn't care whether I had handled a matrimonial case or not. I was hired by Donald Trump to represent him in both of his divorces in the 1990s. Since then, he has been a very good friend and extremely gracious to Rema and me.

Politics aside, I did for him what I do with all clients: vigorously defend their rights according to the law. It doesn't matter if you are Donald Trump going through a divorce, or Charlie Rangel facing House censure. It makes no difference if you are mobster Matty "The Horse" Ianniello fighting charges of extortion, or musician Miles Davis, needing me to literally help you stand before a judge because you are high on the drugs you are being charged with using. If you are my client, I will give you absolutely everything I have. A lawyer has a job to do. It should not matter to any attorney what political affiliation a client has or what skeletons are in his closet. As an attorney, one thing should always remain constant when you decide to take a case: set aside your personal feelings and do your utmost for your client.

Donald was introduced to his future wife, Ivana, at Maxwell's Plum, a Manhattan restaurant and singles bar. Rema and I didn't know him and Ivana when they were married. It was actually their split that brought us together.

When it was announced that Ivana was seeking a divorce, the breakup garnered more publicity than a third World War would have.

According to *People Magazine* columnist Liz Smith, in an article back then about the couple:

> "In a decade of glitz, they were the glitziest; in a decade of greed, they were the greediest: He the scrappy investor who made a fortune wheeling and dealing real estate, she the gregarious, Czech-born outsider who charmed and clawed her way into New York's most refined social circles. As they fashioned an empire in their own image—and plastered their moniker on nearly every piece of steel, brick and glass they owned—they became, as *New York Newsday* columnist James Revson quipped, 'larger than *Dynasty.*' They had it, and they flaunted it in a brash, bold, brazen way that seemed to typify their times."

Ivana was not content with the post-nuptial agreement she had signed that provided the division of property were there to be a divorce. Ivana claimed that since Donald was allegedly keeping a woman, Marla Maples, at the then-Hotel St. Moritz, he never intended to stay married to Ivana. She also pointed to a situation over Christmas where she, Donald, and the family had gone to a ski resort in Aspen, only to find that Donald's "kept woman" was there too. Ivana claimed the agreement was the product of a fraud perpetrated upon her when she agreed to it without knowledge of his supposed true intentions. She wanted a percentage of Donald's overall net worth.

The legal issue was a simple one: was the agreement airtight, as Donald argued, or was it subject to being set aside so that Ivana could get a much larger piece of the pie? For Donald, what complicated the case was that their marriage had produced three children, household names today: Ivanka, Don Jr., and Eric. Donald was, as noted by many, a great father, and he did not want a drawn-out litigation for fear that it would be harmful to their children.

After the split was made public, newspapers reported that a number of lawyers had offered to represent Donald for free just to garner the resultant publicity. Donald described the scene clearly in his book, *The Art of the Comeback*:

"My office resembled an emergency room, but instead of patients, there were lawyers crowding around and offering their services. Some were so eager to become involved in what promised to become one of the most publicized and talked-about divorces in the past twenty-five years that they assured me there would be no legal fees. I interviewed many of these people, but no one satisfied me."

One day, to make up with Rema following an argument she and I had had, I went to Greenwich Village to buy a Valentine's Day gift—a sexy blue negligee. A friend of mine told me this was the go-to store for such an item. As I crossed over historic Eighth Street in Greenwich Village, my beeper went off. I went to the nearest phone booth to call my office.

"You need to call Donald Trump," my secretary said. There was nothing more to the message. I knew who Donald was—a local real estate magnate who managed a good number of commercial buildings in New York—and I knew the enormous publicity surrounding his divorce case, but we'd never met. I called him.

"This is Jay Goldberg. I am returning a call to Donald Trump."

"Please hold," the receptionist said. She put me right through.

"Jay? Donald Trump."

"Yes, Mr. Trump."

"How are you today?"

"I'm fine, thank you."

"Jay, are you familiar with my divorce case?"

"I am," I said, trying to play it cool.

"Would you like to be involved in it?" he asked.

"Yes, I would."

I answered him that quickly. I knew how big his case already was and how much bigger it was likely going to be.

"Edward S. Gordon recommended you," he said.

"That was very kind of him," I replied.

Gordon was one of Donald's trusted friends and one of my former clients. He had shown Donald a local magazine article from the year before titled: "Courtroom Killers: The Lawyers Other Lawyers Most Admire, Fear, and Talk About." The article rated me "The best pure trial lawyer in town," while another attorney interviewed for the story said I was his "idea of a prosecutor's nightmare." I was truly humbled by the accolades, but the truth was that I had zero matrimonial litigation experience. That, however, didn't matter to Donald. All it took for him to know I was his guy, he later told me, was reading the title of the article.

"Can you be here at my office at three o'clock today? he asked.

"Yes, sir. I will see you then."

After hanging up, I bought Rema's negligee to make amends in my marriage, then I headed to Donald's office to help him end his.

I learned that Gordon had recommended to Donald that he use two lawyers: Stanford Lotwin, who specialized in matrimonial cases, and me, for litigation and trial purposes. Lotwin and I met for the first time in Donald's office, and Donald asked me what I thought of Lotwin right in front of the man.

"Well, from what I know, he is the biggest matrimonial lawyer there is, and judges are in awe of his work," I said. Of course, I didn't know if this was true, but it was the thing for one attorney to say about another when they are about to work together, right? I swear, when I finished, Lotwin had grown a foot taller.

Then Donald turned to Lotwin and asked him what he thought of me as a trial lawyer.

"I have never seen Jay try a case; I am not familiar with him," Lotwin said.

Gee, thanks a ton, Lotwin.

As time proceeded, Lotwin showed that my blind assessment of him was accurate. He was, without question, a major matrimonial practitioner with a tremendous amount of skill. And I assume he came to think highly of me given that Trump gravitated toward me as the lead in all aspects of the case.

Once word of the divorce broke, Ivana quickly hired a public relations firm to help her spin the story of the divorce in her favor. Realizing the effect this media attention would have on his children, Donald instructed me to offer Ivana a settlement despite the fact that he had what I believed to be an iron-clad post-nuptial agreement. I did as he asked, but I also told him I wanted to counter her PR campaign with one of my own. On one of our days in court,

I stood on the steps of the courthouse with TV cameras rolling as I held up a placard of a 10-million-dollar check signed by Donald.

"We have offered Ivana's counsel a check for ten million dollars to settle this case right now," I said. I also stated that, as part of the settlement, Donald was prepared to give her additional monies and property.

"If Mrs. Trump doesn't accept the check," I continued, "she will rue the day she rejected the offer, especially considering the money she will pay to her counsel for a wasted effort."

Ivana did not take the bait; she turned down our offer. She was willing to settle, but not for that amount. When we met with the judge in her chambers, a judge who had a reputation for being prejudiced against men in matrimonial cases, she tried to persuade Donald to settle for an amount he considered inappropriate. He refused. She continued to press. Donald had finally had enough.

"You are full of shit!" he shouted to the judge in response to a statement she'd made. "I'm done here!" He grabbed his coat off the back of his chair and stormed out as we all watched in stunned silence. I would never advise my client to try to make a point by speaking to a judge that way; I was caught off guard. We all were. Even the judge appeared shocked that someone would speak to her in that tone, yet she remained professional. She took no retaliatory action and simply said the case would go to trial.

As the case proceeded toward trial, I submitted a brief that stated, as a matter of law, Donald's extramarital affair did not render the post-nuptial agreement infirm. Since Ivana had a lawyer when she signed the agreement, it should be treated as virtually encased in cement. I feared the worst given Donald's outburst in the judge's chambers, but the judge took the brief under advisement...and she agreed with it.

She sided with Donald and upheld the agreement Ivana signed. However, she also ruled that any restriction on Ivana's right to describe the circumstances of the marriage was void as a restriction on the right of free speech. In other words, Ivana was free to write a tell-all book about their marriage. This ruling with respect to First Amendment rights was in my view meritless and subject to review by the Appellate Division.

With the property dispute essentially settled by the judge's ruling, still to be negotiated was the monthly spousal support and support for their three children. Counsel from both sides, along with Donald and Ivana, entered into what became an all-night negotiation at my office. It hadn't gone well from the start, and we were still so far apart in demands after a few long hours that Donald's patience had expired. He had an outburst that was nearly identical to the one he'd had in the judge's chambers.

"I'm tired of this!" Donald exclaimed as he stood up and headed toward the door. "I'm fed up with this whole scene!" He walked out and slammed the door behind him, leaving all of us shocked once again. As I would find out a minute or so later when I went to look for him in the halls, he hadn't just left the room, he had left the building. I made numerous calls to him over the next several minutes to try to lure him back since we couldn't negotiate anything without his approval. When he finally answered, he was still upset.

"Jay, I said I'm done!" were the first words out of his mouth.

"Mr. Trump, I know you're upset, but we need you here to get this settled. Her team wants to get this ironed out as much as you do."

"No, they don't!" he exclaimed. I certainly understood his skepticism given how poorly the negotiations had been going.

"I assure you that they do," I replied. "Please, let's get this done tonight."

After a little more discussion, he agreed to return. When he reentered the room, nobody said anything to him. We simply got right back to work. Was the whole storming-out thing an act? In retrospect, I believe maybe it was. Much to his credit, though, it worked. It helped speed up the process by getting everyone at the table refocused. It took a few more hours, but we came to an agreement.

"In discussions Friday that went from five p.m. to midnight," reported the *Baltimore Sun*, "Donald and Ivana met face to face in the Park Avenue law office of Jay Goldberg, who represents Donald. Things were testy for a while. But, Mr. Goldberg said, 'As with all final divorce negotiations things started off hot, and then reason overcame emotion.'"

That major battle was finished, but we still had another one to fight.

Ivana soon signed a contract with a publisher to write a book, which in part would discuss details of the marriage. I brought an action to enjoin her, despite the trial court's ruling that she had a First Amendment right to do so. The appellate justices allowed the argument to be televised, which of course created a circus atmosphere. The courtroom was filled. There were people waiting to get in if anyone left. All of this, of course, just to see Donald. Onlookers waited until the session ended and sought his autograph. I must say, as someone who has walked with Robert F. Kennedy and spoken with President Kennedy, the attention that Trump garnered when people saw him was extraordinary.

The appellate division came down with a decision months later, reversing the trial court. It sustained the right of Donald to an injunction against Ivana, ensuring that the agreement not to discuss the details of her marriage was in all respects proper and enforceable. Ivana retained a premier attorney dealing with matters such as free speech and sought review in the court of appeals, but she still lost. That application was rejected, and the decision of the appellate division in Donald's favor stood as the final ruling in the matter. There would be no tell-all book.

Donald and I became close after that, and Rema and I sat in the first row at the Plaza Hotel, then one of Donald's properties, along with Donald's parents when he married Marla Maples. The wedding and reception were truly lavish.

Prior to the marriage, I had Marla sign what I referred to as a "Sunset Agreement." This agreement provided that if Donald and Marla were married for less than an agreed upon period of time, Marla would receive a set amount of money and they would amicably divorce.

Unfortunately, after just a few years, the parties decided to split.

Donald exercised the agreement, brought an action for divorce, and relied on the provision for the distribution of property. Marla went to court in an attempt to set aside the agreement, but she was unsuccessful since she had an attorney when the agreement was signed. That was the last action I would have to take regarding their marriage.

Years later, Rema and I met Donald's first wife in his office. Ivana was there to discuss her belief that Donald should increase the amount he was paying for the support of the children. The two who once couldn't agree on much of anything actually maintained a good relationship after their divorce. When Ivana saw us, she was very kind and affable. One might not expect that from the ex-wife of your client, but she was very pleased with how I had handled issues between them. So much so that...

"I want you to have this," she said to Rema as she removed a brooch from her blouse. Rema was stunned.

"Oh, I can't accept that," Rema said.

"No, I want you to have it," Ivana insisted. "You and Jay have been very fair to me, and that means a lot to me and our children."

The pin's diamonds weren't real—it was costume jewelry that Ivana had designed herself—but it looked like it was worth a million bucks. It was fairly large and in the shape of a spider. In fact, it was so dazzling that it caused quite a stir about a week later when Rema and I were at a restaurant having dinner with the president of Sony and several other people. Rema had worn the brooch, and the woman sitting next to her, whom we did not know, appeared very uncomfortable with Rema's presence. She slid her chair away from Rema as much as she could, but she was still very agitated. She finally told the person she was with that she wanted to change seats. Rema was puzzled.

"Is there something wrong?" Rema asked her.

"That pin," the woman said, looking at it as if it were a live tarantula.

"What's wrong with it?" Rema asked.

"I have arachnophobia," the woman said.

"Arachno-what?"

"I don't like spiders!" the woman exclaimed angrily.

Rema looked at her like she was insane. How could someone be so afraid of something that obviously wasn't real? But, not wanting to cause a scene, Rema took off the brooch and placed it in her purse.

Imagine a piece of jewelry so vibrant that it scares someone like that.

It was incredible that Ivana, the woman I had fought against for my client, was now a friend. Giving Rema that piece of jewelry was such a kind gesture. And it was proof that anyone, even a one-time adversary, can recognize hard work and professionalism when they see it.

CHAPTER 15

DEFENDING DONALD FROM NEW YORK TO VEGAS

WHAT FOLLOWS IS AN ACCOUNT of just some of the many cases I have handled on behalf of Donald.

If ever there were a case that truly concerned him, it was one brought by Steve Wynn, the proverbial king of Las Vegas. He owned the Golden Nugget and the Bellagio hotels. The Bellagio was a gem, right in the middle of the Las Vegas strip. The case was brought in the U.S. District Court in Nevada. Wynn claimed that Donald had improperly interfered with Wynn's contractual rights by employing Wynn's casino manager to run Donald's casino at the Taj Mahal Hotel in Atlantic City.

Things were not going well for Donald in that case. His efforts to get it dismissed for lack of venue failed. Depositions were ordered. Donald had paid a great deal of money in legal fees to his Las Vegas counsel. He asked me to fly there to see what I could do. I did as he asked, though I wasn't exactly welcomed with open arms when I arrived.

To Donald's Las Vegas attorneys, I was an interloper from New York—how terrible, right? I was to be avoided. My role, from their view, was to sit in the corner, not talk, and guard the books at lunch time. And I mean that in the literal sense, for when they went to lunch, I was not invited. But it didn't matter to me what they thought; I knew who I was. I was not there to vindicate myself, but to aid Donald if I could. Whatever harsh words were directed toward me, I simply ignored them.

Wynn had a "white shoe" highly-respected Las Vegas firm and a distinguished New York litigator, Tom Puccio, as his attorneys. Depositions revealed that Puccio had tape recorded most, if not all, of Donald's witnesses. So smug was the Wynn side for accomplishing this that now, with what they had gathered, they believed they had Donald on the ropes.

But nobody knew what I knew.

"Excuse me, gentlemen," I said, speaking up from the corner of the room I'd been banished to. Most of them didn't even look at me. A couple of them rolled their eyes, like I was the little brother intruding on their secret clubhouse meeting.

"What is it, Mr. Goldberg?" one of them reluctantly asked.

"Mr. Wynn, I'm sorry," I said, "but your case is over."

Now they *all* looked at me, a few with arrogant grins.

"What the hell are you talking about?" one of Wynn's attorneys exclaimed.

"Mr. Wynn is facing a federal criminal sentence of up to fifteen years if he goes forward with this plan of attack," I stated confidently.

They were all becoming furious with me. Even Trump's other attorneys looked at me skeptically.

"Let me explain," I said, rising from my seat and turning their conference room into my theatre. "Nevada and New York are the same in terms of authorizing eavesdropping. If one party consents to being recorded—that is, if one party is aware of the recording by wearing a body recorder or placing a recording device in a room— the conversation is admissible.

"Of course," Puccio said. "This is why the recordings we have are entirely legal."

"But during the deposition of a key witness," I continued, "it had been brought out that eavesdropping devices were planted in fountain pens and in the hands of a clock, and that other sophisticated methods were used to record the conversations. And the federal wiretap statute prohibits the use of sophisticated equipment to record conversations."

I went on to say that the federal statute had been interpreted as overriding state law. A violation of that federal statute, as I earlier explained, carried a multi-year prison sentence.

"Thank you for your input, Mr. Goldberg," that same attorney of Wynn's stated. Trump's Vegas attorneys were now whispering to each other, and I knew why: they knew I was correct.

"I think we need to adjourn for the day," one of Wynn's attorneys said after my performance. "Let's plan to meet back here tomorrow." But I knew there would be no tomorrow. I was confident that Wynn's legal team would take to heart everything I had said and agree that the risk of going forward was too grave.

Later that evening, in my room at the Venetian Hotel, my phone rang. It was a partner of Wynn's Las Vegas firm.

"We've gone over what you said in the meeting and have discussed the situation with Mr. Wynn," he said. "We have decided to discontinue this action against Mr. Trump with prejudice." He followed through by stating this before U.S. District Judge Philip M. Pro. Wynn and his counsel gave me a general release in Donald's favor.

When I left Las Vegas, I felt as though I were wearing a ten-gallon white hat. When I returned to New York, I went straight to Donald's office to collect my fee. He paid on the spot.

"How did you do it?" Donald said.

"It's what you hired me to do," I vaguely replied. There really was no secret other than I knew the law. From all the reading I'd done over the years about everything related to the law, I knew they could not record witnesses in the manner in which they had. The law is large, and it does not stop changing. A good attorney must respect that and never stop educating himself on it. I had an edge over every attorney in that room before I'd even walked in. Yet they were so smug that they didn't even think I was worthy enough to sit at their lunch table.

In another case, as Donald was building a seventy-story structure opposite the United Nations building, Senator Daniel Patrick Moynihan, Walter Cronkite, and the Secretary General of the U.N. opposed the construction. They cited a zoning provision that they believed required Donald to demolish the fifty stories he had already built because the base of the construction violated the applicable zoning regulation. Donald's building cast a shadow on the U.N. building, and for that simple reason, there was a campaign to block full construction of what was to be an enormous hotel.

Donald was beside himself. He had called in the leading zoning law experts, as well as other lawyers, who found no way around the zoning limitation as to the height of the building.

I sat and listened to Trump's zoning lawyers as they pondered over the archaic provisions of the zoning law. After several hours of reviewing the laws, I developed a defense, which, if accepted by the judge, would not require that the building be reduced in height even if it were not constructed properly at the base. Donald's position was sustained in the state supreme court and the building was allowed to be completed. It stands today seventy-two stories tall as the Trump World Tower.

How did Donald, a kid from Queens, become so successful in Manhattan?

Donald had made a name for himself by remarkably saving the Commodore Hotel, an old world vintage hotel neglected for so long that it was on the verge of being placed in receivership. In the 1970s, when New York City was on the brink of bankruptcy, Trump was looking to purchase a piece of property in Manhattan. His father had built successful residential buildings in Queens and Brooklyn, but the Trump family had no presence in Manhattan. He approached Penn Central, which owned four hotels in the midtown area. Three of the hotels were already successful. Recognizing how much more expensive they would be to purchase, Trump set his sights on the only unsuccessful property owned by Penn Central— the Commodore Hotel.

Donald saw the true value of the property, given its location, adjoining Grand Central at 42nd Street and Park Avenue. The hotel had fallen into such disrepair that the city had considered demolishing it. Donald saw the potential for buying the building and restoring it to a luxury hotel.

Victor Palmieri of Penn Central later told reporters, "Buying the Commodore at a time when even the Chrysler Building was in receivership is like fighting for a seat on the Titanic while it's sinking." Trump, being the savvy businessman he already was (though only in his thirties), used to his advantage the fact that New York City, and particularly midtown Manhattan, were in decay. He negotiated a low purchase price along with distinctly favorable loan packages and tax breaks from the city, which owned the land upon which the Commodore stood.

In the 1980s, the Pritzker family, major developers in Chicago, purchased a fifty percent interest with Trump in the property. It was agreed that the hotel would be renamed the "Grand Hyatt." The agreement Donald had with the Pritzkers was that if they made a capital call for monies to improve the Grand Hyatt and if Trump could not meet the call, his interest in the hotel would diminish from that of a fifty percent owner. The same was true if Donald made a capital call and the Pritzkers could not meet it.

Soon after purchasing their interest, the Pritzkers made a demand that the hotel be upgraded, redecorated, and a health club be installed, turning it into a truly luxurious hotel. The capital call was for eighty million dollars, of which Donald would have to come up with forty million dollars or lose his equal status. Here was a hotel that had won Donald the plaudits of the public and the real estate industry, but now he stood on the verge of losing his equal interest in it. Donald was horrified.

The case was assigned to an arbitrator who was decidedly against Donald. His hostility and anger toward us both were patent. After twenty-five sessions with the arbitrator—yes, twenty-five— in which the Pritzkers' attorneys laid out the improvements they intended to make in order to turn it into a "super luxury" hotel, word had filtered back to us that the arbitrator had decided to impose an enormous award to the Pritzkers. The lawyers for the Pritzkers had presented some twelve thousand pages of documents, along with testimony, that outlined the improvements they intended to make to every room, bathroom, kitchen, and lobby.

When all seemed lost, I decided to look at the ground lease Donald had with the city. It referred to a rider that we could not find. I went to the municipal building's real estate division and requisitioned the full agreement, riders and all. Miraculously, it seemed, one rider stated that the hotel was always to be run as a "convention hotel." A change in the class—for example, to a luxury hotel—would result in a forfeiture of the entire property to the city. It was exactly what we needed. The Appellate Division, in a 5–0 decision, accepted my position. As a result, Donald, did not have to contribute to the capital call at all. Eventually, the Pritzkers bought out Trump's interest in the hotel for 140 million dollars.

Donald called me another time to help him in a clash between him and a trustee for the creditors of Conseco Inc., an insurance company which was in bankruptcy in Chicago and in a dispute with Donald. The trustee was interested in gathering all of the assets owed to Conseco and was going to sue Donald for his alleged failure to meet financial obligations owed to Conseco.

I wasn't able to do much for Donald because I was in the midst of a trial in federal court. Needless to say, the judge would not grant me a one-month adjournment to involve myself in Donald's case (it doesn't hurt to ask, right?). So Donald turned to another law firm in New York to handle his affair, but I came into it during a brief hiatus from my federal trial—and I entered at a very critical point with information that turned a certain defeat into victory.

Donald and Conseco had together bought the General Motors Building at the end of the 1990s for more than 800 million dollars. The trustee wanted to rid itself of the building under an agreement that gave Conseco the right to require Donald to sell his interest so that the trustee would have an asset to inform the district court in Chicago that Conseco could recover from bankruptcy because the creditors were paid off. Donald resisted the need to sell his interest, claiming the prerequisites the agreement laid out had not been met to force him to sell. The agreement provided that in case of any dispute, the matter should proceed to arbitration.

The parties repaired to a three-person panel, where the only impartial arbitrator was the Honorable George Pratt, a former judge of the U. S. Court of Appeals for the Second Circuit who had left the bench to return to private practice with a respected firm. Each party selected their own arbitrator, but the American Arbitration Association chose the impartial Pratt. The proceeding required all three panel members to affirm that they and their firm had never had an adversarial relationship with either party before taking on the role of an arbitrator.

The case did not go well for Donald. The law firm that represented him tried its best, but on a day in June, Judge Pratt was prepared to read a decision for himself and one partial arbitrator—

not Donald's, unfortunately, but the one selected by the creditors. It was a twenty-page opinion contrary to what Donald had urged.

However, in the very early stages of Donald's case I had retained a private investigator to find out whether Judge Pratt had joined a firm that had ever represented a litigant in an action against Donald or his family. It may have been a long shot, but I wanted for Donald and his team every possible option available to contest an adverse ruling.

Wouldn't you know it, my investigator found that Judge Pratt's firm, without his knowledge and years before he joined the firm, had in fact represented a litigant in a suit against Donald's father. As Judge Pratt was reading his opinion, the American Arbitration Association representative advised that the Association had decided to abort the proceeding by reason of Judge Pratt's firm, even though Judge Pratt had no prior knowledge. It raised the possibility that in the public's view he might be prejudiced. A mistrial was declared. I had done my job for Donald and returned to my federal trial.

You will notice in all of my cases defending Donald's business interests, and as you will see in many of my cases defending other clients, that we were able to win because of something I had dug up that no other attorney had even considered. This is where all of the reading I do and my firm grasp of the law come into play. When defending your client, you should be working tirelessly for him or her. I wouldn't have won any of those cases for Donald if I hadn't kept fighting tooth and nail, turning over rocks that nobody else had thought to turn. You may not always win. I haven't always won. But it was never due to lack of effort.

My relationships with clients don't always transfer to outside of the courtroom, and oftentimes they shouldn't, but Donald has become a very loyal friend.

I attended prizefights with him in Atlantic City after he would call and say, "Would you like to go to the fights by helicopter? I'll have you home tonight when they are over." One time I went to opening day with him at Yankee Stadium. In the car with us on our way to the game were Henry Kissinger, Mayor Rudolph Giuliani, and team owner George Steinbrenner. When we exited the car and entered the stadium, fans couldn't have cared less about Giuliani. I don't think many of them knew who Kissinger was. Even Steinbrenner wasn't the top attraction. It was Donald who they were all calling for and trying to get autographs from.

One of my favorite stories about Donald—trivial, yet funny, and a reflection of the man I know—was when Rema and I had invited him to our home in the Hamptons one summer for a party. He spent the night at our house and, in the morning, wanted nothing for breakfast but a bowl of cornflakes.

"Do you want anything with it," Rema asked. "Any fruit or something?"

"No, thank you," he said as he poured milk over his cereal. "I'll just take two teaspoons of sugar."

Rema scooped two teaspoons onto the cereal, and Donald ate it all.

Later in the day, when Rema needed sugar for something, she took it from the same bowl she had scooped it from that morning. When she tasted it, she was mortified.

Oh my gosh! she thought to herself. *What did I do?*

She realized that the bowl she had scooped Donald's sugar from didn't contain sugar at all. She had instead scattered two hefty teaspoons of salt over Donald's cornflakes. But you know what? Not only did he not say a word about it to Rema so as not to embarrass her, but he ate every last salty flake. He was the consummate gentleman.

CHAPTER 16

DONALD'S PRESIDENCY

SINCE BECOMING PRESIDENT, DONALD AND I have spoken repeatedly. I am not at liberty to say what he said, if it were in the context of an attorney-client relationship. But, if I view the subject, as I told him, as one for publication, he would find it agreeable.

One of my recent contacts with Donald was one hot and sunny afternoon in the summer of 2017. Rema and I were walking north on Third Avenue at 58th Street, heading home after a trip to the movie theatre. Just as we crossed the street, my cell phone rang. Those who know me know that I am not technologically savvy—just hitting the right button to answer my cell phone can be a challenge every time, assuming I can even find the phone. After fumbling through all of my pockets, I finally got it.

"Hello?"

"Jay Goldberg?"

"Yes."

"This is the office of the president. Please hold."

"Who is it?" Rema asked.

"I think it's..."

"Jay!" the voice boomed on the other end. "It's Donald."

"Hello, Donald."

"Jay, where are you? What are you doing?"

"I'm in the city with Rema, coming back from the movie theatre."

"I mean work related," he said.

"I'm involved in the heaviest case of my life with five different law firms," I told him. He did not say specifically why he was asking, but I knew.

Four weeks prior to this phone call, a congressman faithful to Donald had arranged for me to fly to Washington to meet a member of Donald's legal staff. What conversations we had, I cannot divulge.

All I can say is they had sought my legal guidance in some matters, and Donald was calling hoping that I would return to Washington to continue to assist them.

"I'm sorry, Donald," I said. "You know how much I love you, but I am working nonstop on this case. I simply don't have the time."

"But I could really use you here, Jay," he said.

"I'm sorry, I am just too busy."

"Okay," he replied. "Please put Rema on the phone."

I smiled and handed Rema the phone. This was a standard tactic among a lot of my clients—*If Jay says no, ask Rema.*

"Hi Donald," she said. She politely let him state his case as we continued walking toward home. "No, Donald, I'm sorry, he just has too much going on right now." And when Rema says that's the way it is, nobody questions her. Donald accepted her answer, wished her well, and we continued our walk home.

Upon reflection, I think what I was most grateful for about that phone call, besides my good friend calling to ask for my assistance, was that it came about five minutes *after* we had left the theatre. Obviously, I hadn't turned off the ringer. Can you imagine the disturbance I would have caused inside, unable to find my phone in the dark to stop the incessant ringing? Had we still been inside, I definitely would have answered it because I don't know how to do anything with my phone other than answer it or let it ring. How would I have reacted with the other patrons, no doubt, cursing at me and throwing their popcorn at me for taking the call? Would I have yelled, "I'm sorry, but I am talking to the president?" That's actually exactly what I would have done, and I'm sure Donald would have gotten a good laugh. Fortunately, that didn't happen, and Rema and I are able to continue to frequent our favorite movie theatre.

There was a time when the issue of testifying before Robert Mueller's team arose. Mueller was the Special Counsel investigating Russian interference in the 2016 Presidential election, appointed by the Deputy Attorney General Rod Rosenstein. When Attorney

General Jeff Sessions recused himself in the Russian Probe, Rosenstein filled his role.

The House Committee found there was no collusion. Interference there was, but no collusion by Trump and his top aides. But, that didn't satisfy the intelligentsia, for they latched onto the Republican Senate finding that there had to be collusion, though none was specified. It could not be specified involving Trump himself, for he had been investigated according to James Comey since May 2016. One would say enough is enough, particularly when the President is confronted with such monumental issues as a proposed meeting with the North Korean dictator. It does not serve the government well to present to Kim Jong Un a crippled leader who lacks the support of his own countrymen/women, but the bicoastal attack on Trump continues.

I told Trump I worried about Michael Cohen, for the cases are replete with instances where persons facing substantial prison time tell the prosecutor what he wants to hear in an effort to secure a lenient sentence. Certain people just do not see themselves doing jail time. They cannot see themselves walking down the corridor with inmates clanging their canteens against the bars yelling, "You are going to be my wife." A famous judge has said that false testimony of persons facing jail time "corrupts our system." It happens all too frequently.

And so, we get to the issue of whether Trump should testify. Trey Gowdy, a respected member of the House Intelligence Committee, has said that if Trump has nothing to hide, and I am sure he doesn't, then he should testify. This is a naïve piece of advice. I told the president not to testify. I did not believe that the goal of the Mueller group was to get information; rather, it was to get Trump. I urged him to resist testifying, and if this takes a judicial proceeding, he should resist efforts to subpoena him.

That brings us to the subject of the perjury trap. A witness may tell the truth, but if there be one or more "cooperating witnesses" the government will claim that your client gave false, knowingly corrupt testimony. The perjury-trap doctrine refers to the practice of securing a perjury indictment by having a witness testify under regarding an issue that is not material to the investigation, for the purpose of having them say something that can be contradicted by a cooperator. It is a form of entrapment, and so it must be affirmatively proven by the defendant. That means that the defendant must overcome the presumption that the prosecutor is acting in good faith.

One may ask, is Trump likely to follow the advice of his counsel, in this case Emmet Flood, aided by Giuliani. I am confident they are strong-willed enough to carry the day. *The New York Times Magazine* on July 9, 2017 had it right—there are all kinds of lawyers who represented Donald Trump. The article is entitled, "All the President's Lawyers: Donald Trump's life and career have been defined by his legal battles." But there are times when, however correct he may be, obligation to another client makes it impossible to give it all to a client like Donald who is in need of competent counsel. He first turned to New York lawyers to guide him through the hurdles presented by Washington insiders. I told him it was a mistake to rely on counsel other than those familiar with District of Columbia practice. He soon found that to be so when his first lawyer, a New York practitioner of note took a misstep, and so, he had to turn to legal counsel with offices in Washington.

My record with him has been one of total compliance with my wishes. I fit in perfectly to the Trump maxim, "Don't tell me how it can't be done, tell me how it can be done." In Jonathan Mahler's *New York Times Magazine* article he says that I had replaced Roy Cohn as Trump's lawyer of consequence. But there was a big difference, Trump never ever asked me to do something that was improper. He never turned to me to "fix something" as a favor to him.

That is why I find it difficult to understand that I had represented Donald for some twenty-two years and I never heard of the name of Michael Cohen. I never saw him. I never met with him.

It is for all this, that Ty Cobb, Counselor to the White House, Office of the President, wrote: "Deeply grateful for your loyalty to the President. He has abiding respect for you and great affection. You are a prince! Deeply grateful my friend! Honored to know you!"

Politicians and Businessmen

CHAPTER 17

PASSING ON A NOTORIOUS DICTATOR

I RECEIVED A PHONE CALL one day several years ago during the war in Iraq from the U.S.

Secretary of State. I had never had relations with him previously, but he called because he said I had been recommended to him.

"Mr. Goldberg," he said, "I would like to have the U.N. Ambassador to the Office of War Crimes in the Hague (a city in the Netherlands that is home to the U.N.'s International Court of Justice) meet with you to discuss an opportunity."

I had no idea what this was about and he wouldn't tell me, but a U.N. ambassador? And at the encouragement of the secretary of state?

"Of course I will meet with him," I said. "It would be an honor."

The ambassador flew to New York and we met at the Harvard Club. We chatted about our families for a few minutes before getting down to business. He told me that a country in the Middle East had a leader who was going to be prosecuted at the Court in the Hague. He made it clear that since the U.S was not a member country of the Court, the attorneys from the U.S. could serve only as assistants to the chief counsel, and he wanted me to be part of that team to advise them on how to handle the case. He told me that I would have to take up temporary residence in the Middle East country, which was known for its sandstorms, not to mention a war. I would also have to learn the country's language and customs.

"It's intriguing," I said, "but I will have to discuss this with my wife."

I brought the offer home to Rema, though I already knew what her answer would be.

"Wow, the desert?" she said. "But where would I go for my art class?"

Well, that's not exactly the answer I was expecting, but close enough.

Rema is an artist. A fantastic one. Her work is displayed all over our home and in the homes of many friends. No, missing her art class was not why we didn't go to the Middle East. Her point was that as intriguing and adventurous as the idea of living in a foreign country was, it was simply too much of a change and too far away. I know she would have done it if I had insisted—heck, she moved to Gary, Indiana, in the dead of winter without any hesitation because she knew it's what I wanted. But uprooting ourselves to move to a foreign country at this stage in our lives was much different. We weren't so young anymore. The work the ambassador was asking me to do was extremely important to our government, but it would have been too much of an interruption in our lives.

The most difficult part about turning it down was the unique challenge it presented and the headlines it would have received. That's because the leader they wanted me to advise them about prosecuting was none other than Saddam Hussein, president of Iraq. Hussein had not been detained yet but, obviously, our government and others were anticipating his capture soon.

I was truly honored that our government leaders would think to turn to me for help in such a matter. While this would be a much better story had I actually gone to Iraq, I still tell it to show how important it is to be flexible as an attorney, something that could help many young attorneys today set themselves apart from their fellow lawyers.

In one day it was not unusual for me to take a call from someone like this, a call from a mobster, a call from a celebrity, and a call from some Average Joe nobody knew. People called me because they felt I could help them. They didn't worry about my "specialty," because my specialty is, and always has been, the law. When you read it and study it and consume like you do food on a daily basis, and when you are committed to giving your client your best, you can defend just about anybody for any reason.

Having that widespread legal knowledge can also help you determine what you are best at and what is best for you to pursue. I had so many important cases I was working on here in the U.S. when I met with the ambassador, that I knew leaving those cases to take an advisory role for our government in a foreign country was not the ideal situation for me. It is easy to get caught up in the potential glitz and glamour and notoriety of a case involving a celebrity, politician, or someone or something else that is going to garner a lot of attention—which the case against Hussein certainly would have. But don't be blinded by the bright lights. If it's for you, do it. If it's not, don't be afraid to say no.

Advising the government would have done nothing for me, and it would have left my clients here at home without the person they had hired during their most vulnerable times. What I have also learned about myself is that I am at my best not when I am working in a consultory role, but when I am at center stage in the courtroom, my theater.

CHAPTER 18

DR. ARMAND HAMMER AND THE MILLION DOLLAR PAINTING

DR. ARMAND HAMMER WAS PRESIDENT of Occidental Petroleum and former confidant of Vladimir Lenin, Winston Churchill, and Franklin Delano Roosevelt. He was heralded as the most influential businessman of his day. Carl Blumay has written the definitive account of Armand Hammer in a book titled, *The Dark Side of Power: The Real Armand Hammer*. Another book written with respect to this giant's reach is *Dossier: The Secret History of Armand Hammer* by Edward J. Epstein.

Hammer graduated from the Columbia School of Physicians and Surgeons and became a doctor. Rather than practice, he found his way to the Soviet Union at the time of the Russian Revolution and formed a close relationship with Lenin. With Lenin's consent, Hammer opened a number of businesses in Russia. In time, he was not only a confidant of Lenin, but he had also established warm and respected relationships with Churchill and FDR.

Hammer was celebrated as one of the all-time greatest entrepreneurs. He turned the nearly bankrupt Occidental Petroleum into one of the world's most powerful companies. He was a deft business wheeler and dealer, known at times to be ruthless. He maintained contacts in Saudi Arabia so that he could tap into the country's oil reserves. He was renowned for the deals he struck, some of which would not withstand today's Foreign Corrupt Practices Act, since bribery was sometimes his mainstay. He conducted shrewd and manipulative business deals, used sly moves to win political favors from five American presidents, and performed self-serving manipulation of the media. His bribery and scheming led to many brushes with the law. He was relentless in his efforts to acquire additional companies. He maintained friendships with kings, princes, and leaders of many nations.

Dr. Hammer was also a major art collector. His wife had signed a waiver of her right to community property with respect to the Hammers' multibillion dollar art collection. After his wife died in 1989, her niece and only heir, Joan Weiss, sued him in the Los Angeles County Superior Court to establish that the waiver signed by his deceased wife had been coerced, and that she, as the only heir, was entitled to an interest in half of the Hammer art collection. Mrs. Hammer had left Weiss fifteen million dollars, but Weiss claimed she was entitled to much more. The art collection included works by such artists as Renoir, Manet, Rubens, Vermeer, van Gogh, Rembrandt, Degas, Sargent, Monet, Picasso, Cassatt, El Greco, and the famous portrait of George Washington by Gilbert Stuart. He also owned Leonardo da Vinci's Codex Leicester, a collection of famous scientific writings. The value of the entire collection was believed to be up to 450 million dollars.

According to Blumay, Dr. Hammer engaged in a several-month search to find someone he considered to be "the best trial attorney in America" to represent him in the California action brought by Joan Weiss. Hammer said, according to Blumay, that this was the most important case of his life, because it involved his moral character in dealing with his departed wife.

It was now the summer of 1990 and I happened to be in California representing country music legends Willie Nelson, Waylon Jennings, Kris Kristofferson, and Johnny Cash in the Highwaymen case—a fascinating case that I will discuss a bit later—when the judge's law clerk came out with a message for me to call Dr. Hammer. I'd never met the man and had no ties to him that I knew of. As I stated, it wasn't unusual for me to get calls from just about anybody—though being handed a message from a clerk in the midst of a trial to call a well-known person I'd never met was a first.

I called Hammer's office to find out he wanted to meet with me about possibly representing him. His office was not far from the courthouse, so I drove over. There were guards at the entrance to Occidental Petroleum, and they directed me to a reserved parking spot. I went up to Dr. Hammer's suite on the fiftieth floor. I entered his office, but he was not there. I was told to make myself comfortable and that he would be returning soon. A few minutes after walking around his office where he had several pictures of himself with many famous people, including Lenin, Churchill, and Roosevelt, an announcement came over the intercom.

"Dr. Hammer has arrived in the building," the voice said. This was meant, I assume, to convey to everybody to give full attention to their work, or at least appear to be doing so. I'm sure it also fed his ego.

When he came into his office, he introduced himself and got right to the point.

"Mr. Goldberg, I have spoken to other lawyers and to the American Bar Association to find someone who can help me," he said. "You have been recommended as a very fine trial lawyer."

"Thank you, sir," I said.

"I have also spoken with Donald Trump, who said you have represented him. And I would be honored if I could say that Jay Goldberg is my lawyer."

I was taken aback, but didn't hesitate to answer.

"I would be honored to represent you," I said, still unsure of what the case entailed.

When he finally told me about it, he said he would have to get approval from his board of directors to hire me. I returned the next day and was hired without ever meeting anyone on the board. I'm pretty sure he *told* them he was retaining me rather than *asking* them—he was the king—but he was simply following the necessary process for approval.

He and I flew together to New York on his private jet. We discussed the circumstances of his wife signing the waiver of her community property interest, at which time he showed me something of significant importance: a letter to him from his wife, which freely acknowledged the waiver she had signed and her belief that what she was doing was justified by the benefits Dr. Hammer had conferred to her with respect to other monies and property.

Joan Weiss, the niece and woman suing him, did not know of this letter when she commenced the action against Dr. Hammer.

Dr. Hammer asked my wife and me to have dinner with him at his home in Greenwich Village. From the outside, it appeared to be two non-descript joined structures on West Fourth Street. No one passing by would possibly think it was Dr. Hammer's residence. When we ate, he told us that we were eating on china given to him by Lenin.

"Oh wow," Rema exclaimed. "John Lennon?"

Spoken like a true New Yorker.

"Vladimir Lenin," Hammer clarified with a grin.

Over dinner we discussed the case, the letter ratifying what Mrs. Hammer had done regarding her waiver of community property, and his desire to build a grand museum to house his paintings and make them available to the public.

Following that meeting, I traveled to California, was admitted to practice for this case, and conducted a hearing before the judge as to the competency of Mrs. Hammer. I prepared for it carefully. To me, the matter was a simple one. At the hearing, I showed Ms. Weiss the waiver signed by Mrs. Hammer. Once learning of the letter, the fireworks began:

1. She called a treating doctor who opined that at the time of the signing of the letter, Mrs. Hammer had diminished capacity.
2. There were other witnesses called to dispute the legitimacy of the letter.
3. The court was confronted with a battle of experts.
4. Briefs were submitted.
5. There were, ultimately, thousands of pages of depositions and hundreds of thousands of exhibits.

What I had thought was a simple matter wasn't simple at all. She was not going to go down without a fight. But neither were we.

In November of that same year, with the case still in full motion, Dr. Hammer showed his appreciation for my work thus far by inviting Rema and me to the grand opening of a gleaming white marble art museum he had constructed in the Westwood section of Los Angeles. The opening was a true gala with pieces from his collection on the walls. Dr. Hammer had also set up a dais on which I sat, along with the mayor and various other people Dr. Hammer considered of great importance, including movie stars.

About a month after the gala, when Rema and I were in Europe on vacation, I received a startling phone call: Dr. Hammer had passed away. When we returned home soon after, I called Hammer's local counsel and told him that I wanted certain things done to proceed with the conclusion of the litigation.

"What are you talking about?" he asked.

"What do you mean what am I talking about?" I replied.

"You don't understand," he said. "Dr. Hammer has died, which means you are off the case."

"Off the case? Why?"

"The attorneys for his estate are taking over all litigation," he said. "I'm sorry, but your services are no longer needed."

I was shocked, but there was nothing I could do. I was told to box up my documents for them and send them my bill, so I did.

Four long years later, in 1994, as the defense for Dr. Hammer's estate was about to present its case regarding the art collection, Judge Henry W. Shatford of the Los Angeles County Superior Court granted the defense's motion to dismiss the case. According to a *Los Angeles Times* article, Shatford said in an interview, "The plaintiff was not able to put up a shred of evidence supporting the contention" that Dr. Hammer had deceived his wife. Weiss appealed the case and, five years later, in 1999, according to another *Los Angeles Times* article, "The 2nd District Court of Appeal ruled that Weiss had failed to prove to the trial court that Hammer misled his wife about the money he made."

In other words, my plan for defense nine years earlier had held up—twice.

But there is one more compelling story to this case.

So pleased with the way I had defended him in just the few months we worked together, Dr. Hammer showed me his appreciation by sending me, as a gift, an oil painting of a scene in Shanghai, China. I don't have a strong eye for art, so I didn't know anything about this painting. It looked nice, but the value? I had no idea. I hung it on my office wall and never gave it any more thought. That is, until one day when Rema and I were walking through New York City near our home and passed another art gallery of his, the Hammer Gallery. It was my day off, and I was dressed down in jeans and an old shirt. For the fun of it, I decided to stop in. Two young ladies greeted us.

"Hi, I'm Jay Goldberg. I served as Dr. Hammer's attorney years ago in the case involving his artwork."

Imagine someone dressed as I was, walking into such a sophisticated place, claiming to be the former attorney of one of the world's wealthiest and most famous businessmen. The two women looked me up and down, no doubt questioning my claim.

"How can we help you?" one of them asked.

"Well, before he died, he gave me a painting by a Chinese artist. I have no idea who the artist is or what it may be worth, but I wondered if someone might be able to tell me more about it."

The women looked at each other for a moment in silence. I think they were still unsure about me, but I also felt like I'd said something that struck a chord.

"Why don't you give us your name and number and we will have the director contact you next week," one of them said.

I did as they suggested.

The following Monday, my phone rang. It was the director of the gallery.

"Can I stop by and take a look at your artwork?" he asked.

"Certainly," I said.

When he arrived, his eyes instantly gravitated to the wall where the painting in question hung. I hadn't told him that was the painting, but he knew, which told me that I likely had something pretty significant. He walked over to it to get a closer look. It didn't take him but a few seconds to realize what I had.

"I will write you a check right now for this painting," he said. "How does 1.2 million dollars sound?"

Gulp.

"Did you say 1.2 million dollars?"

"Yes, sir. The artist is Chen Yifei. He is highly regarded in China. He died at a young age, and China is in the market to regain as much of its original art as it can."

Given that startling information, it probably would have been smart of me to turn down his offer and get the work appraised, maybe try to sell it through an auction house such as Sotheby's or even take it to China myself, but I had no interest in running around pursuing the market. This had been a gift. Any amount would have been pure profit. And 1.2 million dollars seemed like a good "any amount" to me.

The director wrote me the check on the spot, I cashed it the next day, and I said a quiet but exuberant "Thank you!" to Dr. Hammer.

I was not happy that I had been dismissed from the case so many years earlier, but this painting obviously signified how much Dr. Hammer appreciated the work I had done for him in such a short time. Most importantly, in the end, my defense strategy worked, even if I wasn't there to witness it.

CHAPTER 19

TAKING ON TWO GOVERNORS

NEW YORK STATE, LIKE SO many other states, was in desperate need of money as we suffered a deep recession in the early 1990s. So what did the state try to do about it? What a lot of states were doing or were about to try to do: legalize gambling. But, in New York, they were trying to do it without changing any state laws that prohibited it.

The passage of the 1988 federal Indian Gaming Regulatory Act established a legal method by which states and tribes nationwide could negotiate tribal land gambling through a treaty, even though New York's laws and constitution prohibited casino type gambling.

In 1993, Governor Mario M. Cuomo utilized the Act by entering into a compact with the St. Regis Mohawk tribe. This was followed by similar action from Governor George Pataki in 1998. The compact permitted the Mohawks to operate casino-type gambling, such as poker, blackjack, roulette, and slot machines. The plan was for a 500 million dollar Las Vegas-style casino in the Catskills.

Some members of the legislature frowned upon the actions of governors Cuomo and Pataki. Soon, every group of people desiring to partake in gambling revenues magically became Indians and claimed that the land they owned was tribal land.

Keith Wright, a Democrat in the New York State Assembly, acting for himself and a group of other members of the Assembly, and the Senate leader, acting for himself and a group of other members of the Senate, came to see me. They asked if I would represent all of them in their argument that, without legislative authority, the governors were acting contrary to the tripartite form of government. That form would require, so it was claimed, an agreement of this kind to be approved by the executive, legislative, and judiciary branches, or with an amendment to the state constitution. It was not a statute that barred commercial, casino-type gambling—no, it was the New York State Constitution, which, for more than one hundred years, had prohibited that type of gambling. The only gambling that was permitted was for charitable purposes and at horse racing tracks.

With the state constitution on our side, we won our argument.

Justice Joseph C. Teresi of the State Supreme Court in Albany ruled that agreements on behalf of the state had to have legislative approval, and governors Cuomo and Pataki had acted in excess of their authority. According to a *New York Times* article the day after the ruling, Justice Teresi said the governors "crossed the line of executive power and entered into the domain of the Legislature without proper mandate or authority."

I was quoted in that same article: "It seems to put an end to Sullivan County gambling for the near future. The ruling affirms the power of the legislature to speak for the people."

The decision was a shocker to gambling interests. So much money had been spent to equip tribal lands to open casinos, but the court came to the rescue of those who opposed this type of gambling that appeals to persons willing to spend whatever it takes "to beat the house," which of course they never do. The victories in both cases were carried in a summary insert in the February 2004 *New York Law Journal* under the heading "Top Cases of 2003."

Unfortunately, though, the victories were short-lived. Justice Teresi said Pataki would have to obtain legislative approval in order to sign a compact with the Mohawks.

So he did.

Gambling forces went before the court the next year after the legislature had authorized the governor to enter into agreements with Indian tribes. In its ruling, the Court of Appeals authorized the broadest expansion of gambling in state history, leaving in considerable question just what the anti-gambling provision in the state constitution meant. It was ruled that Indian tribes were like sovereign entities, and within the confines of their lands they could have any kind of gambling they wished. The way the gambling interests came to prevail, and what it meant for New Yorkers concerned about encouraging gambling, became the subject of a February 2006 *New York Law Journal* article entitled "Top Trials of 2005." We took the case to the U.S. Supreme Court, but the court refused to hear it, meaning the federal Indian Gaming Regulatory Act would win over the state's constitutional prohibition of gambling.

I had had a hunch that, with all the money that had been put in to opening these casinos, my efforts in the end could go for naught.

But did they?

I took pride in vindicating the tripartite form of government, which restricts the actions of the governor acting alone in critical matters. I won because the governors had no right to do what they did on their own, and it forced them to seek approval from the legislature. My victory in the casino issue didn't last long, but the long-term victory of forcing New York governors to follow their own constitution in matters such as this remains intact today.

CHAPTER 20

HON. CHARLES B. RANGEL, CONGRESSMAN— RAILROADED!

AS A REWARD FOR "BREAKING" the quiz show scandal case, District Attorney Hogan assigned to me an intern, a young lawyer named Charles Rangel.

Charlie was not a typical intern given that he was a couple years older than I. He had spent a number of years in the Army, where he earned a Purple Heart and a Bronze Star with valor in the Korean War. He was handsome, well-spoken, and extremely intelligent. After leaving the DA's office, he served in the New York State Assembly before unseating the legendary Adam Clayton Powell Jr. in a congressional primary election, en route to being elected to the U.S. House of Representatives. Over the next forty-four years the Democrat would become the chairman of the influential Ways and Means Committee, become a founding member of the Congressional Black Caucus, and be responsible for major contributions to economic development and the rebirth of Harlem. When he left Congress, he was the third ranking member of the House.

One time, while attending a Congressional Subcommittee Hearing, the subcommittee chairman, Rema, and I had lunch in the congressional dining room. Congressman Rangel was there and handed me this note he'd written: "It was indeed my good fortune that District Attorney Hogan assigned me to you. You provided me with my first real experience in the law. What I learned while working with you has stayed with me all these years." My feelings toward him were mutual. He was a good and hard-working man during our time together in the DA's office.

In late 2010, Charlie came to see me about hiring me. He was deeply upset at the recent punishment he'd been given by the House of Representatives. Three years earlier he had been accused of ethical improprieties and tax violations. The allegations concerned improperly renting rent-stabilized apartments in the city, soliciting donations for City College of New York using office personnel to address and send letters, and failing to disclose rental income from property he owned in the Dominican Republic. In mid-2010, the House Ethics Committee, to whom the matter was referred, empaneled an adjudicatory subcommittee of eight members to act as impartial fact finders. They each swore they would act as judges do—take testimony and hear proof only in the subcommittee hearing room, and use only that evidence to determine whether the alleged improprieties were proven to the clear and convincing standard. If that were the finding, they would make a recommendation of punishment to the full House Ethics Committee which, if necessary, would recommend discipline.

In November 2010, the subcommittee found by clear and convincing evidence that the allegations had been proven, and it recommended that the full House Ethics Committee advise the full House that censure should be imposed. The House Ethics Committee conceded that there was no evidence of corruption, but nonetheless, on December 2, 2010, Charlie received as punishment a "censure," which is one step removed from expulsion from the House.

Seven months after his censure, an undated memorandum authored by the chief counsel of the House Ethics Committee and subcommittee was unearthed. It stated: (a) that he had previous communications with the Chair regarding wrongdoing of two errant members of his staff, who furnished information to four Republican members of the eight-member subcommittee. This information was not shared with the Democratic members; (b) that this was only one of several examples of misconduct by these staffers and the four Republican members of the subcommittee; (c) that some of the information furnished to these members was incorrect; (d) that this misconduct may have been motivated by racial prejudice;

149

(e) that it was obvious that evidence was received outside the hearing room in violation of the rules; (f) that the promise of the committee rules requiring any hearing to be conducted in a fair and impartial way assuring protection of procedural due process rights had been ignored; (g) that if Rangel had called a witness, the Chief Counsel would have recommended dismissal of all charges; and (h) shockingly, binders had been prepared for and distributed to only the Republican members of the committee. The cover of the binders read as follows: "NUCLEAR OPTION: Do Not Ask Unless Things Go Bad."

The chair of the subcommittee was also the chair of the full committee. She had falsely represented to the remaining committee members and to the full House that the hearings had been conducted in compliance with the promise of the committee rules and comported with all aspects of due process.

I listened to this extraordinary story Charlie told me, and I was convinced without any hesitation that he had been denied rights guaranteed by the Constitution. I told him that, with fair treatment, I could prevail in a suit brought in the U.S. District Court for the District of Columbia to set aside the finding and punishment. Experienced colleagues warned me not to take anything for granted, for the courts there provide their own rules when dealing with an attack on a member of Congress or a congressional committee, but I was confident.

Charlie told me that before I could officially sign on to represent him, I would have to go down to Washington to visit with the chairman of the Congressional Black Caucus, Congressman Emanuel Cleaver (D-MO) for approval. I went with my associate, Alex Huot, who worked closely with me on the case, to meet with Cleaver. When we reached his office door in the U.S. Capitol building, Cleaver rushed toward us from behind his desk before we could walk in. He put his index finger to his lips, warning us against saying anything. He signaled for us to follow him.

"We're going to my private office," he whispered.

That's interesting, I thought. *He has another office here? And why is he whispering?*

We followed him down the hall to an unmarked door. He opened it, flipped the light switch, and motioned for us to go in ahead of him.

"Are you kidding?" I said.

He shook his head. It was no joke. We cautiously stepped in, and he followed us, closing the door behind him.

We were standing in a broom closet no larger than six feet wide by eight feet long.

There we were, three grown and professional men in suits, shoulder to shoulder, way too close for anyone's comfort, standing among several mops, buckets, towels, rolls of toilet paper, and jugs of whatever chemicals they used to clean the hall floors of one of the most powerful buildings in the world.

"Pardon the close quarters," Cleaver said matter-of-factly. "You never know who could be listening."

Welcome to twenty-first century Washington, D.C., where the lack of trust toward each other forces your representatives to conduct meetings in this manner.

I moved a mop away from me to the corner and slid aside with my foot a couple buckets to give myself a few more inches of space. We proceeded to talk about the case, in which there was really nothing secretive at all. Feeling claustrophobic while inhaling fumes that are confined to a closet for a reason, Alex and I explained the case as quickly as we could and handed the congressman copies of our proposed papers.

"Are we finished here?" I asked, trying to speak and not breathe at the same time.

"I think we are," the congressman said.

He opened the closet door and we exited. A few people happened to be walking by when we came out, and not a single one of them gave us a look—which made me wonder how many other closets in the building were currently occupied.

A week later, Charlie called to say that the Congressional Black Caucus had approved our representation of him. I assume the vote was held in that same closet.

As I would later learn, being on the merit side of a case does not ensure victory. More things come into play in a case brought in Washington against a sitting congressman or congressional committee than anywhere else. We would be on the meritorious side of the controversy, but on the losing side of the political ramifications that a victory would bring. Justice took a backseat to politics, and so the case stands as a monument to how the transaction of court business is played out in the nation's capital.

Before I explain what happened in the case, know this: while most every lawyer will tell you that because of the Speech or Debate Clause (Article I, Section 6, Clause 1 of the U.S. Constitution), members of Congress, when Congress is in session, cannot be held accountable in the court of law for what they say or do—that is absolutely wrong. Courts have the power to decide whether the conduct complained of is shielded by the Speech or Debate Clause, even when the words or actions are uttered or done during a time when Congress is in session. This includes the power to determine whether procedural due process has been followed in the course of a congressional hearing. The immunities "were not written into the Constitution simply for the personal or private benefit of members of Congress, but to protect the integrity of the legislative process." The immunities extend to things that are "generally done" in a committee hearing or on the floor of Congress.

In a case of Charlie's kind, according to case law, if he suffered injury (in this case, censure), and if the injury were fairly traceable to the actions of the wrongdoing subcommittee members, he had a right to have this redressed by court action. Implementation of committee rules must satisfy constitutional protections. Charlie had a right to the enforcement of his constitutional protections by a hearing conducted in an impartial manner within a fair procedural framework.

The case law is that legislative/investigative adjudicatory subcommittee fact-finding hearings are subject to judicial review if they are not within the sphere of legitimate legislative/investigative activity. In this case, an offending member secretly meeting with two Ethics Committee staffers and sharing what he learns outside the hearing room with his three other Republican colleagues (according to that memorandum authored by the chief counsel of the Ethics Committee and subcommittee) is not legitimate legislative/investigative conduct protected by the Speech or Debate Clause. It corrupts and obstructs the purpose and goal of a committee proceeding under 18 U.S.C. § 1505.

We brought the suit to set aside the censure, which was fairly traceable to the misconduct of the subcommittee. We specifically sought oral argument and fully expected this request to be granted. But we heard nothing from the district court. We sent the court several more letters, repeatedly stating our request. Every single one went unanswered.

Since the chief counsel had argued that the misconduct we had specified was only partial, we asked for discovery of what other wrongdoing occurred during Charlie's hearing. Again, there was no response from the court.

We called the judge's chambers, and our calls were transferred to the deputy clerk, where we pleaded for the judge to listen to us. Still no response.

The judge, John D. Bates, was a close friend of U.S. Supreme Court Chief Justice John Roberts. Bates had been appointed chief judge of the Administrative Office of the Courts and of the Foreign Intelligence Surveillance Act ("FISA") court. He obviously feared no repercussion from a total denial of a right to be heard on a matter as pressing as this one. He saw no need for discovery, for the misconduct of the Republican members—which led to the erroneous conduct of the full committee and the mistaken belief by the full House that all proceedings were conducted fairly, impartially, and in satisfaction of Charlie's right to procedural due process—was shielded by the Speech or Debate Clause.

We appealed the decision of the district court to the Court of Appeals. The Court of Appeals rejected Charlie's effort, also citing the Speech or Debate Clause. While we were given the opportunity to argue our case, the court did little analysis and added to the mistaken view of Judge Bates. We filed a petition for certiorari with the U.S. Supreme Court. It was denied.

We'd gone as high as we could go. The matter, shockingly, was over.

Congressman Charles B. Rangel, member of the House since 1971, was left with a censure on his record.

It broke my heart that we lost this case, for two reasons: It was an extreme miscarriage of justice, and my long-time friend, who had served our country honorably for nearly a half-century, was forced to accept such a preposterous fate.

How could the misconduct of the subcommittee, which did not happen on the floor of Congress and was not part of a legislative act, be protected by the Speech or Debate Clause? My specialty is constitutional law, and there is no question that the clause should not have applied. It was a case of me knowing more than the people in charge of making the decisions, but their ignorance won out because of their positions.

I apologized profusely to my former intern, my state's congressman, my friend. He was railroaded. We both knew it. But there was nothing more we could do.

Fortunately, the voters of New York knew what a good man Charlie was, and he was reelected in 2012 and 2014 before retiring in 2017.

Just a few months after his retirement, my phone rang. It was Charlie.

"Jay, I just want you to know I love you," he said.

"I love you, too, Charlie," I replied.

Odd? Maybe to many, but not to me. That was just the kind of man Charlie was.

He told me that he was enjoying retirement, and he said he wanted to call to thank me again—not only for what I had done for him as an interning lawyer in Hogan's office decades earlier, but for fighting to have his censure removed. We didn't win, but he never cried about it or let it define who he was. He recognized my good effort, knew the justice system didn't give him a fair shake, and that was it. He moved on, won two more elections, and served the people he represented with honor and dignity. He is a good person, a true man, and an even better friend.

CHAPTER 21

MY REJECTION OF ENTRY INTO POLITICS

WITH MY SUCCESS WORKING FOR the Kennedys and as an assistant district attorney, it was no surprise to me that some people wanted me to run for office. I was connected to politics through much of my work, but being an actual politician was not something that was of great appeal to me. I was approached twice about running. The first time I answered with an immediate and firm "No, thank you." The second time I considered it for about a couple weeks—until I tried to literally kick in a potential voter's door and realized I probably didn't have the temperament for the job.

It was early in my career when I'd been asked by a local group to run for district attorney of Bronx County. I decided against it immediately because it would have been an interruption in my life plan to be a premier trial lawyer in all different phases of the law. I had recently started my own firm, and I wanted to build it into something grand. It was an easy decision that public office was not for me.

About a year later, though, I was recruited hard by the Reform Democratic Club to run for an open state senate seat in the Riverdale section of the Bronx. The Reform Movement was an outgrowth of those who opposed regular Democratic forces in the Bronx that traced back to Edward "Boss" Flynn, who ruled with an iron fist and was a confidant of Franklin Delano Roosevelt. The Reform Party was eagerly pressing to have a candidate in the senate race, and they had decided, without my knowledge, that I was their guy.

One evening at about ten o'clock, roughly a dozen Reform Party members and leaders came to my home unannounced to push me to run. It was like a spontaneous mini campaign rally in my living room. They even had a mockup campaign poster to show me, putting the cart way before the horse. This horse initially said no...a few times. But they weren't leaving my home without a yes. Not thinking it through, I went against everything I had told myself the year before about politics and succumbed to their wishes. I told them I would test the waters to see if it was the right thing for me.

It wasn't. I mean, it *really* wasn't.

One afternoon, soon after the living room rally, I went out with an attorney named Norman Liss, one of the party members who had recruited me, to try a little face-to-face campaigning. I'd obviously never done it before, but how difficult could it be? After all, I'd made my living working with people, many whom I didn't know until they called or walked into my office. Certainly I could use my self-confidence and charm and other people skills to gain the affection of voters.

I walked up to the first house, one completely unfamiliar to me, and politely knocked on the door. An angry dog barked from inside as I patiently waited. After nobody answered, I knocked again; the dog continued to bark. After waiting a few more seconds, I knocked one more time. The dog now wanted to rip off my head. Apparently, so did its owner.

"Who is it?" a woman sharply yelled from the other side.

"My name is Jay Goldberg," I said.

"Not interested!"

I took a deep breath.

"I would like to speak with you for a moment about my candidacy for state senate."

"Go away!"

I looked at Norman. His body language told me to try again.

"Miss..."

"What don't you understand? I said go away!"

Now *I* was getting annoyed.

"If I could just..."

"I said no!"

And with that, I did what no candidate for any office would ever do or has probably ever done: I kicked my big old foot right into her door. Not once. Not twice. But three times in succession. *Bam! Bam! Bam!*

Boy, was that dog angry. Why she didn't open her door after I kicked it and let the dog maul me, I don't know.

"Jay, let's go," Norman said calmly.

That first house was the beginning—and the end—of my state senate campaign.

"I don't think this is for you," Norman said politely as we headed back to the car.

"I guess not," I replied tersely, looking over my shoulder, just daring the woman to show her face. I learned pretty quickly that, unlike a court of law, political campaigning does not allow for both sides to present their cases. That's what had me so worked up. All I wanted to do was give a quick pitch for my candidacy, but I was completely denied. Imagine a judge refusing to let me say anything to defend my client. I'd certainly kick a few courtroom walls, and probably a few heads, if that were to ever happen.

I didn't knock on another door after that rejection. I simply didn't have the patience or tolerance for the job. Norman took me home and thanked me for considering it. Despite petitions my supporters had gathered to put my name on the ballot, they were never submitted. My political career was finished and, quite frankly, I was perfectly fine with that.

I had the personality of a lawyer, not a politician—and there was a front door in the heart of the Bronx with scuff marks on it as clear evidence.

The Entertainers

CHAPTER 22

THE BIRTH OF A JEWISH COWBOY—WAYLON, WILLIE, AND THE GIRL OF MY DREAMS, JESSI

ADAPTABILITY MATTERS, ESPECIALLY IN THE life of an attorney. No two cases will ever be the same. No two clients will ever be the same. No two juries will ever be the same. Adapting can be difficult, but with fortitude, one cannot only accept it, but prosper. Pivots will often have to be made to achieve the most satisfying result which, in my work, has often led to new and fascinating clients. My path to working for Waylon Jennings and Willie Nelson is a perfect example.

An acquaintance had referred an attorney to me, who was a partner at a respected firm. He had been married twenty-three years when he took his wife and children to Cannes in the French Riviera. While walking alone on the beach one night, he met a French beauty. She spoke no English, but he was "taken" with her, which led to secretive meetings that took place during the month he was on vacation with his family. He fell in love with her, left his family on the spot, divorced his wife, brought this new woman to New York, and married her.

Though many, including I, may disagree with his personal choices, he still had a right to see his children, which his wife refused to grant him after he left them. As a result, he brought a lawsuit to secure his rights in family court in New York County. After a good deal of hard-fought litigation, the judge worked out a settlement that gave my client virtually all that he had sought.

Given that "victory," my client asked me if I would help his friend, Neil Reshen, who had run into some trouble. Reshen was being investigated for allegedly having stolen money from a company whose businesses included music publishing and mass media. I met with Reshen and discussed his situation. I learned, from him and through my own research, that he was a well-regarded negotiator with major record labels on behalf of a number of music stars.

One of the first questions he asked me was, "Academically speaking, of course, can you tell me which country has no extradition treaty with the United States?" I told him that I did know of one country—the Ivory Coast—but there was always the risk that he might be eaten by one or more members of the populous. It was a joke, but also maybe a subtle message to stay put and trust me and the law.

We addressed his criminal case by my traveling to California, meeting with the assistant U.S. Attorney, and entering a negotiated plea before a U.S. district judge, who had originally practiced in New York. The judge and I hit it off immediately. We had mutual friends, which can never hurt during a case, for we are only human. The court accepted the plea bargain worked out between the assistants and me. Reshen would agree to pay back money in return for serving a probationary period and supervised release. Reshen was overjoyed with the result, which led him to ask me to help some of *his* friends. Remember, this all started with an acquaintance referring me to a friend, who later referred me to a friend. I always say, "Do good work, and people will notice."

Reshen told me that he represented a number of very well-known country-western artists, including Waylon Jennings and Willie Nelson. He asked if I would be interested in representing them in their recurring legal problems, which included some criminal matters. I didn't hesitate to say yes. The truth is, I knew nothing about Waylon and Willie. I might have heard of them, but I'm not even sure of that. I couldn't have told you what they looked like or what they sang. All I knew was that I liked Reshen, and if he was recommending clients to me, I wasn't going to turn him or them down.

Now, I know a lot of attorneys don't take the time to get to know their clients. I'm not talking about digging deep into a client's past, knowing every little nugget they've done right or wrong, or even necessarily becoming good friends with them. I'm talking about simply knowing their personalities—what makes them tick, how to talk with them, how to relate to them, how to make them feel comfortable. After all, they are putting a huge load of trust—and money—into their lawyer. I had a pretty good feeling that dealing with Donald Trump and Dr. Hammer was going to be quite different from dealing with Waylon Jennings and Willie Nelson. As an east coast Jewish lawyer who is normally stiff-dressed in a suit and tie with polished shoes and cuff links, I knew that showing up on Waylon's doorstep looking like that probably would result in him behaving like the woman in the Bronx did when I went out to campaign—and I really didn't want to have to kick in Waylon's door. So I decided it would be a good idea to first immerse myself in his culture.

And if you haven't figured this out about me yet, when I say I'm going to do something, it is to the fullest and absolute extreme.

Rema and I packed our bags and headed to West Texas with a pit stop in Nashville, Tennessee. Our intent was to become a cowgirl and cowboy—to the best of a couple Jewish city-folk's abilities—before meeting my new clients. I know, normal people don't do that, just like a normal person doesn't plant recording devices on crooked cops at his own risk. I guess I'm more of a rare breed than maybe even I thought. From a personal standpoint, country music and the whole lifestyle that came with it were foreign to us, but we were intrigued. From a professional perspective, I will do whatever it takes to serve my clients the way they deserve to be served— even if it means becoming a cowboy.

We traveled to Nashville at Reshen's recommendation to a store famous for its western and rock-n-roll fashions and sequined jackets. It was there where I bought the clothing I felt was necessary to meet with Waylon: a vest, western hat, and two pairs of ridiculously uncomfortable cowboy boots, something my feet had never slipped into before.

From there we jetted to West Texas and saddled right up. West Texas, as I learned, is not for sissies. It is so very different from the rest of the state. One can look for miles and see only large spreads of cattle ranches and oil rigs over the rugged terrain. Some towns have just a general store and a bar. Don't order a Caesar salad or a vegetable platter—you'll likely be laughed at, if not ignored. I asked Waylon once why all his steaks and hamburgers were charred. He said, "We know where it comes from." The food is beef, ribs, grits, and little else. It is known for fast women and country-western music. Barbara Streisand is a no-no. So is Frank Sinatra.

It's also not so easy to blend in if you're an outsider, no matter how hard you try.

One day, dressed in my cowboy gear in my best effort to appear to be "one of them," I went to a honky-tonk bar with Reshen, who had traveled with us to get us acclimated to the area and to introduce us to Waylon. While at the bar, another patron moseyed over to question my presence.

"Who's this guy?" he asked Reshen, who naturally fit in.

"My friend, Jay," Reshen said, keeping my Jewish surname out of it.

"You from around here?" the cowboy asked.

"He is," Reshen said, answering for me as I nodded in agreement.

"Where you from?" the man asked, his suspicion rising.

"He's a roadie," Reshen said.

"A roadie?" the guy said incredulously. "He ain't no roadie!"

"Hey, he's good," Reshen insisted. "He's with me. Don't worry about it."

It was like a scene out of an old black-and-white western film in a saloon. The man gave me a glare as he reluctantly accepted Reshen's claim before slowly backing off. It was my first Texas bar confrontation, and I didn't have to say a word. I am grateful to this day that Reshen was there. If he weren't, a shootout may have been inevitable—and I know at least one of us didn't have a gun.

When Reshen took Rema and me to meet Waylon and his wife, Jessi Colter, a recording star in her own right, I was still decked from head to toe like John Wayne.

"Well hello there, Cowboy," Waylon said in his southern drawl and with a big smile.

"Hello, Mr. Jennings," I replied in my high-pitched, east coast accent. I don't think I fooled him into thinking I was someone other than a Jewish New York lawyer in a Lone Ranger costume, sans the mask, but he seemed to appreciate the effort. Had I been mounted on a horse, my appearance might have been more convincing, but I didn't want to go overboard.

Waylon was born in Littlefield, Texas, a community of some six thousand people. Waylon Jennings Boulevard is named in his honor and is a major thoroughfare in Littlefield. A celebration of his birthday in 2010 was held to recognize his contributions to "Outlaw" country music. And why not? He released critically acclaimed albums *Honky Tonk Heroes, Are You Ready for the Country,* and *Wanted! The Outlaws* with Willie Nelson, Tompall Glaser, and his wife, Jessi. *Wanted! The Outlaws*, was the first platinum country music album. One of his most famous songs was "Mammas Don't Let Your Babies Grow Up to Be Cowboys," with Willie Nelson on their *Waylon & Willie* album. Jessi also had an immensely popular hit, the country-pop crossover "I'm Not Lisa," which hit No. 1 on the Billboard Country Music Chart. Her album, *I'm Jessi Colter*, reached No. 1 on the Country Album Chart. If anyone wants to fall in love with country western music, let he or she listen to any of those albums.

A bit of trivia that only the biggest music fans will know: Waylon began his career playing bass on Buddy Holly's tour in the late 1950s. Early in the tour, Holly chartered a plane to take himself, Jennings, and Ritchie Valens (singer of "La Bamba") to the next stop. The day the plane was set to leave, Waylon was sick with a very bad chest cold and gave up his seat to J.P. "The Big Bopper" Richardson. That night the plane crashed, killing all three musicians and the pilot, a date memorialized as "the day the music died" in the famous Don McLean song "American Pie."

Waylon and Jessi had a son, Shooter, and Rema and I were present at the Jennings's home in Henderson, Tennessee, for Shooter's christening. How time flies and how success follows with it. Shooter Jennings is an honored "Outlaw" country, alternative country, country rock, southern rock, hard rock, and psychedelic rock musician, whose albums have peaked on the Billboard Country charts. He also performs frequently alongside his mother.

Overall, Rema and I spent about a month in West Texas. I ate a lot of steak. I wore my boots nearly every day, ending each evening with new and painful blisters on my feet. I learned how to shoot a gun. I lassoed some calves. Okay, maybe I didn't do that last one, but I was about as deep into the culture as any Manhattanite had likely ever been. I loved the life. It was completely alien to me, but it fit in with what I loved to do as a lawyer—represent anyone at anytime. Another way the courtroom was my theater was that I could easily change characters. I could represent the future president of the United States in a divorce one day, and a country music star against drug charges the next. I loved the challenge of each unique role.

One of my first and most notable defenses of Waylon occurred while he was working in Nashville. He had an addiction to cocaine, which was no secret to me or anybody else, including the Drug Enforcement Administration. The DEA had been put on notice by an informant that a messenger would be delivering a large quantity of cocaine from Waylon's manager's Connecticut office to the hotel in Nashville where Waylon was staying. When the agents believed that the delivery had been made, six of them burst into the room, and Waylon was caught red handed attempting to flush the cocaine down the toilet. He was arrested on the spot. Jessi called me immediately.

"Jay, they arrested Waylon!" she cried. Like any spouse, she was frightened and in a state of panic.

"What happened?" I asked.

After she rambled through the few details she had, I told her not to worry.

"I'll take care of it," I said. "I can already tell you, based on what you have told me, that there is a major problem with what the DEA did."

I caught the first flight I could out of New York to Nashville and met with Waylon. I got the facts from him and did my own research, and I knew we would beat the charges. That's not to say that Waylon was clean of any wrongdoing, but there is a legal procedure that must be followed by law enforcement, and they chose not to do it.

"Waylon," I said, "the DEA had information nearly a week in advance that this package was going to be coming to you. That means that what they seized was illegal, a violation of search and seizure. Simply put, they entered your room without a warrant, which they could have easily secured if they had followed protocol."

"Hoss," he said, "your strategy sounds like a plan. I hope it works."

"It will," I said.

Of course, no attorney knows for sure, but this was Nashville and Waylon Jennings, not Washington and Charlie Rangel. I felt comfortable that Waylon would get more of a fair shake than Charlie did in D.C. And I was correct.

The case, in almost no time, was dismissed.

On another occasion, the U.S. Attorney in Tyler, Texas, was investigating a doctor whom the attorney believed was illegally prescribing drugs to members of the Dallas Cowboys football team, as well as to other celebrities. Waylon was subpoenaed in the case. He sent a private plane to New York to pick me up and transport me to Nashville to pick him up. We then proceeded together to Tyler. I recall the case vividly because the judge presiding over the grand jury was Judge William Wayne Justice, an eminent scholar. When the plane arrived in Tyler, we were met at the airport by the U.S. Attorney himself.

"Mr. Jennings," it's a pleasure to meet you," he said.

I knew right away that we had a shot at getting Waylon out of this. The attorney was star struck. I could see it in his eyes and hear it in his voice. And it took him less than a minute to prove me right.

"Mr. Goldberg, I would be happy to excuse Mr. Jennings's appearance before the grand jury if the two of you would consider coming to my home for some coffee and cake and a little discussion about the music business," he said.

I had no idea what the attorney's interest was in the music business, but all we had to do was say yes and this case would be over.

"Yes," I said, not bothering to consult with Waylon. We never had to step foot in the courthouse. On our way back to the airport from the attorney's home, Waylon was ecstatic at what had just transpired.

"Hoss, you did a mighty fine job," he said. "I'm gonna get you present."

"Waylon," I said, "I did nothing but drink coffee and have a Danish. I don't need a present."

"Well, you just let me worry about that," he said.

Four days later, Rema and I went to the train station in Tarrytown, New York, where Waylon had instructed us to meet his "driver."

"Driver?" I asked him. "Driver of what?"

Driver of a brand-new gold Mercedes.

"Waylon! What are you doing!" I yelled when I got home and called him.

"I told you I was gonna get you a gift," he said.

"For coffee and a Danish?"

"For coffee and a Danish," he repeated.

"But do you know the taxes I'll have to pay on this thing?" I really was beyond grateful...but, seriously, the taxes.

"If you don't want it, I'll arrange to bring it back," he said.

What would you do?

One thing is clear: entertainers, businessmen, politicians, anyone with money...they won't hesitate to show their generosity when you've done something to help them, especially if it involves protecting their assets or keeping them out of jail. And it is often difficult to say no when that generosity is nice and shiny with four wheels.

I kept the car.

Late in his career, Waylon joined the television series *The Dukes of Hazard* as the balladeer. I negotiated his contract. The show ran close to ten years. He wrote and sang the theme song, "Good Ol' Boys," which became a big hit. It was the twelfth single he'd released to reach number one on the Billboard country music chart.

In the latter days of his life, Waylon kicked the cocaine habit that had plagued him for so long. He did it "cold turkey." We were friends for more than twenty years. He died on February 13, 2002. After his death, Jessi resumed her career. In 2017, still going strong, she performed a concert in Manhattan and invited Rema and me to the show. Before Jessi started singing that night, she asked that the spotlight be shined on us. We didn't know what was happening.

"Please, everybody, join me in a round of applause for my good friend, Jay Goldberg, and his wife, Rema. Jay was responsible on more than one occasion for saving Waylon's life."

The crowd applauded. We didn't know what to say or do, so we politely stood and waved. It was such a generous gesture and an enormous honor. In fact, I'd have to say in many ways it was even bigger than a new gold Mercedes.

CHAPTER 23

JUST WILLIE

WHILE WILLIE NELSON HAD TREMENDOUS success recording duets with Waylon, it was his solo work that made him famous. Some of Willie's most celebrated solo recordings include "On the Road Again," "You Were Always on My Mind," and "Whiskey River." With his trademark long hair, bandana, and voice that one only needs to hear a few notes of to know it's him, Willie was inducted into the Country Music Hall of Fame in 1993, one of countless honors he has received the last eight decades.

I met Willie about the same time I met Waylon. My first case with Willie was when he was subpoenaed as a witness before a U.S. grand jury sitting in Dallas to find out whether he knew performers who had sold or used cocaine, as well as their supplier. It was no secret to anybody that Willie loved his marijuana, but he was not a user of the hard drugs for which he had been subpoenaed.

The government, nonetheless, assumed Willie's prominence in country music would lead them to the users and suppliers of such hardcore narcotics. Unlike when I worked with Waylon, there was no offer of coffee and Danish to let Willie out of this. He had to repeatedly testify, and each time he told the grand jury that he was unaware of any such information about other stars.

Willie's two standard answers to just about every question asked of him were "I don't know of any such persons" and "I don't remember knowing of any such persons." I didn't advise him to answer in that manner—he was telling the truth as he knew it. And it infuriated the U.S. Attorney. He was so upset, in fact, that he told me he was considering bringing "obstruction of justice" charges against Willie. It was absurd, but there wasn't much I could do about it at that moment. He said to call him in a week to see if such charges would be filed.

"I'm telling them the truth," Willie told me when I revealed this to him.

"I know," I said. "Let's just wait a week and see what they determine. I promise you we'll fight any charges they bring, and we *will* win."

A week later, I called the prosecutor to discuss the matter. I was ready to argue out of the gate but, surprisingly, I didn't have to.

"You know," he said, "I was on the fence as to whether to ask the grand jury to return an indictment. I hope you appreciate that."

"Of course I do," I said, staying on his good side, at least until I heard which side of the fence he decided to fall on.

"You may not know this, Jay, but I lived in Chicago at the time when you received so much publicity for cleaning up crime and corruption in the Lake County, Indiana, area."

"I didn't know that," I said. What were the chances?

"Out of respect for you and what you did back then for our area, I have decided not to seek a prosecution of Willie."

I was blown away. Something that had happened so many years earlier, something that had nothing to do with Dallas or Willie Nelson or the drug users and suppliers the attorney was trying to stop, had possibly saved a country music legend from prison. It was another glaring example of good work recognized and remembered.

"I truly appreciate that," I told him, as we continued to talk about the "good old days" in Gary. I had expected this case was going to be long and drawn out, for I didn't think the attorney was going to let Willie get off so easily, but it turned out I had already done my job for Willie—in Gary, Indiana, in the 1960s.

"Willie," I said when I called him with the good news, "they have decided not to pursue any charges against you. It's over."

"That sounds fine," he said. Don't mistake Willie's ho-hum response for a lack of appreciation. Willie was a very distant and reserved person by nature. He was not the emotional type. No matter whether things were going wrong or right, his demeanor would be the same. While Waylon would have bear-hugged me the next time he saw me after winning a case for him, and while Donald Trump would have exclaimed "Holy shit!" at such good news, Willie

171

politely shook my hand and quietly said thank you. And I was mighty fine with that. I had done my job. The man was happy.

About a month later, Willie decided to have a party at his Colorado home, which stood on one of the highest mountainsides outside of Denver.

"I'd like you and Rema to come," he said when he called.

I didn't know what the party was for, but I imagined this was the equivalent of Waylon's gold Mercedes. Inviting me to his home for a party was his way of thanking me for what I had done for him. Whatever the reason, I didn't care. When Willie Nelson calls you and says to come visit, why ask any questions? You just go, right?

When we arrived, Willie was elegantly dressed in an all-white suit with a tail and a top hat. Soon after Rema and I walked in, he led us to the living room, put his arm around my waist, and asked the crowd of several dozen people for their attention.

"I want you all to know just how well this fine man from New York represented me in court down in Dallas," he said. "This party is in his honor because this is what you do for someone who may have just saved your professional life."

The crowd applauded, clanking together their glasses of booze and raising their joints in my honor. I was stunned. I'm guessing Willie would have thrown a party that night whether he knew Rema and me or not, because Willie liked to throw parties, but to give us as the reason for it was a true honor.

Rema and I mingled with the guests throughout the night and had a marvelous time. While the marijuana was plentiful, the only contact with it Rema and I had was through the secondhand smoke. If this party had been on Willie's narrow and confined tour bus, we'd have ended up with enough smoke in our systems to have us arrested. Fortunately, it wasn't bad given how large his house was.

We spent the night at Willie's, as did many of his guests. Some had private quarters like Rema and I, while others were sprawled out on his couches and floors—pretty much wherever they had landed when the marijuana and drinks told their bodies enough was enough.

The next morning, as most everybody remained passed out until well past noon, Rema and I were up by about eight o'clock. The house was deathly silent, with the exception of the soothing sound of an acoustic guitar being strummed from the back of the house that we could hear through our open bedroom window. I don't know that I can paint a picture with words that will do this justice, but as Rema and I stepped over bodies in the house to follow the music, we eventually came upon Willie sitting in a chair on his back porch. I'm not sure he had ever gone to sleep. Still in his white pants from the night before, along with a tee shirt and bandana, Willie had his eyes closed as he hummed each chord he played. It was if he was trying to find just the right sound that only someone with his talent could detect. Rema and I quietly tiptoed across the porch and sat on a nearby rock to soak in the moment.

"Well, good morning, Goldbergs," he said with a gentle smile as he opened his eyes.

"Good morning," we said.

"Are we interrupting?" Rema asked.

"No, no, not at all," he replied.

He strummed a few more notes, as if he were trying to return to the musical space he'd been immersed in before we had come out.

"I've wanted to try something new," he said. "Tell me what you think of this."

What happened next was one of the most spiritual moments I've ever experienced. Breathing in the crisp cool air, surrounded by the Rocky Mountains on three sides and Willie Nelson on the other, we watched and listened as this legend of country music tenderly brought the guitar strings to life. He produced an intro that sounded all too familiar, but one I couldn't pinpoint until he sang the iconic lyrics to a song I heard so many times before, though they never sounded quite like when he sang them.

"Georgia on My Mind" was written in 1930 by Stuart Gorrell and Hoagy Carmichael, though most people associate it with Ray Charles, who recorded it in 1960. It was one of those songs that, after Ray Charles recorded it, would be recorded many times by singers of all genres. But Rema and I had never heard it played like this. Of course, we'd also never received a private performance by the artist himself.

Willie played through the entire song. I swear, he could have recorded it right then and there on the first take in front of us and it would have become a number one hit. Rema and I applauded when he finished.

"Willie, I think you need to record that," Rema said to him.

"You think so?" he replied.

Not that I'm going to claim he wouldn't have recorded it if Rema hadn't said that, but it was wonderful to hear that he would record it a few weeks later. The song would vault to number one on the Billboard country music chart. Willie would later receive a Grammy Award for the song as Best Male Country Vocalist Performance.

And to think, it began on his back porch in front of Rema and me.

As happy of an ending as that may sound, Willie's need for legal defense would resurface. About twelve years after that first case, the Internal Revenue Service descended without notice upon Willie's Texas home and seized much of his professional equipment, including his guitar, sheet music, and record collection. They also served him with a hefty multimillion dollar tax bill, most of which was interest and penalties. He called me for help, claiming that the bulk of the unpaid taxes was the result of his investing in tax shelters on the advice of accountants. Through a number of negotiating sessions with the government, I worked out an acceptable settlement and arranged for him to retrieve his property the government had seized. While the government initially moved with a heavy hand, the IRS came to realize the unpopularity of what it had done, and it was only too anxious to settle the matter.

Like everything else he'd faced in life, Willie took it all in stride. Determined to pay off his debt, and showing his sense of humor, he released a disc of songs on an album titled *The IRS Tapes: Who'll Buy My Memories?* He also appeared in several humorous television commercials, including one for tax preparers H&R Block. According to a *Rolling Stone* magazine article, Willie said of the IRS: "They didn't bother me, they didn't come out and confiscate anything other than that first day, and they didn't show up at every gig and demand money. I appreciated that. And we teamed up and put out a record." The magazine went on to state: "Attesting to the Zen attitude he had adopted about it all, the T-shirt he wore on the LP cover, which featured Nelson in a black cowboy hat, summed up the situation nicely in just two words: 'Shit happens.'"

I represented Willie again several years later in litigation in Connecticut. There wasn't much to the case, but I bring it up because, as I sat next to him during his deposition, I noticed an aura around him. Yes, I'd recognized it before, especially on his back porch in Colorado, but what struck me this time was that I knew outside the courthouse there were hundreds and maybe even thousands of people on the street waiting to catch a glimpse of him. If this were somewhere in the south I would have understood it, but Connecticut? When we left the courthouse, many people received more than a glimpse. Willie was generous, kind, and warm, sometimes to a fault, and he took a lot of time to sign autographs for as many people as he could. Finally, when he was ready, we got into our car to head out.

"Willie," I said to him as he continued to wave to fans through the window, "I just saw a big movie star in the airport this week refuse to sign autographs for people because he said it was his day off. Why do you do what you do?"

"Because these are my people," he said in the Zen-like manner *Rolling Stone* had talked about years earlier. "Without them, I am nobody."

Now in his 80s, Willie continues to perform regularly. One night, when he was about to play at Nassau Coliseum in New York, I stopped by his hotel to say hello and wish him luck.

"Jay, come with me," he said.

We got into his limo and were driven to the back of the arena where we would enter. I realized it was pretty close to show time. Most performers I know arrive very early to prepare. Not Willie. He prepares by relaxing in his hotel room. Once he leaves that hotel, he is ready to go. When we entered the door of the arena, one of the security members led him to the stage. Waiting for Willie was one of his roadies, who handed him his guitar.

"Here we go," he said to me with a smile, and he walked right on stage to an audience of more than ten thousand fans. It happened that quickly.

As an attorney who knows his stuff, I'm pretty calm and confident when I head into a case. But Willie takes "calm and confident" to an entirely different level.

CHAPTER 24

THE HIGHWAYMEN VERSUS THE HIGHWAYMEN

I RECEIVED A CALL ONE afternoon from Waylon. He needed my help, and fast. He and his buddies—Willie, Johnny Cash, and Kris Kristofferson—were scheduled to perform a concert that was in danger of being canceled due to litigation over their group name.

The four country music legends had formed a group called the Highwaymen, and they were booked to play a concert at the Universal Amphitheatre in Los Angeles. They had released an album entitled "Highwayman" four years prior and were very popular. The event was widely publicized, and tickets for the show sold out in the first hour.

An article in *The New York Times* gave me sole credit for the outcome of the case, but that was not accurate. I consulted with Peter Parcher, an extraordinary lawyer of great skill and attorney for The Rolling Stones, asking that he come aboard. He brought in Gerry Margolis, a partner at Manatt, Phelps & Phillips. All three of us dropped what we were doing to fly to Los Angeles, for the concert was in less than a week.

The case began when an action for an injunction was brought in the U.S. District Court for the Middle District of California under the Lanham Act, which "...protects the owner of a federally registered trademark against the use of similar marks if such use is likely to result in consumer confusion..." according to the Cornell Law School website. Those filing for the injunction were members of a group also known as the Highwaymen, an old folk group of five students from Wesleyan College in Middletown, Connecticut, that had formed some thirty years earlier. They actually were somewhat popular for a couple of years back in the day, when they had recorded two hit songs: "Michael," which rose to number one on the pop chart, and "Cottonfields." Both sold more than a million copies. The group had also appeared on *The Ed Sullivan Show* and on *The Tonight Show Starring Johnny Carson.*

To add a twist to this case, one of the group's members was Stephen Trott, who was at the time of the injunction the chief judge of the U.S. Court of Appeals for the Ninth Circuit. He had previously been the U.S. Attorney in Los Angeles and the U.S. representative to INTERPOL. In other words, his standing in the legal community, especially where this case was being heard, was of the highest caliber. According to *The New York Times*, what made the matter even more interesting was that any appeal from the U.S. district judge would go before the Ninth Circuit where Chief Judge Trott was a member. To boost their case, the original Highwaymen claimed that they intended to release a compact disc of their old material. The matter was set for argument.

Sitting within five feet of our defense table and intending to argue the case for the original Highwaymen was Chief Judge Trott himself. U.S. District Judge Robert Takasugi asked me if I wanted the case transferred to another court outside the Ninth Circuit.

"Your honor, I am satisfied with the case being heard before you." A small part of my decision may have been arrogance, for nothing would have been sweeter than defeating a sitting judge in Judge Trott, and on his home turf. But mostly I felt confident that the trial judge would find it inappropriate for Chief Judge Trott and his thirty-year-old group to interfere with the public's appreciation of Waylon, Willie, Johnny, and Kris.

The other two attorneys and I prepared the opposing papers, arguing that the Lanham Act did not apply, for there could be no confusion by members of the public that these four Highwaymen we were representing were the five east coast college students from the early 1960s.

The New York Times reported: "Jay Goldberg of New York, the lawyer for Nelson, Jennings, Cash and Kristofferson...[dismissed] the plaintiffs as a 'defunct band.'" I pointed out that the original

Highwaymen had performed a grand total of once since 1962, and that was at Judge Trott's college reunion.

"I challenge [Judge Trott] to bring any witness who, having purchased a ticket to the Highwaymen's performance in the 1990s, would be confused into believing that when he/she entered the arena, they would see the honorable Stephen Trott strumming a guitar," I argued.

"Only one person in this room would be confused about the two groups," I continued. "That person is Judge Trott."

The judge ruled as I had expected. The court dismissed the challenge to the current Highwaymen's use of the name.

But that wasn't the end. In fact, it was the beginning of something pretty beautiful, brought on by no one other than Waylon.

"Hoss," he said to me after the dismissal of the case, "I'd like to soften the blow a little bit for these guys."

As an attorney who had just gotten him and his buddies exactly what they had wanted, I wasn't enamored with the idea of doing anything more than hopping on a jet back to New York. But, of course, I listened to his idea.

"What if we make them the opening act for our show here in L.A.," he said. "It will be the Highwaymen and the Highwaymen."

Wow.

"Waylon, if you and the others are comfortable making that offer," I said, "then I am certainly all for it."

The group accepted the invitation.

In a *Los Angeles Times* article after the offer, Judge Trott said, "Maybe we should turn the legal system of the U.S. over to Waylon. With a single swipe [Waylon] eliminated all the usual things that go with the resolution of this kind of case." He also said, "I've always said it's too often that we turn to the courts in this country to resolve problems, and this is a classic example. I think [the offer] is wonderful."

It was another case of these "outlaws" being quite contrary to their real personalities. I was so proud of Waylon for his offer, and I was proud to represent the group and help them maintain their name of the Highwaymen.

CHAPTER 25

LYNYRD SKYNYRD AND THE BENEFIT OF SETTLING

A HIGHLY RESPECTED ENTERTAINMENT LAWYER in 1988 referred to me an interesting piece of litigation involving the musical group Lynyrd Skynyrd. The group had achieved great commercial success in the 1970s. Known for such classic songs as "Sweet Home Alabama" and "Free Bird," they quickly became one of the most popular southern rock bands in the world. Tragically, on October 20, 1977, on a flight from South Carolina destined for Louisiana, their plane crashed. Killed were lead singer Ronnie Van Zant, guitarist Steve Gaines, backup singer Cassie Gaines, the pilot and co-pilot, and an assistant road manager. Several others in and associated with the band were seriously injured.

A few months after the crash, Judith Van Zant (Ronnie's widow) and two surviving members of the band orally agreed never to use the name Lynyrd Skynyrd, an agreement that was written in the minutes of a 1978 shareholder's meeting. It was a decision mutually made to not capitalize on the tragedy and to ensure revenue on the earlier records produced. For nearly ten years there was no problem; everyone abided by the contract. Individual members continued to perform during that time, but under names other than Lynyrd Skynyrd.

However, in 1987, the surviving members of the group decided they wanted to reunite to tour and produce a live album using the name Lynyrd Skynyrd. In cooperation with Van Zant's widow (now Judith Van Zant Grondin), the survivors of the crash set up a tribute tour to Lynyrd Skynyrd that was scheduled to be completed by the end of 1987. The tour would honor the deceased band members during the show and songs by the original band would, of course, be performed. The album was to be produced from those performances.

When the album came out, it featured the title *Lynyrd Skynyrd Live*, which was printed in large, bold letters on the cover. At the bottom of the album, in significantly smaller letters, were the words "Lynyrd Skynyrd Tribute Tour 1987." Grondin objected to the album once she saw it—which she said she did not see until it was in record stores—claiming that she did not approve the title or design. The band also later decided to continue its tour into the spring and summer of 1988 to promote the album, something else Grondin said she did not approve.

With the tour in full swing in June of 1988, Grondin sought a preliminary injunction to stop the band from performing and to stop the marketing of the album. She cited as part of her argument the Lanham Act—similar to the Highwaymen case—claiming that a new Lynyrd Skynyrd band and album would cause consumer confusion.

This matter, as important as it was to Grondin to protect her financial interest and the legacy of her deceased husband, was equally important to the surviving members of the group. After all, they had suffered so much physically and emotionally. To prevent them from reuniting and performing as Lynyrd Skynyrd after biding by the oral agreement for nearly ten years seemed heartless to many.

After the plaintiffs presented their case and after I presented the defense for the band, an injunction was granted in part and denied in part. Mostly, our side got what we wanted. Here is what happened:

In terms of the tour, while it was determined that there were minor ways in which a concertgoer not too familiar with the band might be deceived, the judge sided with us. The tour was well under way, tickets had been sold, and it was essentially the same tour as the one in 1987 in terms of how it was conducted on stage. Since Grondin did not object to the 1987 tour and received a percentage of profits from those concerts per the agreement she had made then with the band, it was ruled that the tour could continue.

Regarding the album, it was determined that there could be some confusion to the consumer. While fans of the band knew Ronnie Van Zant was dead, it was possible, given the way the cover was designed, that consumers might think some of the recordings on the album included those featuring Van Zant before his death. While the cover did include the words "Lynyrd Skynyrd Tribute Tour 1987," they were so small across the bottom. The ruling was that the albums currently in the marketplace did not have to be recalled, but the record company would be required to add a sticker to all future *Live* albums sold. The sticker would have to clearly state that the album was a recently recorded performance by the new Lynyrd Skynyrd band.

Remember, this action was a move by Grondin for a preliminary injunction—this was not a negotiation to avoid a trial. After the ruling, the judge set a trial date. However, the feeling among everyone involved was that a trial was not in anybody's best interest. We were all anxious to end the dispute. Van Zant's widow had a right to monies, but the surviving members of the group had a right to perform.

This case shows how important it is for a lawyer to always consider the interest of the parties involved above all else. Trial fees are so very costly that, in the vast majority of cases, justice is best accomplished by putting the parties in a room, virtually locking the doors, and not letting them out until a settlement is affected. You may remember that is how we handled Donald and Ivana Trump's divorce case. Though Donald at one point left the negotiations, we didn't give up and pulled him back in because we knew a settlement was in everybody's best interest.

In the Lynyrd Skynyrd case, it wasn't an easy negotiation, but we did eventually come to a settlement and a trial was avoided. That is not to say that all the parties were overjoyed, for it is often said that in a good settlement, neither party is fully satisfied.

In fact, proof of that statement could still be seen thirty years later.

In 2017, while the band was still going strong as "Lynyrd Skynyrd," touring across the U.S. and in South America, there was an article in the Las Vegas Review-Journal that stated a judge had blocked distribution of a film titled *Street Survivors: The True Story of the Lynyrd Skynyrd Plane Crash*, which was based in part on stories from the band's former drummer Artimus Pyle. According to the article: "The judge said a dispute after surviving band members decided to commemorate the ten-year anniversary of the crash with a tribute tour resulted in an agreement defining when the parties could use the band's name, its history, or the name and likeness of Van Zant."

Three decades had gone by and my work was still in effect.

CHAPTER 26

SAVING HIP-HOP ICON SEAN "PUFFY" COMBS

MY SON AND I WERE walking home one evening and passed a prestigious restaurant. It was about 10:00 p.m. Standing outside the door, having just finished his dinner, was hip-hop mogul Sean "Puffy" Combs. Sean, who was a rapper, song writer, record producer, and actor, also used stage names "Puff Daddy," "Diddy," and "P. Diddy."

"Mr. Goldberg!" he said with a huge smile as we approached him.

"It's good to see you, Sean," I said, shaking his hand. "This is my son."

Sean shook my son's hand before putting his hand on my shoulder. His look turned serious.

"You know what?" he said to my son. "Your father is a great man. He saved me from prison."

Before I go any further, in case you're wondering, yes, the music he performed was completely foreign to me. I didn't listen to it, I couldn't sing it, I couldn't dance to it, I couldn't have even told you who he was until I met him. *Puffy? His name is Puffy?* Frankly, it was the same way with many others I represented—Waylon, Willie, The Rolling Stones, Lynyrd Skynyrd, Miles Davis. I didn't have time to listen to music a whole lot, and when I did, it was more of the classical variety. But it didn't mean I couldn't represent them better than anyone else, which is why my musical tastes mattered none to them.

Sean attended Howard University for two years, majoring in business administration. He dropped out of school to work as an intern at Uptown Records in New York, where he developed famed R&B artists Jodeci and Mary J. Blige. After his time at Uptown, he

183

established Bad Boy Records, taking yet-unknown hip-hop artist Notorious B.I.G.—also known as Biggie—with him. Biggie soon released what remains one of the most iconic hip-hop albums of all-time, *Ready to Die*, and Sean's career began to take off as a result. Bad Boy Records would work with a number of artists after that, including Lil Kim, Usher, Mariah Carey, Boyz II Men, and Aretha Franklin. In 2016, Sean had reported earnings of 116 million dollars. Not bad for a college dropout from Harlem.

Despite Sean's success, trouble seemed to follow him in the early years of his career. While he was the subject of so much fan appeal, he also attracted a lot of police attention. Police were so hostile to his enormous success that I began to feel there was prejudice against him.

My first encounter with him was in 1991 while he was still in college and not yet a household name. Sean had co-organized and co-promoted a charity basketball tournament at City College of New York to raise money for AIDS awareness. A number of hip hop artists were in attendance to play and to give a performance that would follow. The capacity of the gymnasium was about 2,700, but certain promoters sold three thousand tickets to the event in an effort to pocket extra money. The ticketholders bought the tickets not so much for the basketball game, but to see the post-game show.

The overflow crowd of three thousand gathered outside the 138th Street entrance, and they grew unruly. Obviously, the selling of tickets in excess of what was lawfully permitted resulted in chaos. One of the ticketholders broke a glass door to gain entrance. Despite the many police officers and campus security guards, the crowd surged through the doors and rushed into the building toward the gymnasium. Once inside the lobby, they stampeded down the stairs. The crush led to a fatal result: nine people were trampled to death and twenty-nine were injured.

The district attorney considered the case, trying to determine if there was any criminal conduct on the part of Sean in the tragedy. I argued vehemently that Sean was not aware of the amount of sales, and that he had actually gone above and beyond his duty in trying to provide a safe environment. There were sixty-six officers outside the gym, thirty security officers provided by the college, and another twenty security personnel hired by the promoters. In fact, one of Sean's business lawyers would say several years later in 1998, during a trial in which Sean was a witness in a lawsuit filed against City College by some of the victims, that Sean hired extra security for the event even though security was not his responsibility. In time, the prosecutor agreed with my analysis. I was notified that there was insufficient evidence to warrant an indictment against him. No charges were filed.

"City College is something I deal with every day of my life," Sean told a *New York Times* reporter during that 1998 trial. "But the things that I deal with can in no way measure up to the pain that the families deal with. I just pray for the families and pray for the children who lost their lives every day."

Rema and I went to Sean's home to give him the news. Biggie was also there.

"I talked to the D.A.," I said. "You're a free man."

"It's over?" Sean asked.

"There won't be any charges filed," I reiterated. I knew it wasn't completely "over" from a litigation standpoint. Civil lawsuits were likely to be filed against him by victims and families of victims. Whether or not there are criminal charges filed, suits seeking monetary compensation are generally filed, especially in matters that involve anyone who has money. Sean wasn't as popular yet as he would soon become, but he was getting close. He would settle more than one suit in relation to the case in the coming years, but I had done for him what mattered most—I kept him out of prison.

Sean would continue during his career to have run-ins with police and other authorities. Detectives from Los Angeles came to my office in 1997 to question him as to whether he had any knowledge of the people involved in the murders of Tupac Shakur and Biggie.

Tupac was a rapper and actor from the west coast. *Rolling Stone* magazine ranked him 86th among the 100 Greatest Artists of All Time, and he was inducted into the Rock and Roll Hall of Fame in 2017. He achieved his success despite facing a lot of adversity in his life. He grew up around several family members who had serious criminal pasts. He was heavily involved in the west coast/east coast hip-hop feud, which often pitted him against Biggie and, at times, resulted in violence or the threat of violence between their factions. Tupac was the victim of a drive-by shooting after a boxing match in Las Vegas on September 7, 1996. He was shot four times and died six days later.

Biggie was killed in Los Angeles, also in a drive-by shooting, six months later. Sean was part of Biggie's entourage that night, but he was riding in a separate car when Biggie was killed.

Sean spoke to the detectives in my office, clearly stating that he knew nothing about who was responsible for either of their deaths. Soon after that meeting, despite his claim, Sean was subpoenaed to appear before a federal grand jury in Washington, D.C., to give testimony with respect to his knowledge of the deaths of both men. I accompanied him, and on two occasions, he left the grand jury room to ask for my advice.

Due to attorney-client privilege, I cannot discuss what Sean asked me, but I will say there is no question in my mind that he had no knowledge of who committed the murders of either man. There are times as an attorney when you know everything about your client, and there are times you know very little. There are times when a client will plead innocence, and other times when he is simply looking for you to limit the potential punishment he will receive. In Sean's case, through numerous conversations with him, I had no doubt that he was telling me and the L.A. detectives the truth. He felt that authorities often went after him because of his skin color, and in some cases I couldn't disagree. That is why I defended him.

As in the case of the City College deaths, and as I had expected, no charges were filed against Sean regarding the deaths of Tupac or Biggie. Their murders remain unsolved to this day.

Also in the 1990s, Sean asked for my help defending him against claims of violence made by Steve Stoute, a record executive and president of the Urban Music Division at Interscope Geffen A&M Records.

If you're wondering how innocent a person like Sean could be when so many serious charges are made against him, consider this case. Fed up with the way people were treating him and trying to take advantage of him, I decided to not only defend him against Stoute's claims, but defend him by proving his innocence.

Stoute, like Sean, managed a number of leading hip-hop artists, and they often competed for clients. In one case, there was a music video production in which the two decided to partner. After the production, Sean, who had been filmed in the video nailed to a cross, decided he didn't want that scene in, but Stoute included it anyway. According to Stoute, Sean was so angry that he and three men went to Stoute's office and beat him with a chair and liquor bottle. Stoute filed charges, and Sean was charged with felonious assault and criminal mischief. He faced seven years in prison.

Sean and I had several face-to-face conversations about this case.

"I'm telling you, Jay," he insisted, "I did not lay a hand on that man. Neither did my guys."

I knew Sean had a volatile personality, so to hear one guy say there was significant violence and the other say there was none at all initially left me in a tenuous spot on how to strategically defend my client. But those meetings with him convinced me he was telling the truth.

"I believe you, Sean," I said. "And I'm going to prove your innocence."

"How are you going to do that?" he asked.

I can't say that I knew right away exactly how I was going to do it, but it became clear to me when one afternoon when I received a call at my office from Stout's lawyer, Tom Puccio. Puccio was one of the city's most prominent attorneys, and the attorney who represented Steve Wynn and illegally recorded people when I was representing Donald Trump. Puccio practiced in a way that was close to the line, even though as a prosecutor he was known as an effective and thorough investigator. Stoute had sued Sean for fifty million dollars, and Puccio wanted to discuss a settlement.

"Let me call my client and see what he says. I will let you know soon," I said.

But I was confident something shady was going on, so confident that I wasn't afraid to go public with my gut feeling.

According to a *New York Post* article about the case: "Stoute said an apparently contrite Combs has made overtures to him, but he's not interested. 'He reached out to me – I didn't reach back out to him,' Stoute snapped. 'The only thing he can do for me is go to jail.' Combs' lawyer, Jay Goldberg, said: 'I view this as a shakedown.'"

I called Sean and Puccio the next day and arranged for the four of us to meet late in the evening at a steakhouse near my office. According to that same *Post* article: "'There was a demand made by Steve Stoute to look the other way for $50 million,'" Goldberg said. 'It finally went down to $12 million.' Stoute responded: 'I never told anyone for $12 million I'd drop all charges – that's extortion.'"

Exactly!

Which is why, when we met at the restaurant, I had my briefcase with me. And guess what I had in my briefcase?

I recorded the entire meeting.

We had barely ordered our drinks when I realized Stoute and Puccio had no interest in a complaint against Sean for purported violence against Stoute. Their intention was clear: were Sean to pay an agreed upon sum of money, Stoute would immediately change his testimony. It was confirmed by Stoute during this meeting that Sean and his men never touched him, not with their own hands, a chair, or a liquor bottle. He said Sean threatened him—which Sean did not deny. But a threat versus whacking someone in the head with a fist and three objects aren't even in the same legal sphere.

"We will let you know our decision tomorrow," I said to our opponents as we left the restaurant. I didn't tip my hand at all, though I think they thought they were about to hit a multimillion dollar payday.

The next morning I took the tape to the assistant district attorney and played the tape. I thought it was an open and shut case. But she thought otherwise.

"We're proceeding with the case," she said.

"What?"

"Nothing has changed," she insisted.

"What are you talking about? Were you not listening to the tape?"

"Oh, I was listening, and the charges stand."

"You could end this man's career," I said.

"If that happens, he can always drive a bus when he gets out," she retorted.

I don't know what she had against Sean, or why she viewed driving a bus as a bad thing. So I took the tape to another assistant DA, someone I knew well, and played it for him. He knew immediately after listening to it that their case was finished, and he convinced his ignorant colleague of that.

When we got to the courthouse for Sean's probable cause hearing, it seemed like all of the personnel in the building were waiting to get Sean's autograph or photo. Court officers were included among the throngs of fans. It was so chaotic that I found myself separated from Sean in our effort to get to the courtroom.

When we finally got there and the matter was before the judge, who had been informed by the assistant DAs of the damning evidence I had on tape, Sean pleaded guilty to harassment and was sentenced to one day of "anger management" classes. The claims of violence were dismissed. This nightmare was over.

According to the *Post*, Stoute and Sean were friends again and the "wheels of friendship were reportedly regreased with a $500,000 payment from Combs to Stoute. After the payment was made, Stoute told prosecutors 'he didn't want the defendant to be convicted of a crime, and conveyed that he and Sean had worked out their differences,' according to a law-enforcement source. Combs' case was quickly disposed of during an appearance in Manhattan Criminal Court."

That was not true.

There was no payment. The article says nothing about the recording from the restaurant that I had because the reporter did not know about it. Stoute's camp spun the story the way they wanted. The truth was that Stoute tried to extort money from Sean, and I caught him. Stoute did not receive a dime from my client.

It was a sweet victory, not only because I'd outsmarted Puccio and his client who was willing to put a man behind bars for not getting his undue payday, but because I'd defeated a prosecuting attorney who, for whatever reason, disliked my client so much that she was willing to ignore evidence in order to prosecute him.

Soon after the Stoute incident, I represented Sean once more when he was arrested on a complaint that he had assaulted a *New York Post* photographer. The photographer had waited outside Sean's office into the late hours to take pictures of him leaving. It is hard to understand from reading the cold pages of this book how starstruck some members of the public were and how insistent the paparazzi could be. I was astounded at what many of my clients had to deal with each day, multiple times a day.

The photographer claimed that Sean was accompanied by two other people when he left his office, one of whom threatened the photographer with a gun. The charge was again assault in the second degree. When the police responded, of course no gun was found. I was present when the police later interviewed the photographer, and I didn't trust him one bit, so I had my investigator examine his background. My investigation disclosed that the photographer had been a former New York City public school teacher who had been fired by the board of education for chasing a student down the street with a gun. Yes, you read that correctly. Not with a camera like he did for the *Post*, but with a gun. It was enough to scare the assistant DA, who immediately dismissed the charges.

With his legal problems behind him, Sean was free to dedicate his time and talent to his work. He released his first album, *No Way Out*, which was certified platinum seven times, and he released a number of other commercially successful albums. He has won three Grammy Awards, two MTV Video Music Awards, and started a clothing line for which he earned a Council of Fashion Designers of America Award. He was said to be the richest figure in hip hop music during the 2000s. In 2002, he was number 12 on the *Fortune* magazine top 40 money-making entrepreneurs under 40, and in 2012, *Forbes* ranked him 50th among money-making musical artists.

His career has not been confined to just music. He has appeared as the lead on Broadway in the Tennessee Williams play *A Raisin in the Sun*, and in a number of movies as well.

Sean remains a dear friend, but I did have one gripe with him recently. Every summer he holds a gala affair at his mansion in Southampton known as the "White Party" where all who attend must wear white. Though I consider Sean to be a wonderful friend, not once has he invited me to the White Party.

"Sean," I asked him one day, "why have you never invited Rema and me to your party?"

The hip-hop icon, who is roughly thirty-seven years my junior, laughed at me.

"Jay," he said, "our party usually starts about one a.m. And I am guessing that is at least three hours after you have gone to bed."

I had no further questions.

CHAPTER 27

GETTING MICK JAGGER SOME SATISFACTION

I REPRESENTED THE FIRST MANAGER of the Rolling Stones, an Englishman named Andrew Loog Oldham. He was a salesman in a men's clothing store—a London Barneys type store—in the early 1960s. He truly had a winning personality.

One day while working, in walked Mick Jagger, then an unknown musician and performer. Oldham and Jagger struck up a conversation. Jagger said that he was part of a music group giving a concert at a London arena. He invited Oldham to be his guest. Oldham went, recognized their enormous talent, met with the group afterward, and offered to manage them.

But Oldham and the Stones would make a terrible mistake: they would allow Allen Klein to become co-manager. Klein had managed the legendary Sam Cooke and was well known in the industry as a solid negotiator of record contracts. He was a music entrepreneur with talent, but he also had an extremely poor reputation for honesty and true devotion to a client's interests. He was said to be rock 'n' roll's most ruthless manipulator, one who ignored his managerial obligation to pay performers their share from record sales, and one who would later in life serve jail time for tax evasion. Klein would also manage the Beatles and become one of the leading managers in rock music. But, before long, it became apparent that he would be better known as the one who broke up the Beatles.

Klein eventually bought out Oldham's share of the management rights in the late 1960s. It was in the early 1980s that Oldham came to me and said that Klein contractually still owed him money from the Stones's success after Oldham had left the group. I had determined that since the Stones—who had employed Klein as their manager through 1970—knew Oldham was owed this money, they too were liable for Klein's debt to Oldham.

Before I could file suit to enforce Oldham's rights, the Stones's lawyer, Peter Parcher, a very successful entertainment lawyer and litigator who would later help me in the Highwaymen case, came to my home to talk about the issues in dispute. Klein not only owed Oldham money but, not surprising, he'd also withheld money from the Stones. In fact, the Stones had been in constant litigation with Klein since about 1971, right after they fired him to hire someone else. There were multiple suits that spanned more than a decade. The Stones often won those suits and received money they were owed, but they could never actually break their contract with Klein.

Parcher and I came to an amicable agreement that the Stones would pay monies to Oldham that he was owed by Klein. Parcher's intent was to then go after Klein for that money. After filing suit in U.S. District Court in Manhattan, Parcher feared that with the liberal rules of discovery (such as gathering depositions), the matter would not reach the point of trial for several years. A delay such as that would be exactly what Klein would want, hoping that the Stones would decide to settle for an agreement largely in Klein's favor rather than have the case drag out. That's why Parcher called me.

"Jay, I'd like you to join us on our case against Klein," he said.

This was quite an unusual move. Parcher wanted me to help him try to get what his clients felt they were owed by Klein so that his clients could then pay my client what Klein owed him. With Oldham's approval, and after my firm's accountant went over the financial records and determined that our case against Klein was solid, I didn't hesitate to say yes.

Before the trial, Parcher brought Mick Jagger to my office one afternoon since Mick would be called to testify. I had never seen Mick. I'd never heard him sing. I knew none of his songs. But I knew he was somebody special when word had spread that he was coming to my office. There were five thousand women who worked in the building who congregated outside my office. Okay, that number might be a bit of an exaggeration, but it was quite the chaotic scene as women screamed, cried, and nearly fainted at his presence. Once Parcher and Mick were able to squeeze through the insanity and into my office, Parcher introduced us. Mick was very polite, soft-spoken, and quite intelligent.

"What a scene out there," I said, breaking the ice as I shook his hand.

"Yes, a bit crazy," he said. That was quite the understatement. Though I knew little about Mick, it was obvious to me by his tranquil demeanor that such attention was typical for him.

"Has music always been your life?" I asked.

"I actually spent some time as a student at the London School of Economics, but I dropped out to join the band. I guess I made the right move," he said with a smile.

He talked about what they had been through with Klein over the years, and that they simply wanted what was rightfully theirs. He didn't speak in a vengeful tone, but in more of a moral one.

"Andrew (Oldham) and I met in London a long time ago, and he helped us a lot," he said. Mick said he and the band simply wanted to make things right for themselves and Oldham, and then move on to the next chapter of their storied careers.

I believe Parcher asked for my assistance in their case primarily because he felt, based on my reputation and the respect judges had for me, that I would be able to convince the trial judge that pretrial discovery (depositions and such) was not in order. The parties knew each other too well for us to waste time on that. We wanted the case set for immediate trial.

Parcher's hunch was correct.

When it came time to appear before the court, as Parcher and I walked up the stairs to the courthouse with Mick, there were throngs of screaming fans, including dozens of courthouse workers, who apparently dropped their office duties to see this legend. Court officers were necessary to enable us to get through the mass of people and take the elevator to the courtroom, which was also filled to capacity. When it came time to appear before the judge, the marshals advised that the court wanted to see us in the robing room. It was there that we argued against pretrial discovery, and the judge agreed. The trial was set for ten days out.

It began on a Monday. The judge took the bench in what was a non-jury trial, and Mick was called as the first witness. Fashionably dressed and appearing relaxed, he walked up to the stand, took his oath, and, as he sat down...

Clunk.

He knocked over the microphone. He clumsily tried to stand it upright, obviously embarrassed by his faux pas.

"Mr. Jagger, you do know how to deal with microphones, don't you?" the judge asked facetiously.

Courtroom observers erupted in laughter.

That was pretty much all of the excitement of the trial. After Mick and others were questioned, the judge called for another conference in the robing room.

"I've heard enough," he said to all of us. "There needs to be an economic divorce." He suggested the Stones end their contract with Klein by buying him out for a nominal amount.

"Negotiate a settlement and you will all be free to go your own ways without owing anybody anything more," he said. So that's what we did.

Oddly enough, the Stones's relationship with Klein improved after the settlement, and they brought him back into the fold to help them celebrate and promote their fortieth anniversary in 2002.

I was grateful to Parcher for allowing me the opportunity to work on his case with him and represent the Rolling Stones. Something I have learned about working with celebrities like Mick is that there is always a story, and oftentimes multiple stories, behind the story we see in public. Most people only know celebrities based on the way the media portrays them, which normally doesn't include much substance. I am fortunate enough to be in a position to dig deeper into their psyches. The crazed fans outside my office and the courthouse saw Mick as a famous singer. My perspective was that he was a sincerely bright man, a former student at the London School of Economics, who happened to also be a damn good musician.

CHAPTER 28

HELPING MILES DAVIS STAND ON HIS OWN TWO FEET

MANY OF MY CLIENTS HAD worldwide acclaim, but maybe none more than Miles Davis. Miles was a trumpeter, considered one of the most influential jazz musicians of the twentieth century. He wasn't just some guy who picked up a horn one day and started playing. He attended Julliard School. He perfected his craft. He would play before sold-out audiences all over the world. From New York City, where there is a street named after him, to Kielce, Poland, where a bronze statue stands in his honor, everybody loved Miles Davis.

Neil Reshen, who referred me to Willie and Waylon, also referred me to Mark Rothbaum, Miles's manager. As talented as Miles was, he had one major flaw that nearly derailed his career several times: an addiction to drugs and alcohol. He was born in 1926. His addiction began in the '40s and continued for more than three decades—heroin, cocaine, prescription drugs, whatever booze he could find. It was an ugly side to a beautiful man, a side that I had to defend four times in front of judges.

When he called me the first time at Rothbaum's recommendation, he sounded sober. He had a case coming up and wanted to get to know the guy who was going to be defending him. Rema and I always knew when it was Miles on the other end of the line by his raspy whisper of a voice.

"Goldberg," he said the first time we spoke. "So you're Jewish?"

"I am," I replied.

"You know, Jewish women love me," he said. "They just love me."

196

Miles was a very handsome man. In his autobiography, he didn't hold back in revealing how much women were attracted to him and the many sexual encounters he had had with them. How many were Jewish, I have no idea, nor did I need to know when he called me that day.

We talked about many things of mutual interest, including his drug addiction. He didn't hide the fact that it was a problem and that it had caused many hardships throughout his career, but sadly he seemed more concerned about how to make it legally go away than he did about kicking the habit.

The first time we appeared in court, everything was normal. He came in, answered the judge's questions, allowed me to work out a deal with the judge that amounted to a slap on the wrist, and the case was over.

"Thank you for everything," he said to me as we left the courthouse.

"You're welcome," I replied. "But you really should work on getting yourself clean."

"I'll be alright," he said with a smile as he headed to his car. I got the sense that he thought this would be the only time we'd encounter each other, but I had a suspicion it would be far from the last. Miles went back to performing as if nothing had happened, entertaining crowds worldwide. But where he went, his habit went, and he inevitably would have to repeatedly call me to get him out of trouble.

The saddest moment for me in our relationship was when, during one case, he arrived at the courthouse higher than a kite. I could see it in his eyes and hear it in his speech, not to mention the fact that he couldn't walk a straight line from the entrance to the courtroom to the table where we were to be seated. When his case was called, the judge asked him to rise. That should have been the easiest part, but Miles sat there as if he didn't know what to do.

"Stand up, Miles," I said, as I put my hand under his bicep to try to help him.

"Mr. Davis, are you okay?" the judge asked.

"He's fine your honor," I said, as Miles leaned nearly all of his weight against me for support.

The judge read the charges and asked Miles what plea he would like to enter. Miles looked at the judge with bewilderment and then looked at me as if to say, "What did he just ask?"

"Miles, focus on the judge," I whispered. "Tell him your plea, Miles."

Still using me for support, he turned to the judge, paused for a moment, and then forced out the word "guilty," in a voice barely audible enough for the court reporter to record. What was fascinating was watching the judge's reaction. Some judges would have reprimanded a man who was obviously under the influence of the very substance he was being charged with abusing, and rightfully so, but this judge appeared very sympathetic, just as past judges had. He extended himself considerably by ignoring Miles's condition and giving him nothing more than probation.

Every time I represented Miles, he could have easily gone to jail, but he didn't because of who he was. Every judge knew him. Every judge loved him. And every judge gave him a break. They felt sorry for him and knew that prison would break him. Miles, like many drug addicts, was a good man with a serious problem. The judges sensed that and always gave him a pass.

As an attorney, I do sometimes say enough is enough to my clients who refuse to help themselves, but I always try to keep in mind what addiction is, as I witnessed its grip on my father in the form of gambling throughout my childhood. To me, addiction is like being covered in metal and standing before a magnet. It pulls you, and you have no choice but to succumb to that force, a force that can only be broken through outside intervention—in Miles's case, intense counseling. I've had clients who came out clean on the other side. Miles tried several times, and he even was clean for periods of time, but the force always pulled him back.

As I helped Miles walk out of court that day, I told him how lucky he was.

"I don't think you understand how fortunate you are to be a free man right now," I said.

"I know," he said, appearing to feel some shame.

"The time is going to come when we are going to run into a judge who won't be sympathetic," I said. "Let me try to find you a doctor who can help."

"I'll take care of it," he slurred. "I really will. I'll try."

But I had no illusions. He was an addict who was going to continue doing what he was doing, and I knew I couldn't help him if he wasn't going to try to help himself.

Miles spent the last years of his life on the West Coast painting. His works were exhibited in a number of museums. He would remain a great friend over the years. He and his beautiful wife, the legendary actress Cicely Tyson, even graced me with their presence at my fiftieth birthday celebration. His website, milesdavis.com, is continually updated and fresh as if he were still alive today. Which, in some respects, he is, given the legacy of his music.

Annual Dinner

N. W. Indiana Crime Commission

You are invited to attend the

CRIME COMMISSION'S THIRD ANNUAL DINNER

Saturday, February 2, 1963

Vogel's Restaurant

WHITING, INDIANA

7:00 P.M.

An award of commendation for performance of special merit will be awarded Mr. Jay Goldberg, former United States Attorney, whose work resulted in the indictments, disclosures and trials of Lake County officials.

Mr. Goldberg will make the principal address of the evening. This will be an unique and important occasion for every citizen of N. W. Indiana interested in good government.

Please indicate your plans to attend this dinner by mailing today, the card enclosed.

Northwest Indiana Crime Commission

UNITED STATES DEPARTMENT OF JUSTICE

WASHINGTON, D. C.

Address Reply to the
Division Indicated
and Refer to Initials and Number

August 17, 1961

Mr. Jay Goldberg
Criminal Division
Department of Justice
Washington, D. C.

Dear Mr. Goldberg:

      As an attorney and counselor at law, you are hereby specially retained and appointed as a Special Attorney, under the authority of the Department of Justice, to assist in the trial of the case or cases growing out of the transactions hereinafter mentioned in which the Government is interested; and in that connection you are specifically directed to file informations and to conduct in the Northern District of Indiana and in any other judicial district where the jurisdiction thereof lies, any kind of legal proceeding, civil or criminal, including grand jury proceedings and proceedings before committing magistrates which United States Attorneys are authorized by law to conduct.

      The Department is informed that various persons, companies, corporations, firms, associations and organizations to the Department unknown have violated in the Northern District of Indiana and in other judicial districts the false statements and conspiracy statutes (Sections 1001 and 371 of Title 18 of the United States Code); the income tax laws (Sections 7201, 7202, 7203, and 7206 of Title 26 of the United States Code) and other criminal laws of the United States and have conspired to commit all such offenses and to defraud the United States Code in violation of Section 371 of Title 18 of the United States Code.

      You are to serve without compensation other than the compensation you are now receiving under existing appointment.

      Please execute the required oath of office and forward a duplicate thereof to the Criminal Division, Department of Justice.

Respectfully,

Robert F. Kennedy
Attorney General

Appointment by Robert F. Kennedy

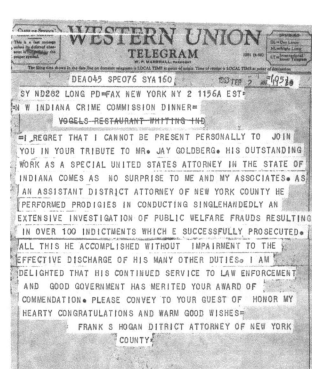

Top: Telegram from Frank Hogan.

Bottom: Carmine Galante, dead with a lit cigar still in his mouth.

Top: U.S. Congressman
Charles B. Rangel and his
wife Alma.

Bottom left: My mother and
sister before going I left to
train for my sparring session
with Rocky Graziano.

Bottom right: Miles Davis and
Cicely Tyson

Court of Appeals, Saratoga Indian Appeal, a victory then won.

Acquittal of the legendary Miss America - Press Photographer's Award of the Year.

Vincent "Jimmy Blue Eyes" Alo, partner of Meyer Lansky, founders of Las Vegas.

Dr. Armand Hammer, a true industrialist.

Doesn't she look great!

Donald during the matrimonial case.

The campaign that could have been.

Matthew "Matty the Horse" Ianniello, King of Midtown Manhattan.

Record - Waylon, a legendary performer.

With Rema, eating the night away at Mar-A-Lago.

A Jewish cowboy living in West Texas, trying to be a good ol' boy.

DONALD JOHN TRUMP

January 9, 2012

Dear Jay:

Thank you for the wonderful note you sent me over the Christmas holiday. I truly appreciate your great words and support.

There has never been a lawyer more important to me than you. It is very important to me that you know that!

Say hi to the fabulous Rema.

With best wishes,

Sincerely,

Donald

Jay Goldberg Esq.
250 Park Avenue
Suite 2020
New York, NY 10177

(Underlining his)

Enduring faith.

Willie and Rema

Rooftop for hamburgers and
frankfurters, his favorite food,
with royalty present.

Willie and Waylon at my birthday party.

With our friend Matty.

Legendary entertainers Miles Davis and Cicely Tyson.

Muhammad Ali, Heavyweight Champion of the World.

THE MAFIA

CHAPTER 29

THE SO-CALLED "MEN OF HONOR"

WHEN ONE ANALYZES THE ENTERTAINMENT industry, films involving gangsters who are romanticized as those who thumb their noses at authority without affecting law abiding citizens are often very popular. There have been very few TV series more popular than *The Sopranos.* And is there a set of movies more popular than *The Godfather* series?

One thing I noticed as I represented the boss of each of the crime families and some of their underlings was that a wise guy had a different voice when speaking to me. His face was at ease, not contorted in any way. He appeared relaxed, even trusting and loving. But if you were to approach him with a business proposition, his voice would harden and his face would twist to demonstrate strength. He would ask, "What's in it for me?" while showing little to no concern for you. He had dual personalities, polar opposites.

Another thing about mobsters is that they all have nicknames. There was Carmine "The Snake" Persico, Vincent "Jimmy Blue Eyes" Alo, Matty "The Horse" Ianniello. As close as I was to Jimmy Blue Eyes, I never asked him where "Jimmy" came from or what "Blue Eyes" meant since his eyes were obviously brown. As their attorney, there were some questions I needed to ask. What wasn't my business I left alone.

Cases against gangsters are invariably "made" by turncoats, or informants. The problem with informants is that even though they begin working with the government, they often find it hard to abandon their criminal ways. This provides fodder for the cross-examiner. I will talk later about the misuse of the Witness Cooperation Agreement—when an informant is given a reduced sentence in return for truthful disclosure to the FBI during examination at pretrial and for truthful testimony during trial. The agreement is often used by the government to mislead jurors, with the concurrence of trial judges, all in an effort to convict a defendant.

The public fascination with the gangster world began following the constitutional prohibition on the sale of alcohol in 1919 with the enactment of the Volstead Act. Bootleggers imported and sold alcohol for consumption, catered to the public's interest in the product, and stood up to authority, all the while engaged in intrigue and open violence with one another for leadership. But, the question remains: Are these "men of honor," as they have often been referred to in movies and books, or are they just people who have gone astray, seeking to garner the most money, with ugliness and offense to the sensibilities of everyday citizens who should be more interested in those who abide by the law and contribute positively to the welfare of society?

I personally have found nothing romantic about them—except for Vincent "Jimmy Blue Eyes" Alo and Matty "The Horse" Ianniello. More on them in a bit.

Many gangsters prey upon fellow gangsters, but their quest for money also intrudes upon law-abiding citizens. Take, for example, my father, who was in the dress manufacturing business. He was also a degenerate gambler. Gamblers are often in desperate need of monies to salvage their business and support their families. The only source of funds is the shylock, i.e., the money lender who lends funds at an enormously exorbitant interest rate. If there is no prompt repayment, the lender employs the efforts of goons to collect outstanding debts. That is why they tried to physically knock down our door when I was a young lad in search of my father. We were lucky. Many instances of death have followed nonpayment of monies owed, causing so much grief to innocent families.

Gangsters have threatened industries, such as the building trade, with illegal labor strikes to extort money. Restaurants are often the victims of "shakedowns" unless "protection" monies are paid. A restaurant owner is sometimes able to avoid paying protection money to a particular member of a crime family by pleading that he is associated with another crime family. And so it goes, wherever money is to be made, "men of honor" intrude upon law abiding citizens to "shake the trees" to obtain ill-gotten gains. No, it is a wrongly held romantic version to view members of organized crime as having a hold on the romantic populous. We should be offended by people who threaten violence to extort monies when their only weapon is the threat of harm.

With all of that said, people may wonder why I have represented members of organized crime. I guess the answer is twofold, part legal and part selfish.

I'm fairly certain that I never represented an innocent mobster, but from a legal standpoint, they had a right to be defended like anyone else. Just because they were guilty of a crime didn't mean they should be put away for a hundred years, as some judges seemed to want to do to them no matter the charges. Also, the government had a duty to prove their case. They had to cross over a certain threshold—beyond a reasonable doubt—and it was my job to keep them honest by making them do it while also trying, in many respects, to save my client's life.

From a selfish standpoint, I did it to make money doing what I loved to do: perform in a courtroom. Most gangsters did not want to plead, but wanted instead to go to trial. I lived for trials. A trial meant more money for my family while also affording me the opportunity for theater.

One day in federal court, I represented Joe "Scarface" Agone. He was being sentenced following a plea of guilty. He stood before the judge in a packed courtroom.

"Mr. Goldberg," the judge said, "Don't you think Mr. Agone should suffer economic loss for his criminal activity?"

I looked at the judge stoically.

"Judge," I said, "I have taken care of that already."

The crowd in the courtroom roared with laughter. But, who knows, maybe the hit in the wallet that my client was levied by the judge wasn't quite as bad as it would have been had I not tossed out that simple one-liner.

Prior to that case, I represented Agone in another case that resulted in an acquittal. He said that he would come to my office the next day to pay me the 100,000 dollars. Sure enough, Agone arrived right on time, but he had no checkbook. Instead, he had a briefcase full of money.

"Here you are, Mr. Goldberg," he said as he opened the black leather case. "Fresh, crisp bills."

Rema, who had stopped by my office at the same time to drop something off, witnessed this. Since my money was her money, she didn't hesitate to make sure Agone was on the up and up. She pulled out the bills and created two stacks, side by side.

"Are you counting it?" I said with a chuckle. She didn't respond and showed no expression. Once all of the bills were in their stacks, she picked them up, one stack resting in each hand. Agone and I watched in silence while she moved her hands up and down, as if she were weighing the money.

"It's not all here," she said, looking first at me, then at Agone.

I thought she was kidding. She wasn't.

"How do you know that?" I asked.

"Because I know," she replied sternly.

I looked over at Agone. I'd be lying if I said I wasn't a little nervous that my wife had just accused a gangster of trying to cheat us out of our payment, but Agone just grinned.

"You're a good one," he said, wagging his finger at my wife. "I thought it was all there, but it's possible I'm a little short. I will have the rest next week. Is that okay?"

Rema said nothing.

"That will be fine," I said.

After Agone left, Rema and I counted the money bill by bill. There was 85,000 dollars.

"You're incredible!" I exclaimed. "Really, how did you know?"

Rema smiled.

"I'll see you at home," she said as she left the office.

I don't know what struck me more: that a client was paying me that much money in bills, or that my wife could simply hold that much cash in her hands and know for certain that it wasn't all there.

CHAPTER 30

JIMMY BLUE EYES, MEYER LANSKY, AND JOHNNY DIO— MAFIA *AMERITAS*

VINCENT "JIMMY BLUE EYES" ALO was extremely well read and knew all there was to know related to public affairs in New York City. Always wearing a sweater vest and sport jacket, one would have thought he was an Ivy League history professor.

Jimmy was like a father figure to Rema and me. He was there at the hospital when I went through two intense surgeries. He was there at the hospital when Rema underwent surgery. He accompanied Rema and me when we went to the agency to adopt our daughter. His influence on us also extended internationally. When Rema and I went to Rome for vacation, he arranged to have us picked up and chauffeured around town. When we continued on to France, he had someone meet us and provide us with "anything you want."

Though he once told us that he carried a bullet in his body from when he was arrested in 1933 for armed robbery, we saw no "gangster" side of him—ever. We aren't fools—we know he may have been involved in many things of which we wouldn't approve. But he showed us nothing but deep affection. He once even gave me marital advice by telling me a story of when some "men of honor" had come to him for help. He turned to his wife and said, "Do you see how when these wise guys come to see me they bow and shake my hand?" to which his wife replied "I don't see why they make such a fuss over you." He said to me, "Jay, always remember that she

221

is your wife, not your mother." Our mothers love us and are always impressed by us; our wives love us and keep us humble.

Jimmy was an overlord of the Genovese crime family and close associate of the late Frank Costello, Vito Genovese, and Lucky Luciano, and he was the partner "assigned" by the mob to monitor Meyer Lansky. Jimmy and Lansky were, according to the government, at the apex of organized crime. Jimmy was considered the more fearsome of the two and was a leader in the mafia with contacts in a number of countries. Lansky was unable to become a member of the Italian Mob because of his religion, but was known as the "Mob's Accountant," "Chairman of the Board," and the "Godfather of the Godfathers."

The two were so big that their relationship was portrayed in *The Godfather Part II* (1974). The character of Jimmy was named Johnny Ola and portrayed by Dominic Chianese. Meyer Lansky was named Hyman Roth and portrayed by Lee Strasberg. They were also the central characters in the movie *The Lost City* (2005), which portrayed them accurately as controlling organized crime, particularly gambling in Cuba at the time of the reign of the Dictator Fulgencio Batista from 1952 to 1959. Lansky was played by Dustin Hoffman. Jimmy was also portrayed by Robert De Niro as the character Victor Tellegio in the movie *American Hustle* (2013).

As a young man, Lansky was a member of the Bugs-Meyer Mob, headed by Bugsy Siegel and Lansky. This organization was the predecessor to Murder Inc. and preyed upon Jewish merchants and other members of the Jewish community in the same way the Black Hand preyed upon Italian Americans. Lanksy's financial wizardry made him a desired member of organized crime. He functioned to the advantage of the Genovese crime family.

There are many books detailing the activities of Lansky and his relationship with Jimmy and the Italian Mob, such as *Little Man: Meyer Lansky and the Gangster Life* by Robert Lacey, *Meyer Lansky: Mogul of the Mob* by Dennis Eisenberg, *But He Was Good to His Mother: The Lives and Crimes of Jewish Gangsters* by Robert A. Rockaway, and *Daughter of the King: Growing Up in Gangland* by Sandra Lansky.

Legend has it that Jimmy, Lansky, and Bugsy Siegel (who was later assassinated), among others, were responsible for turning a tract of sand into what we now know as the Las Vegas strip. They were instrumental in the opening of the Flamingo Hotel, which was financed entirely by mob money. The belief was that Bugsy Siegel had siphoned off a considerable amount of money, causing the construction of the hotel to be built wildly over budget. Today, the hotels are owned by corporate giants. Years ago, every Las Vegas strip hotel was run and controlled by mafia members and their associates.

Jimmy, Lansky, and Frank Costello developed a gambling empire that stretched across more than just the U.S., owning pieces of casinos in Las Vegas, Florida, Cuba, the Bahamas, London, along with a major piece of gambling activity in New York. I recall when I was working for the government and eating at a restaurant in Washington with several FBI agents, one agent said, "Don't look now, but Jimmy Blue Eyes has just walked in." His presence garnered everyone's attention.

One day, Herbert Kaminsky, a well-known fraudster, called my office—I had represented him successfully in two cases. He told me he wanted to send Jimmy to see me so I could represent him. I didn't hesitate to say yes. I knew there was potentially big money in representing mobsters. Who they were and any potential dangers I faced of being associated with them mattered none to me, for I was extremely confident in my ability to properly represent them. I told Kaminsky that I could see Jimmy at 3:00 p.m. the next day.

The following afternoon, into my office shuffled an elderly gentleman with white hair, a short-sleeved cardigan sweater, and a newspaper under his arm. He hardly looked to be the gangster that he was reputed to be. He was very soft-spoken and docile. I was so surprised by his appearance that I excused myself from the room for a moment when he arrived.

"Herbie," I said on the phone to the man who was supposed to send me Jimmy, "who is this guy?"

"What do you mean?" he asked.

"There's a guy in my office claiming to be Jimmy Blue Eyes, but he looks like some elderly retired grandpa on a morning walk. Maybe even a great-grandpa. And his eyes are brown."

Herbie laughed.

"That's him," he assured me. "I know it's not what you expected, but trust me, that's Jimmy."

I returned to the office and apologized for my brief absence.

"So, what can I do for you, Mr. Alo," I said.

"I've been indicted for obstructing an investigation," he said. "Herbie tells me you can help me."

"Tell me about the investigation," I said.

Jimmy talked slowly in a gravelly voice. And, like many Italians are known to do, his hands gestured in sync with his voice.

"The Securities and Exchange Commission was investigating the affairs of Scopitone and Tel-A-Sign stock, which was owned by Al Malnik, a property investor in Florida. Now, keep in mind, Mr. Goldberg, everything I am telling you I didn't know until after I testified," he said.

"I understand," I said.

"When the stock went up, Malnik kept all the money and didn't give any of it to four other people who claimed they had a right to it. They told Malnik that if they didn't get their money, they'd see to it that he wouldn't get any for himself."

"Go on," I said.

"Well, Malnik got scared. So he flies to Italy to see me and begs me to come back to New York to work out a deal between him and these other four guys. So I did. Because I'm a nice guy."

"Of course," I said.

"So, we met at the Warwick Hotel here in Manhattan, I worked out a deal among the men, and that was the end of it. Nobody got hurt and everybody was happy. Except the government."

"Where does the obstruction come in?" I asked.

"Well, four years later, the SEC finds out about this meeting through a snitch and I get subpoenaed to tell them all about it. But, I didn't remember anything about it except that I worked out a deal for them like Malnik asked. I had no recollection of the names Scopitone or Tel-A-Sign. I don't know who besides Malnik arranged the meeting or when exactly it took place or why it was at that hotel. It was four years ago. I can't even remember what I did last week. So, I tell them I can't remember things, and they tell me I'm being evasive.

"You see," he continued as he leaned forward, "the government doesn't like me, so they will try to nail me whenever they can. But I didn't do anything except help a bunch of guys work out a deal. If anything, I helped the government by preventing a bad situation from potentially getting much worse."

The lawyer Jimmy had used during the testimony didn't help matters. Had Jimmy consulted me or many other solid attorneys I know, we would have simply told him to invoke the Fifth Amendment to avoid exposure to prosecution. Instead, he engaged a naïve lawyer who advised him to testify "since he had nothing to hide." But, there is no such thing as an organized crime figure testifying without the odds being all but certain that he will be prosecuted for something he says, refuses to say, or when the government believes it has proof of a false statement, regardless of how important or unimportant it might be.

I took Jimmy's case, and it was assigned to Judge Constance Baker Motley. She had a wonderful record of serving as Borough President of Manhattan, was a close associate of Thurgood Marshall, and prevailed in nine of the ten arguments she had made before the U.S. Supreme Court on the issue of racial discrimination. However, when it came to organized crime and criminal defense lawyers, she took an extraordinarily harsh position. Her presence always reminded me that it was never easy to be a criminal defense lawyer.

For example, in one case I attended as an observer that was tried by defense attorney Fred Hafetz, he wheeled his seemingly crippled defendant into court sitting in a wheelchair. Judge Motley looked at the defendant and said, "Mr. Hafetz, if Mr. Cohen is not out of his wheelchair and at the defense table in ten minutes when I return to the bench I will remand him. Do you understand me?" After she left the bench, I watched Cohen straighten up, get out of the wheelchair without any assistance, and walk to his place at the defense table.

Jimmy's trial was scheduled to begin on a Monday and was expected by the judge to be finished in just five days so that she could preside over the taking of a civil deposition in The Hague. On the Thursday prior to the start of the trial, I wasn't feeling well and went to a doctor who diagnosed me with spinal meningitis, which is an inflammation of the lining of the brain and spinal cord. I was immediately checked in to Mount Sinai Hospital. I notified the court of my condition and sought a delay of Jimmy's case, but the judge selfishly wanted to finish the case so she could have the enjoyment of being in The Hague at the government's expense.

On Friday, one of the judge's law clerks called me.

"If Mr. Alo is not in court on Monday ready to try the case, the judge said he will be remanded," the clerk said.

"Are you kidding?" I asked. "I'm lying in the hospital right now with spinal meningitis!"

"Those are the orders I've been given," the clerk said.

I was horrified at the lack of heart shown by the court. I had my doctor call the judge to explain the situation, but even he was denied. There was nothing more I could do. I had the doctor discharge me after two days, against his will. I was completely disoriented and certainly unable to effectively try a case. We began trial on that Monday. After five days and with the trial still not finished, Judge Motley ordered a rare Saturday court session. The courthouse was not air-conditioned and New York was experiencing a heat wave. It was insufferable for everyone, especially me given my condition. The trial ended with a conviction.

I was so upset that Jimmy was convicted. I never should have tried it, but being that late in the game and with no sympathy from the judge for my condition, I felt that my hands were tied. What also didn't help was that just before Jimmy was sentenced, *The New York Times* ran a false story, obviously fed to them by the government (they often resorted to false "leaks"), that Jimmy had met with the notorious crime boss Frank Costello, who it was claimed controlled a vast gambling empire in the U.S. and was a high-ranking member of the Genovese crime family. The article claimed that the purpose of the alleged meeting was to enlist Costello to oversee Jimmy's gambling interests were Jimmy to be imprisoned, so certain were they that it would happen.

Jimmy was sentenced to five years in prison, and eventually he would be assigned to the Atlanta Federal Penitentiary.

What was so incredible to me after this case was that Jimmy didn't hold a grudge. In fact, he loved me. He couldn't have done any worse with any other lawyer, and yet he remained a champion of my work. After the sentencing, I apologized to him for the outcome, but he remained as calm and gracious as he had been that first day he walked into my office.

"You're not God," he said to me.

"No, I'm not," I replied, "but I still feel like I let you down."

"Hey, listen to me," he said. "You win some and you lose some. You couldn't control the outcome or the judge's insistence that this go forward despite your illness. You did the best you could, and for that I thank you."

Jimmy paid me my money, went to prison, and would later refer me to Johnny Dio, one of his prison mates who desperately needed help. As the years went on, I would become the "go to" attorney for the New York City mafia, and the results were generally mixed, which, given the backgrounds of the men I was representing, wasn't a bad winning percentage. And, no matter the outcome, they always respected my effort, believing that they had the best attorney possible in their corner.

Before Jimmy was sent to Atlanta, he spent time in Manhattan at the Metropolitan Correctional Center. While in the MCC awaiting transfer, Jimmy had discussions with Johnny Dio, who was awaiting trial. Dio was charged with stock fraud in the Manhattan federal court and was being represented by an enormously successful attorney, Joseph Brill. But Brill had told Dio what Dio didn't want to hear: that he had little chance of winning.

"You need to hire Jay Goldberg," Jimmy said to Dio. "He is the best there is. He isn't going to tell you that you can't win."

Dio did as Jimmy suggested. As Brill handed over the case, he reiterated to me that the proof against Dio was overwhelming and that "Johnny has his head in the sand." But I was intrigued by the challenge. How could I do any worse than an attorney who was already waving the white flag?

As soon as I took over, Robert Morvillo, the assistant U.S. Attorney in Manhattan in charge of the Frauds Unit prosecuting the case, called me to his office.

"Johnny needs to cooperate with us," Morvillo said. "The government has never had such overwhelming proof against a member of organized crime. If he cooperates, we'll work something out."

"I appreciate your candor, but Johnny didn't hire me to 'cooperate,'" I said. "I'm sorry, but we can't do that. We'll see you at trial."

Was I being brash? Hell yes! The government had nearly two dozen witnesses. I had Johnny and nobody supporting him. But sometimes that many witnesses against you isn't a bad thing—if your attorney's strength is cross-examination. I had faith that I could cut into the testimony of the witnesses one by one. And I did. After each one told a story with the aid of softball questions from the prosecutor, I stepped to the mound and fired fastballs, curveballs, and anything else they couldn't hit. I painted Johnny as being a guy who was so given to violence that he was simply not smart enough to be a stock swindler. It was a risk—jurors weren't going to take too kindly to a violent man—but I had to trust that they would remember this was about white collar stock fraud, not about breaking somebody's kneecaps.

And they got it!

Johnny was acquitted. It was the first time in seven prosecutions that he'd been acquitted.

"Jimmy Blue Eyes was right about you," Johnny said to me as we exited the courthouse. Johnny did go to prison, but as a visitor, to tell Jimmy what had happened. Jimmy showed little reaction, not surprised that Johnny was a free man.

"I told you," he said to Johnny. Though I had lost Jimmy's case, my victory for Johnny proved that Jimmy's judgment of me was correct.

Years later, after Jimmy was released, I was at the Eden Roc Hotel in Miami Beach, Florida, when Meyer Lansky and Jimmy approached me poolside. I didn't know they were there, and how they knew I was there, I'm not sure. But when you are a couple of gangsters who need legal help, I guess you'll figure out a way to find the person you need.

Like Jimmy, Lansky was an elderly man, though he looked more frail. They were born a couple of years apart at the turn of the century. Dressed down in beachwear, Jimmy introduced me to Lansky.

"Don't believe anything you have read about me," Lansky said.

I laughed.

"None of it?"

"Well, the good stuff is true," he said with a wry smile.

"So, what do you need from me?" I asked.

"The FBI is giving me trouble," he said. "They think I'm in the racket business and that I'm receiving gambling money. They are threatening to subpoena me and make me testify before a federal grand jury. Truth is I'm no more of a gambler than anyone else. I win a little, I lose a little, and that's it. I'm too old to be involved in anything more than that."

"What specifically do they want from you?" I asked.

"They want to know who is sending me money, how I'm getting it, when I'm getting it, all that stuff. But there is no money," he insisted.

I was not so naïve. Despite his claim, I didn't forget that he had been a member of the Bugs-Meyer Mob. In fact, after I told him I'd take his case—I couldn't resist trying to defend an old man being harassed by the FBI—he said, "If you need a cabana, just use number thirty-five or thirty-six. If they give you any trouble, just tell them who sent you."

He hardly seemed retired.

His case was to be heard in the district court for the Southern District of Florida. I could have waited for the subpoena from the FBI and moved to quash it, but I chose to get ahead of them by trying to abort the process before it reached that point. I secured letters from several psychiatrists who supported the view that Lansky was suffering from advanced dementia, and that there was no way he could testify. Was he really suffering from dementia? Based on what the FBI was claiming about him, and based on Lansky's age and what he was stating to be true, it seemed likely...likely enough that the FBI and prosecutor didn't dispute it, and the court agreed.

We were at the same hotel where we'd initially met when I told Lansky he was off the hook. He showed no emotion, simply stating,

"Thank you for the information." I was with him when he told Jimmy, who smiled and politely thanked me for helping his friend.

"Are you ready to go?" Jimmy said to Lansky.

"Yeah, let's get out of here," he replied.

And with that, a very large man who had accompanied Lansky, no doubt his bodyguard, handed a leash to Lansky that had a tiny dog attached to the end of it. The bodyguard went off on his own while the two elderly men—"Jimmy Blue Eyes" and "The Little Man"—strolled into the sunset.

Lansky died in Florida in 1983 at the age of eighty. Jimmy also died in Florida, but in 2001 at the age of ninety-six. I remember Jimmy's parting words to me, when he'd reached an age at which virtually all his friends were gone: "That's the problem with getting old," he said. "When you get to be my age, you are left all alone, for all of your friends have passed on."

How true that is.

CHAPTER 31

HANGING A MAN OUT A WINDOW ISN'T BANK FRAUD

IT WAS THE GOVERNMENT'S VIEW that Matty "The Horse" Ianniello dominated organized criminal activity in New York for decades, especially in the 1960s and 1970s. Criminal defense lawyers were anxious to meet him, for it was said that he was the source of enormous business for those practicing criminal law. I had a dear friend, a great booster, the wonderful Hy Lieberman, who tried multiple times to arrange to have Matty and I meet, but his efforts failed.

When I finally did meet Matty, it was under the strangest of circumstances.

After securing the acquittal of Johnny Dio in the stock fraud case, the government did what the government normally does when it loses a case against a mobster: they bring another case against him.

During his second stock fraud trial, Dio's co-defendant, Louis Ostrow, was represented by eighty-year-old criminal defense attorney Maurice Edelbaum. The presiding judge was Chief Judge of the Manhattan federal court, David Edelstein, who had a reputation of demonstrating terrible hostility towards criminal defense lawyers and "professional" criminal defendants. The Dio case lasted for a month before jury deliberations began. They were lengthy and would continue until ten o'clock each night, when marshals would take the jurors home.

One winter night at 7:00 p.m., while the jury was deliberating and the judge was upstairs in his chambers, Edelbaum complained to the clerk and me that he was suffering from cardiac spasms. We laid him out on one of the empty benches. He did not want me to call an ambulance, but he did want to go home for the evening. He felt that he could be adequately treated at home and be in shape for the next morning. On several occasions I called chambers—at 7:00 p.m., 8:30 p.m., and 9:30 p.m.—to ask the judge's law clerk to have the judge come down and send the jury home for the evening because of Edelbaum's physical infirmity. But Edelstein refused. At 10:00 p.m., he finally came down and discharged the jury. So very cruel was his behavior I thought, but who would have the courage to say that to a judge?

Well...

The judge called Edelbaum and me into the robing room after the jury left. He was angry that Edelbaum had wanted to leave early. While smoking his pipe, he said to Edelbaum, "If you want to continue to practice in this court, you will have to commit yourself to being present in the courtroom until I discharge the jury at ten p.m." Edelbaum was a broken man when the judge made this statement. Of course, I was just an observer, for the judge wasn't speaking to me or directing any of his comments my way. However, I was deeply offended by the harshness of his declaration to someone who was obviously suffering.

I stood before the judge and, with the court reporter present, said: "Judge Edelstein, you say that deliberations have to run in effect at all times until ten o'clock. Well, I think the record should show that when it suited your purpose, you stood here last night in a tuxedo, complete with a bow tie and patent leather shoes and dismissed the jury at seven o'clock so that you could take your wife to a dinner-dance."

The judge almost swallowed his pipe. Edelbaum gaped at me in awe. He could not believe that another lawyer would have come to his rescue the way I had done and would say what I had said to a federal judge. Quite frankly, I hadn't planned to say such a thing, but defending my colleague was the right thing to do. The next day, deliberations proceeded until 6:00 p.m., when the jury was discharged. On the third day of deliberations, both defendants were acquitted of participating in a stock fraud.

Edelbaum, in the hallway after the verdict, told me that in two months he had a case before Chief Judge Mishler in the Brooklyn federal court. The charge was bank fraud. The allegation was that the defendants supposedly controlled the Bank of Miami Beach and used deposited funds for their own purposes. He said he intended to represent Ben Cohen, and asked whether I would be interested in representing the other defendant, Matty. I was thrilled to be able to do so, and thought back to how hard and often Hy Lieberman had tried to hook me up with "The Horse." Now, simply because I spoke up in defense of a fellow attorney, it was finally going to happen.

Matty's demeanor was similar to that of Jimmy Blue Eyes and Johnny Dio, and his reputation for being a "man of honor" was even greater. According to a 2007 *Washington Post* article, Matty was "a decorated World War II veteran. In the 1970s, he joined authorities searching for a six-year-old named Etan Patz after the boy disappeared on a Manhattan street. He was a businessman in a world where brutality often spoke loudest, operating like a CEO rather than a street thug." He was also called "a good earner" and "a stand-up guy" who was "helpful to people he liked." He didn't resort to violence, but instead "skimmed" millions of dollars to build his financial empire.

Matty was a very jolly guy, Santa Claus-like, who trusted me immediately because he had been referred to me by Edelbaum, in whom Matty had tremendous faith.

When we arrived at court in Brooklyn, part of the government's proof was that when Matty had gone to Florida to get a true accounting of the bank's operation, he was not satisfied with his partner Phil Simon's response. Simon had the obligation to keep the records relating to the bank's operation. Matty, it was alleged, proceeded to hold Simon out of the tenth-floor window of the bank building by the legs in order to get him to tell the truth about what had been earned and expended by the bank. While there was more important evidence for the jury to consider, it was the sensational image of a grown man holding another grown man out of a window that captured the attention of the jurors—and likely why by mid-afternoon they had acquitted both defendants.

Did Matty hold Simon out the window? There is no doubt in my mind that he did. But the government made a big mistake presenting that evidence. As I would point out to the jury, this case was about bank fraud. How does hanging a man out a window indicate bank fraud? Matty wasn't charged with a violent crime. The fact that he held a man out a window was irrelevant. And the jury agreed. Despite the other evidence, which I thought was pretty overwhelming against Matty and his co-defendant, I had blasted a hole in the credibility of the government's case.

Following his acquittal, I drove with Matty to Manhattan. He parked his car, exited, and casually walked up Mulberry Street with his jacket slung over his shoulder. People in this Italian section of town had somehow already learned of the verdict and were hanging out their windows waving at him and congratulating him on the victory. This is how revered he was. In many cases, the government couldn't find a witness to testify against him, not because they were afraid of him, but because of how beloved he was by his community. I stated that there was nothing romantic about the mafia, but I made an exception for Matty. He was a gentleman who ruled with a soft touch and never raised his voice, endearing him to everyone who met him.

I never saw Matty angry except on one occasion. It was one evening when we were working alone at my office. He called a restaurant in which he supposedly had a financial interest and ordered veal parmesan sandwiches to be delivered. When they were delivered, they were cold.

"This is unacceptable!" he exclaimed to me.

"I'm okay with it," I said, hungry and anxious to eat.

"No!" he said. "You're not eating this. It's not right."

Matty called the restaurant and asked for the chef. I don't know what was said, for it was all said in Italian. But by Matty's tone, it didn't sound like he was thanking the chef for a delicious meal. My hunch was confirmed when Matty ended the conversation in English with: "Just tell me, chef, whether you think you can cook under water!" With that, Matty hung up, smiled at me, and said "Okay, let's get back to work."

About fifteen minutes later, hot veal parmesan sandwiches arrived. I said Matty was not known for his violence. Maybe that's because his threats were so effective.

As a side note, years had passed since I had almost made Chief Judge Edelstein swallow his pipe when I addressed his unfair comments toward fellow attorney Maurice Edelbaum. I was out on a walk about to buy that negligee for Rema; you recall my beeper went off and, when I called the office, I was told to call Donald Trump. Donald had told me that his good friend, Edward S. Gordon, had recommended me to represent him in his divorce with Ivana. Well, I found out later that Gordon wasn't the only one.

Cindy Adams, who for decades had been a major columnist for the *New York Post*, told Donald that she had a friend who lived on her floor in her apartment building who could give Donald an assessment as to whether he should use me. When Donald consulted her friend, he said that Donald should definitely hire me because I was a "fine, strong-willed, and aggressive attorney."

That friend was Chief Judge David Edelstein.

CHAPTER 32

BETTING ON THE WRONG "HORSE"

I'VE MENTIONED THAT THERE COULD be potential danger bringing another lawyer into a case to assist you as "of counsel." Why? Because it is possible the lawyer you bring in will go behind your back and make incendiary remarks about your work to the client to try to influence the client to dump you. Professionalism and a sense of morality in such cases are often overtaken by the quest for money. You must always keep your eye not only on the prosecutor, but on your co-counsel. It's sad to say, but true, as you will read in this story in which my co-counsel nearly lost his life from fifty-six floors above Manhattan.

The Teamsters Union transports goods throughout the U.S. and is considered one of the most powerful unions in the country. The union is divided into locals. New Jersey Union Local 560 was notorious for acts of violence. Sam Provenzano was the international vice president of the union and his brother, Nunzio, was president. The dangerous killing machine in the family was Anthony "Tony Pro" Provenzano. It was rumored that he disposed of bodies in Brother Moscato's landfill in Newark, New Jersey. The leaders of the Union Local 560 were allegedly members of the Genovese crime family.

Matty asked me to represent Tony Pro in a case in which Tony was charged with extortion and making threats to local businesses. I chose a young lawyer, one who is today extremely prominent, to assist me. Prior to trial, we all met at Matty's office: me, the young lawyer, Matty, Sam, and Nunzio, and several of their henchmen. Matty sat at the head of the table.

"Who is this?" he asked me, nodding toward my assistant.

I introduced them. "He is going to be helping me with this case since it's going to require a lot of work," I said.

Matty trusted me, but something about this young attorney didn't sit well with him.

"Before we start the meeting," Matty said, looking at my assistant, "I would like you to deliver a message to Tony."

"Deliver a message? You mean in jail?"

"Yes."

"Now?"

"Yes."

Tony had lost a prior case when he was represented by Maurice Edelbaum and was now housed at the federal Metropolitan Correctional Center. Matty took the young attorney aside and whispered something to him, leaving me out of the conversation. The attorney said he'd be back as soon as he could and dashed out the door.

"What was that about?" I asked.

"It's nothing," Matty assured me. "We'll all know soon enough."

I was perplexed, but I just let it go. *Just Matty being Matty* was my thought. We talked somewhat about the case while my assistant was gone, but it was more just idle chatter as I didn't want to delve too deep into our strategy without him there. About an hour later my assistant returned.

"You're back!" Matty said. "So, what did Tony say?"

"He said that he would like me to be the lead attorney on this case, not Mr. Goldberg."

I honestly showed no reaction to this statement because it was so absurd. These Mafia men knew me. I determined immediately that Matty must have told him to ask Tony who he would like as the lead attorney to test the attorney's trustworthiness. He failed. More than he knew.

Matty went berserk.

He slammed his fists on the table, stood up, and walked toward the attorney. He had that "My veal parmesan sandwich is cold!" look on his face. He was fuming. Nunzio also stood up and was walking toward the attorney from the other side, following Matty's lead.

"Wait, guys, what's going on?" the attorney asked, realizing he may be in some trouble.

"You're a liar!" Matty screamed.

"Guys, guys, let me explain," the attorney said.

"You just did," Matty replied.

"No, wait, guys..."

Matty grabbed the attorney's left arm and Nunzio the right. They escorted him, against his will, toward the window. The attorney let his body go limp as he begged them to release him. They continued to drag him, ignoring his plea. I finally spoke up.

"Matty! Nunzio! C'mon, let the guy go. He's learned his lesson."

"Yeah! Yeah! I've learned my lesson!" the attorney insisted.

"He lied to me!" Matty cried. "Tony knows you are his lawyer and would have never said that this guy should take over!"

Nunzio let go of the attorney's arm to open the window, high enough for a human body to easily fit through. The two gangsters then yanked the resisting attorney to the edge of it and forced his head out the window so he could clearly see the view below from fifty-six floors up. The attorney by now had stopped talking and begging and resorted to just blood-curdling screams. I was confident they weren't really going to toss him out...but with these guys, one never knows for sure.

"Matty, please let him go!" I yelled above the screams.

"Why should I? He cannot be trusted."

"He *can* be trusted," I exclaimed. "Look, I wouldn't have brought him into the fold if I didn't think he could help us. Let him go and let's get to work."

Matty looked at Nunzio, paused for a moment, then threw the attorney backward and away from the window. The attorney fell down, scrambled on the floor toward me, stood up, and said "Thank you." I'm not sure who the thank you was intended for—probably all of us.

"Now, are you finished screwing around?" I calmly asked him.

"Yeah, yeah, of course," he said as he straightened his tie and took a seat. "I'm sorry about that," he whispered to me. "I thought the Provenzanos were in charge of this. I guess I bet on the wrong horse."

I don't think a pun was intended given how rattled he was, but it was a fitting line.

I kept the attorney on the case because I knew I could trust him after he had stared death in the face. I also didn't want to start over with a new lawyer. He was good, he just needed to know his role. Unfortunately for him, it was a tough lesson.

This was a multiple-defendant case. Tony was at the center of it, but he had several alleged co-conspirators who had been charged. As tough of an attorney as I am, the government wins the majority of its cases against gangsters. And, in this case, the evidence against all of them was overwhelming. At one point during the trial, when we were on lunch recess and things weren't going our way, Tony called me into a side room to speak to me privately. Gus Newman, a wonderful and skillful lawyer and counsel to one of the co-defendants, was with me when I was summoned.

"If my wife comes looking for me later," I said, "tell her to check Brother Moscato's dump."

Tony and I discussed some strategy and, while I had his one-on-one attention, I discussed my fees. I normally asked for money at various points throughout the trial. A chunk of his was due.

"I'd like to be paid this Wednesday," I said. "Or, you could pay me early on Monday or Tuesday. But do not come to me with money on Thursday or Friday." It was my way of saying "Don't be late." His bodyguard, a six-foot four-inch brute who was in the room with us, began to move toward me—nobody bossed his boss around. But Tony put up his hand, signaling the giant to stay put.

"You will get your money," Tony said. "Just keep fighting for me."

That night, that same body guard came to my home and delivered the money without incident.

A few days later, all of the defendants, including Tony, were convicted. But, again, nobody harbored any ill feelings toward me.

"You tried," Matty stated, and he said nothing more. He knew the cards were heavily stacked against Tony and his cohorts.

I must tell the reader a few things about the character of Matty:

If Matty referred a client to me, he would tell the client that he is to call and report on my "performance" *after* my closing argument but *before* the verdict. He did this apparently because he believed that following the closing argument for the defense, the defendant would be extremely complimentary of my performance, but not necessarily after the verdict. Following this procedure, if the referred client wanted to call Matty to discuss a gripe he had with me, Matty would not speak to him because the client had declared himself after I had summed up. How clever was this?

If I lost a case after receiving good reviews from my client in step one, Matty was perfectly fine with it.

If Matty told me my money would be paid in three weeks, I could be sure that at the end of the third week an envelope would be delivered to my office. There would be no delays or excuses; Matty's word was his bond.

If I were about to direct extended comments to the court, perhaps seeking recusal for a show of bias, Matty would say to me, "Remember Harvard Law School." This was to remind me of the need to be restrained, yet direct, and not to resort to any invective.

Matty's behavior sharply contrasted with the pretrial, trial, and post-trial behavior of so many other clients, those who weren't gangsters. I can't tell you how many times, if I represented someone and went to trial and lost their case, it would be *I* who would be blamed for losing the case, not their obvious guilt and the overwhelming evidence against them. They would get hostile toward me and sometimes refuse to pay. I tried to choose men and women with spines to represent. When I lost a case for a notorious gangster like Matty, he still paid. When I lost Charlie Rangel's case, he still loved me. If I didn't get Donald Trump everything he wanted, he was still my friend.

It bears noting that one winter, on the same day that Matty was acquitted in one case, mafia leader John Gotti was remanded in a separate case, both in the Brooklyn federal court. On the front page of the *New York Post* the headline read, "Gotti's Gotta Go, but Matty Can Horse Around." Included was a picture of Matty walking down the courthouse steps wearing a coon-skinned hat with me at his side.

When I was in Washington D.C., on another case, I visited the chief of the Organized Crime Section of the Department of Justice. He said that no figure in organized crime benefitted from so many acquittals as Matty. I may not have won them all for Matty or his associates, but I made their lives better than they would have been. Matty's entire adult life was spent in and out of prison. The last three years were spent in freedom at his Long Island home. He died at the age of ninety-two.

CHAPTER 33

"NO ONE WILL EVER KILL ME..."

AN ARTICLE POSTED TO CNN.COM on June 4, 2014, entitled "14 Of The Most Ruthless Gangsters In U.S. History" listed Carmine Galante as one of the most vicious members of organized crime. He was known as "Lilo" and "Cigar." Galante was the boss of the Bonanno crime family. One person told me that when Galante walked up Mulberry Street, some people ducked into the cellar or a store so that they would not be seen by him, unlike when Matty walked up that street and people hung out their windows to cheer him.

My path to representing Galante went through Mike Sabella.

Sabella was a captain in the Bonanno crime family. He had referred Alphonse Esposito to me. Esposito and two others were on trial in the Brooklyn federal court for being on the payroll of a dress business, while having no-show jobs in order to hide their proceeds from organized crime.

Judge Edward Neaher had entertained my motion to dismiss, but he decided he was going to withhold judgment as to my client, Esposito, until the end of the trial. In other words, for reasons unknown to me, we'd have to go through the entire trial, *then* the judge would decide if he were going to dismiss the charges.

After the trial, while the jury was deliberating, the judge granted the motion to dismiss under Rule 29 of the Federal Rules of Criminal Procedure. The other two defendants remained and the jury convicted both.

The foreman of the jury gave the judge a note to the effect that they had also convicted Esposito—but he was long gone, for the jury did not know his motion to dismiss had been granted. Sabella was so pleased with the result that he asked me to represent Carmine Galante.

Sabella told me that Galante was in Miami, Florida, represented by Roy Cohn, and was to appear before U.S. District Judge Sidney Aronovitz for sentencing. Galante had been found guilty of contempt for refusal to obey an order to respond to questions before a grand jury. He had not been granted immunity, but the prosecutor represented to the court that Galante could provide information as to a suspected extortion plot and other violations of the Hobbs Act, without incriminating himself.

Besides being found guilty, Galante had another huge problem.

His attorney, Cohn, had met a waiter at the hotel where he and Galante were staying, and he ran off with him to the Bahamas. Cohn had chosen his newfound lover over representing Galante. The gangster known as "The Godfather" was left behind to deal with the sentencing on his own. Rarely had I ever heard of an attorney abandoning his client, especially for that reason and a client with such a high profile, but that's exactly what Cohn did.

I hopped on a plane to Miami within hours after Sabella's call. When I arrived at the hotel, one of Galante's bodyguards opened the door to the suite. I found Galante sitting in a corner shaking like an abandoned puppy.

"Are you Jay Goldberg?" Galante asked.

"Yes."

"Oh, thank God you're here," he said with a tremble in his voice as he approached me. "You have no idea how happy I am to see you."

"I'm glad I can help," I said. "Don't worry, I will take care of you."

It was incredible to see this vicious killer, one of the most feared mafia members on the planet, huddled in a corner in fear because his lawyer ran away with a new boyfriend.

The publicity surrounding the presence of Galante intrigued the people of Miami so much so that an enormous crowd gathered at the courthouse the morning he was to be sentenced, waiting to catch a glimpse of this feared New York gangster.

I made the necessary motion to set aside the contempt, arguing that since no immunity had been conferred upon my client, he had every right to invoke his privilege against self-incrimination. The judge summarily denied my motion and imposed the maximum sentence of five years. I appeared to have done nothing for Galante.

"That's it?" he said, looking at me as if I'd let him down.

"No, that's not it," I said. "This is far from over. This ruling was based on your past, not on the law."

"I'm trusting you," he said.

"As you should. We will appeal this immediately to the U.S. Court of Appeals. But for now, let's get you out of here and away from the media."

The crowd outside the Miami courthouse had grown larger and restless. Journalists, photographers, and television crews were stationed along the streets, eager to catch a glimpse of Galante. But I was in no mood for my client to be forced to participate in their circus, so I conceived a plan. One of Galante's associates was about the same size as Galante.

"Carmine, you're going to go out the back door with the U.S. Marshals into a car. But let me and your associate go out the front first to distract everyone."

I advised the associate to pull his jacket up to a point where his face was covered, and the two of us left the courthouse through the front door. Cameras were flashing as we swiftly walked down the street. TV crews and reporters were chasing us.

"C'mon, let's go!" I urged the associate, pretending I was a character on some TV crime show. We crossed the block to another street with people yelling and following after us, calling out for Galante. Meanwhile, Carmine slipped out the back with the marshals, completely unnoticed.

When we got several blocks away from the courthouse, with a huge crowd still around us, I stopped and had the associate reveal his true identity.

"What can I do for you all?" he said with a smile to the media as he unzipped his coat. It was an unscripted line that made this theatre lover proud.

"Hey, who are you?" one reporter shouted.

"That's not him!" another exclaimed.

"Carmine? Oh, he went out the back of the courthouse," I said nonchalantly.

We'd duped them, and they were outraged. And I didn't care one bit.

When I met the next day with Galante, I told him I'd handle his appeal by writing the brief and arguing it, if the Fifth Circuit issued a directive for oral argument. I submitted the brief and, without oral argument, the court reversed the finding of contempt on the ground that Galante had every right to refuse to answer where there was no grant of immunity. The Court wrote:

"Appellant, who was nationally reputed to be a leader of organized crime, was not clearly mistaken in believing he had reasonable cause to fear incrimination in answering grand jury questions about presiding over and settling an underworld dispute over stolen property, and he therefore did not capriciously invoke his Fifth Amendment privilege and was improperly adjudicated in contempt."

From that day forward, I was Galante's lawyer.

After this result and Galante's release from custody, he repaired to his vacation home in Hampton Bays, New York, on Long Island, to where he invited Rema and me to spend some time. He was proud to show off the field of cabbage that he was growing on the east side of the house and the beautiful roses that he had planted on the west side of the house.

"Let me show you the heads of cabbage I have grown," he said.

"As long as we don't find an actual human head among them," Rema quipped.

Fortunately, Galante laughed. And we found no human heads.

Most leaders of the New York crime families "represented" that they were against the narcotics trade. Galante, however, acted brazenly in defiance of others. He not only dealt in narcotics, he refused to share his profits. He was assassinated in broad daylight by three masked men on July 12, 1979, while having lunch at Joe and Mary's, his favorite Italian restaurant in Brooklyn. The newspapers published a picture of him stretched out and dead, his cigar still clenched in his mouth, lit and emitting smoke.

How ironic it was, because although he was aware he had many enemies, he, once said to me, "No one will ever kill me, they wouldn't dare."

CHAPTER 34

THE CROSS-EXAMINATION THAT SAVED JOSEPH GAMBINO

JOSEPH GAMBINO WAS CARLO GAMBINO'S relative. Carlo was the founder of the Gambino crime family, a powerful force in the underworld that would give rise in later years to the infamous John Gotti.

I was asked to defend Joseph against the charge that he controlled gambling in the state of Connecticut and was a lucrative provider of funds for the Family. The nexus to the charges were calls made to phones within the district, as well as monies paid in Brooklyn and Queens. It appeared at the outset that the trial was going to be particularly difficult for me, mainly because Joseph's name made it impossible to deny his relationship to the Family.

But the government messed up big time.

Not only did they not do a full and accurate search of Joseph's automobile, which would have likely provided all of the proof they needed that he was in control of gambling in Connecticut, but they put Salvatore "Sammy the Bull" Gravano on the stand.

Sammy was their main witness, and one of my favorite men ever to cross-examine. In another case, in which I represented Pat Conte, second in command to Gotti and responsible for the importation of heroin from Sicily, I got to cross-examine Gravano. The government had put on an overwhelming case before a jury and the Judge I. Leo Glasser, but five minutes into the deliberation, the jury sent out a note that stated they were hopelessly deadlocked because two of the jurors claimed they would never convict anyone on the basis of Gravano's testimony. Judge Glasser was livid. He had been on the bench twenty years and had never had a hung jury, but since I seemed to have a hold on Gravano, a hung jury was declared. Conte was tried a second time, used another lawyer, and was convicted.

So, here I was again with the opportunity to cross-examine Gravano, this time for the sake of Joseph Gambino.

An excerpt of the cross-examination, taken from Professor John Iannuzzi's book *Cross-Examination: The Mosaic Art,* follows. It has been used in a number of trial advocacy courses, including at Pace University Law School and Fordham School of Law. The *National Law Journal* wrote: "If not for defense attorney Jay Goldberg's methodical destruction of Mr. Gravano showing that he was not telling even the same story, no less the truth, then Mr. Gravano would still be selling his versions in the way that 'professional anti-Communists' created testimony to order in the 1950s. Goldberg's client was acquitted."

Notice that each question in my cross-examination is closed ended, which means that the question does not permit an answer that is a narrative harmful to the questioner. If there is proper cadence, it should be as though the questioner was testifying, i.e., "You did this, then you did this, then you did this, with the result being...etc."

Q: Sir, you told us when you were arrested on December 11, 1990, you were charged with committing three murders, is that right?

A: Yes.

Q: You told us that as you understood it, if you were convicted for those three murders—you could spend the rest of your life in jail, is that right?

A: Yes.

Q: You were forty-six then?

A: Yes.

Q: With a normal life expectancy, you could have spent more than twenty-five years in jail, is that right?

A: Yes.

Q: But you also have been involved in the killing of twenty-two human beings?

A: Yes, nineteen murders.

Q: Am I right about that?

A: I said yes.

Q: By reason of the arrangement that you made with the government, you face twenty years in jail—maximum twenty years in jail for taking the lives of twenty-two human beings. Isn't that right?

A: Yes.

Q: Is there a low end, a minimum period of time that the learned sentencing judge must incarcerate you?

A: No.

Q: As a matter of fact, under the agreement that you worked out with the government, you replaced an exposure of twenty-two life sentences for the twenty-two murders with a possibility, if luck be with you, for doing no additional time other than the six months you have served? Is that so, zero on the low end, isn't that a true statement?

A: The judge isn't bound by the guidelines.

Q: The plea agreement permits the judge, be he so inclined, to impose a probationary period, a zero term of incarceration, correct?

A: Yes.

Q: Have you not said within the last several weeks that, if luck be with you, that you could be on the street by Christmas, have you said that?

A: I don't think I said if luck be with me.

Q: Forget the luck. If fate be with you, you hope to be with us again as early as the Christmas season, have you said that?

A: I believe I wasn't asked that way, but...

Q: Well, I will ask you, given the festive mood of Christmas, is it your hope, as you sit here, that by Christmas you will be free, that's your hope, isn't that so?

A: My hope is to be free one day, yes.

Q: Yes, and you have said as recently as the last two weeks, you made reference to the month of December as your hoped for goal of freedom, is that so, for these twenty-two murders?

A: I think that's what my lawyer represented.

Q: And what did you say in response to what the lawyer said?

A: Yes, I hope to be out at the earliest possible date.

Q: The earliest at least after you testify, is that right?

A: I'm not to be sentenced in December, so it is actually a wrong date, but...

Q: Let me see how I understand this. When you called the government or the FBI on October 24, 1990, you were sitting in a prison, which Mr. Mearns refers to as the M.C.C. the Metropolitan Correctional Center, right?

A: Yes.

Q: Facing this prospect of twenty-two life sentences without parole, correct?

A: I believe that's what the sentence would have been.

Q: And you picked up the phone and you called the government. Is that right, or the FBI?

A: Yes.

Q: Did you make that call because you had some conversion, some change of direction in the way in which you had lived your life? Is that why you picked up that telephone?

A: No.

Q: Okay. You picked up that phone to try to work a deal for yourself. Is that true?

A: I guess you could put it that way.

Q: Because when you went down on October 24, you met an FBI agent, I think you told us several FBI agents, and the United States Attorney himself, Mr. Maloney. Is that correct?

A: Yes.

Q: And you talked to them about the possibility that you wanted to come clean with your life of crime. Is that correct?

A: I believe I said something to the effect that I was turning my back on my life and I was changing direction.

Q: Changing direction, that was October 24, 1991, is that right, and you told that to Mr. Maloney? Is that right?

A: I believe that's the date.

Q: Did you tell Mr. Maloney that, despite the statement that you made to him that you wanted to turn your back on crime in your "other life" that you were going to go back to the M.C.C. to commit further extortionate credit collections, did you tell that to him?

A: No.

Q: But there is no question that after you left Mr. Maloney's office, when you told him that you wanted to turn your back on your former life, you uttered those words intending for him to believe that you could now be trusted to turn your back on your former life, isn't that so, that is why you uttered those words to him, isn't that true?

A: No.

Q: When you said to Mr. Maloney, I am here because I want to turn my back on my former life you intended to convey to him that it was your intention to change your way of life, isn't that a fair statement?

A: I don't know if that is what was running through my head at this particular point.

Q: As a matter of fact, despite what you said to Mr. Maloney, for the next few weeks after you went back to the M.C.C. you proceeded to arrange collections, or extortionate credit collections between October 24, 1991, and November 8, 1991, when you left the M.C.C., isn't that true?

A: No.

Q: You testified at another trial at page 4232 that the shylocking business you were involved in continued right up until the time that you were arrested, correct?

A: Yes.

Q: In fact you even continued while you were in the M.C.C., did you not?

A: Yes.

Q: Mr. Gravano, until I reached for a transcript, I recall the question on the floor had been, did you, sir, not after leaving Mr. Maloney's office on October 24, 1991, until November 8, 1991, when you left the prison, you left the M.C.C. did you not continue to engage in loan-sharking, you said no. Isn't that right?

A: I just answered you, it is, yes.

Q: The monies that you collected between the time that you first met with the United States Attorney himself, and members of the FBI until the time you left the M.C.C. over this two-week period you never arranged to give that money back through any help of the government for the victims, did you, yes or no?

A: Never came to me.

Q: Never came to you?

A: It was collected by the people on the street.

Q: I see.

A: I just never stopped it.

Q: When you were arrested you had hundreds of thousands of dollars in the bank, didn't you?

A: Two hundred thousand.

Q: Two hundred thousand? None of those monies was ever used by you to make any of your victims whole? Do you know what "whole" means, to repair the damage that you had caused, am I correct?

A: Shylock customers? I don't know what you are talking about.

Q: That is one set of victims?

A: No.

Q: Is that 200,000 dollars that you had in the bank account, that is not the whole of your wealth as of the time that you were arrested, correct?

A: No.

Q: You had additional money, right?

A: Yes.

Q: You didn't work that out, any deal or arrangement with the government to turn back as a condition of this plea of guilty any of that money to either the victims, the government of the United States, namely, the IRS or any other agency of the government, correct?

A: No.

Q: And you've said that when you went to the government on October 24, 1991, you told the United States Attorney that you wanted to turn your back on your former life, is that right?

A: I don't know if I told him that. You asked me what I did. I don't think I told the U.S. Attorney that, but that is what my motive was for, that is what I did.

Q: But your plea agreement provides that your cooperation is only for a period of two years, isn't that so?

A: I don't believe so.

Q: This is not a time limit on the time set for your cooperation provided for in the plea agreement, yes or no?

A: I believe it is not a cooperation, it is testifying. Cooperation goes on, I believe, indefinitely.

Q: Do I understand at the expiration of this two years of testifying, you feel yourself free to go back, should you be favored with a return to the street to your former life is that what you understand the two-year word means?

A: I don't believe so.

Q: But that was a term that was suggested to the government by your lawyer, isn't that right, the two-year limit on testifying, the government never said to you, you only have to testify, Sammy, for just a two-year period. The government never said to you?

A: No.

Q: That was something that you insisted upon as a condition, of facing the prospect of getting no time for the killing of twenty-two human beings, correct, that was your idea to put a time limit?

A: Yes.

Q: And let me ask you something. Did the government ever say to you, listen, Salvatore Gravano, you can keep all the ill-gotten gains that you have made from loan-sharking, gambling, labor racketeering, murder, or was it your lawyer who argued in your presence with the government that there should be, no restitution required for you, whose idea was it that you can keep the money?

A: It was never discussed.

Q: They never said to you, Mr. Gravano. You are a person who I think went to the eighth grade?

A: Approximately.

Q: Correct. You were trained as a ladies hairdresser, is that right?

A: No, I was never a hairdresser.

Q: Wasn't that your training?

A: No.

Q: Did you ever go to hairdressing school?

A: Yes.

Q: Was it ladies hairdressers?

A: It was hair cutting.

Q: Hair cutting, okay. And the government never said to you, listen from your humble beginnings, and there was a period of time, was there not, when you reported, you and your wife in the year 1982 a mere 24,000 dollars and change in taxable income, right?

A: I believe so. That is what the numbers are.

Q: So now—here you are in December of 1991 a millionaire, correct?

(No response.)

Q: And you described yourself as a millionaire, have you not, at the time of your arrest?

A: Yes.

Q: Did the government ever say to you: Listen, Gravano, it is clear to us that this fortune which you have amassed has not been through hard legitimate work, but has been through evil doings, and you should provide a fund for the victims who remain on the earth, as well as other people who have suffered financial loss. Did the government ever say that to you?

A: No.

Q: You certainly never offered it, right, as part of cleansing your soul, you never said it to the government, listen I want to make my peace?

A: I didn't cleanse myself. I never said I cleansed my soul. The answer to that is, no, as well.

Q: You are here, sir, because you will do what it takes, you will spare no words or statement if you feel that it can increase your chances to return to the streets, isn't that a fair statement?

A: No.

Q: Are you here because you feel conscience stricken over your participation in the murder or demise of twenty-two human beings, you are not here for that reason, are you?

A: I am here because I was debriefed about what I know in this case, and I said exactly what I know. I am compelled to be here.

Q: Are you not, sir, as you sit here, in any way restrained or upset by any feeling of conscience about the loss of life, for example, for Joe Colucci who you say you killed, is that right?

A: Sure.

Q: You are. As a matter of fact, Joe Colucci had been your friend, is that right?

A: Yes.

Q: You are here having taken an oath, hoping—this is what I am asking you—hoping that this jury will trust your word, isn't that a fair statement?

A: I am here to say the facts of what I know.

Q: And you want the jury to trust, isn't that a fair statement, of what you say, isn't that correct?

A: That is not my job. I am here to tell the truth of what I know.

Q: You told other people who you knew, in the course of your life, things, for example, you had conversations with Louie Milito shortly before his death, that he could trust you, that there would be no harm coming to him from you. Didn't you say that in words or substance to Louie Milito?

A: Sure.

Q: You gave him your word?

A: Sure.

Q: You knew Louie Milito all your life?

A: If he would have acted a certain way.

Q: You knew Louie Milito and Louie Milito knew you longer than these ladies and gentlemen know you?

A: He was a friend of mine and he was a man.

Q: Let me finish my question.

Q: Louie Milito knew you longer than this jury knows you, isn't that so?

A: Of course.

Q: Louie Milito knew you for fifteen or more years, isn't that so?

A: At least twenty.

Q: Were you a friend of his family?

A: Yes.

Q: You told Louie Milito to meet you at a particular location, is that correct?

A: Yes.

Q: You planned to murder him or have him murdered, isn't that a fair statement

A: There came a point, yes.

Q: Well, when you called him, did you call him on the phone?

A: No.

Q: Did you have someone call him?

A: Someone else called him.

Q: The mission was to cause him no alarm in asking him to come to that place, isn't that right, wherever it was?

A: That is true.

Q: But the man without question did. Before this man departed his home in Staten Island and journeyed for the last time in his life to a given location, the plan was set in motion to murder him, isn't that right?

A: Yes.

Q: As you sit here do you have any feeling of conscience with respect to his murder?

A: Yes, absolutely.

Q: And once you murdered him, or participated in his murder, did you go to his wife and daughter and tell them that you would help find the person who had murdered Louie Milito, did you do that, yes or no?

A: They came to me. I did tell them that, yes.

Q: As far as you could tell, they believed in you; is that right?

A: They believed I would help them.

Q: They trusted your word, is that right? Right? Is that a fair statement as far as you could glean?

A: Yes.

Q: They felt, as far as you could glean from the way they looked up at you after you said that you would help them, that they had faith in you, is that right?

A: Yes.

Q: All the while, sir, unbeknownst to them, you had killed the husband of Mrs. Milito and the father, obviously, of Ms. Milito, correct?

A: Yes.

Q: You had been in a business venture with Louie Milito before he met his demise isn't that so?

A: Yes.

Q: You have said, have you not, on one or more occasions that you never killed in a fit of rage, did you ever say that to anyone?

A: Yes.

Q: In other words, your murders were done not out of anger, but they are planned in terms of what it could mean for you in terms of your pocketbook, isn't that so?

A: Yes.

Q: Do I understand, sir, that at the tail end of your examination, you told this jury that you had pleaded guilty to two instances where you actually obstructed justice by intruding into the jury box to fix the outcome of a case, is that what you pleaded guilty to?

A: Yes.

Q: One of those cases involved Eddie Lino?

A: Yes.

Q: Was that a drug case?

A: Yes.

Q: Was it a federal case?

A: Yes.

Q: Was it in this very building?

A: I would imagine so.

Q: You intruded in effect into the jury box by bribery and corruption of a person who had been sworn as a juror to render justice, is that right, you did that?

A: I was a go-between for the captain in our Family and the people in the jury, yes.

Q: You pleaded guilty to doing that, isn't that so?

A: I participated, yes.

Q: You did that on one or more occasions, correct, yes or no?

A: Yes.

Q: But you say to this jury that they can trust your word, that you are telling the truth, is that what you are saying?

A: I said that I am here according to my deal telling the truth from what I know.

Q: Did it ever figure into your consideration to say to the government you have charged me with crimes. I will tell all that I know and throw myself on the mercy of the Court. I don't need a plea agreement. Did you ever say that to the government?

A: No, I don't believe so.

Q: In other words, you have been involved in business deals in the course of your life, have you not?

A: Yes.

Q: At times you have been represented by lawyers in business deals, is that right?

A: Yes.

Q: Here too you have a lawyer, is that right?

A: Yes.

Q: You didn't go in and say to the government listen, I have killed twenty-two human beings. I have done labor racketeering, extortion, armed robberies, gone on stickups, or did stickups, armed robberies. I want to turn my back on my former life. I will tell you all that I know. And I have

257

full confidence in the judicial system that I will get what is coming to me. Did you ever say that to the government?

A: Not in those words, but that is what I did.

Q: That is what you did. But you told us that on December 11, 1990, a judge, a magistrate or a judge of the District Court had decided that you were such a threat to the community that you weren't even granted bail following your arrest on December 11, 1990, isn't that so?

A: Yes.

Q: You were such a threat to the community that you now hope to rejoin by Christmas, that you were put in prison without any chance of bail following December 11, 1990, is that right?

A: Yes.

Q: And you are telling the ladies and gentlemen of this jury that you harbored not one single scintilla of thought of going in, and telling these people, Mr. Dowling and Mr. Gabriel and members of the prosecution team, all the terrible things that you had done in your life, trusting without any limits being put upon the judge to deal with you as his learned wisdom dictated, you never did that, did you?

A: No.

Q: Sir, this judge is no longer authorized under the law to give you a life sentence, isn't that so?

A: I believe so.

Q: In other words, by agreement between you and your lawyer and the government, the learned judge is no longer able to sentence you to any life sentence for taking the lives of twenty-two people, correct?

A: I believe it is a cap of twenty years.

Q: Cap of twenty, which means if things really go bad for you, the judge in a maximum can sentence you to twenty years, correct?

A: I believe that is the high top level.

Q: Now, sir, was there ever a time when you conveyed to someone that the result of your upbringing was such that it led you into a life of crime, did you ever say anything of that kind to anyone that you were such a product?

A: I said I grew up in the tough neighborhood.

Q: Did you just say it was a tough neighborhood, or did you tell a jury that you were a product of a ghetto life, did you say that to a jury, yes or no?

A: Yes.

Q: When you said that you were a product of a ghetto life, you were trying to get sympathy when you uttered those words in front of a jury, isn't that so?

A: No. Absolutely not.

Q: But you were not the product of a ghetto upbringing, were you?

A: What I did was correct my answer there, and I said that it was not exactly ghetto, but it was a tough neighborhood.

Q: Your parents were hard-working honest people, who worked fifteen hours a day in a dress factory. They bought a 6,000 dollar bungalow in the country, correct?

A: What I said is I grew up in a tough neighborhood with rough guys. We stole, we robbed, we quit school. That is what I said. It had no reflection on my mother and father or their business or how they worked. I never said I came from a broken home or bad home, I never did.

Q: Were there other siblings in that family aside from yourself?

A: Yes, I have two sisters.

Q: There are others in the family aside from you, is that right, two sisters you said?

A: Two sisters.

Q: And did anyone within your family structure, to your recollection, engage in the kind of conduct that you have outlined for this jury?

A: No.

Q: Let me ask you, if you will, to recall a man by the name of Frank Fialla, does that name strike a bell with you?

A: Yes.

Q: Is he one of the people who met his demise on June 27, 1982, through your actions?

A: Yes.

Q: When Mr. Fialla died he was involved in some potential business transaction with you, is that right?

A: Yes.

Q: In other words, there you were the seller and he was the purchaser of some disco, is that what was planned, is that right?

A: A building and disco.

Q: A building, a disco. There was some 650,000 dollars involved, is that right?

A: Yes.

Q: You arranged for him to be murdered, is that right?

A: Yes.

Q: Then there came a point in time when you are left with monies because his death that had to be reported on a tax return, is that a fair statement?

A: Yes.

Q: I am going to show you a document previously furnished by me to the government, and ask that it be marked defendant's Exhibit D for identification. Am I correct that Fialla died, was murdered, after he had given you 650,000 dollars, is that correct?

A: The money was in escrow.

Q: I see. And then there came a point where you met with your tax preparer and had to prepare a tax return to explain that 650,000 dollars, correct?

A: Yes.

Q: I am going to show you, and I take it, your wife's name is Deborah?

A: Yes.

Q: I am going to show you a document which has been furnished to me by the government pursuant to law, and ask you is this your tax return for the year 1983?

A: Yes, I believe so.

GOLDBERG: I am going to offer it in evidence.

COURT: It will be received.

Q: Now, sir, let us take a look at how the 650,000 dollars is explained. This is, now I am going to read it, with Your Honor's permission. And in your tax return that you signed, this is how you explained how you kept the 650,000 dollars, this is what you say: "Deal did not go through until January '83. Deal was aborted by purchaser." I am reading from the document. What you are saying there, is that you kept the 650,000 dollars because the deal was aborted by Mr. Fialla to purchase it, do you understand that?

A: That is not so.

Q: That is in the document. As matter of fact, the deal didn't go through because you aborted Mr. Fialla, isn't that a better statement?

A: No.

Q: Well, the deal didn't go through as you tell the Internal Revenue Service, deal did not go through because the deal was aborted by the purchaser. The purchaser was Mr. Fialla, is that right?

A: It did not go through in 1982 or '83.

Q: This is your tax return, can you read it to the jury with His Honor's permission, it says within the parenthesis?

A: I rather you read it.

Q: You rather I read it, okay. Deal did not go through until January 1987. Deal aborted by the purchaser. You were telling the Internal Revenue Service that the reason the deal didn't go through, is that Mr. Fialla had aborted the deal, had pulled out of the deal, you understand that by the use of that language? It is an accounting term. When in fact, as I said earlier you are the person who arranged the abortion of the purchaser, isn't that a better statement?

A: The abortion?

Q: The end, the demise of Mr. Fialla, the purchaser, isn't that what happened in this case?

A: Yes. And then the deal did not go through.

Q: Because it would be very difficult to have him show up at a closing because of all the dirt on him, isn't that a fair statement?

A: So then the money went back to the family and the estate. It is because you make—

Q: Isn't that right, Mr. Gravano? The deal was not "aborted" by the purchaser, as you wrote on your tax return, because you the seller arranged for him to be aborted?

A: Yeah, all right.

It didn't take long for the jury to deliberate. Joseph was acquitted because they did not believe a word Gravano said. As my reward aside from my fee, Joseph, being of Sicilian birth, cooked me a two-week supply of pasta con le sarde.

CHAPTER 35

TESTING THE WITNESS COOPERATION AGREEMENT

FOR YEARS, I WAGED A virtual solitary battle to have courts recognize that prosecutors often would hold back information helpful to the defense. After all, they do debrief informants, and if one could get a hold of the debriefing notes, there would be an enormous amount of wrongdoing revealed that a private detective would have trouble unearthing on his own. A witness for the prosecution is required to set forth all of his wrongdoing. One must work to disgorge the information.

One judge, Marvin Frankel, U.S. District Judge, Southern District of New York, adopted my view in *United States v. Agone*, 302 F. Supp. 1258 (1969). He accepted my position, while other judges made the absolutely silly statement that "the prosecutor is aware of his obligation," and left it to the judgment of the adversary.

Alive with this is the Witness Cooperation Agreement. It is important for the practitioner to seek remedies for what I describe below. In 1935, Victor McLaglen gave an award-winning performance in the now classic film *The Informer*. Initially, the term "informer" had a pejorative connotation. However, over time, prosecutors embraced the term as a positive one. One may suspect that, from a prosecutorial standpoint, the term is well chosen and believed to embody a positive force.

The first of the questioned provisions of a Witness Cooperation Agreement requires the witness to be debriefed by an agency such as the FBI concerning his knowledge and participation in any criminal activity. The witness, at the debriefing session, must "give complete, truthful and accurate information." But it is the government alone that determines whether the witness has given truthful and accurate information.

This provision was made a part of the cooperation agreement to wrongly convey the impression that when the government calls the witness to the stand, it has determined (through methods of verification not disclosed) that the witness has performed as agreed to in the debriefing session. This provision was inserted into the cooperation agreement for the prohibited purpose of allowing the government to vouch for the credibility of the witness. The undue harm to the defense is apparent.

What is most disturbing is the second questioned provision, commonly referred to by counsel as the "penalty provision." It provides that if the witness gives false testimony, he may be prosecuted for any and all crimes the government is aware of, which may be many more than those covered by the agreement. At trial, the prosecutor invariably asks the witness whether he understands the penalty that would result from untruthful testimony. The witness responds that he understands the substantial penalty, lest there be complete, accurate, and truthful testimony. Any juror hearing this, or reading this provision in the cooperation agreement, would be of the view that few witnesses would ever risk such harm.

However, counsel should make a vigorous argument against its use in court and in the jury room during deliberations. The judge, government counsel, and defense counsel all know that this penalty provision has never been enforced, but the jury does not know this is the case. Few know that the real purpose of having this provision was to chill cross-examination.

Given the purpose of these provisions and, in particular, the lack of enforcement of the so-called "penalty provision," the court should not permit reference to either provision by any witness, and the document should certainly not go into the jury room during deliberations. Were a court to disagree with this, the government should be required, at a hearing pursuant to Fed. R. Evid. 104, to show whether any witness it had later determined to have given false testimony *was thereafter prosecuted for all crimes known to the government.* If the government fails to do so—and it *will* fail even if the court has the prosecutor canvas all judicial districts in the U.S. in which the penalty provisions exist—the court should then not permit testimony about these provisions or any reference to the agreement in the closing argument, or to permit it to go into the jury room during deliberations.

A defendant should seek a hearing under Rule 104 to test the bona fides of the agreement. The best way to do this is to have a *defense* Witness Cooperation Agreement for your witness, which mirrors, as far as possible, the government's agreement, only instead your witness will suffer the loss of a large amount of property if you determine he is not being accurate, complete, and truthful. You could be sure that the government will seek a Rule 104 motion to test the trustworthiness of your agreement, and then you will be in a better position to argue that the government's agreement should be tested for bona fides as well. You will have the same kind of bolstering argument that the government has during its closing argument: "Why would he lie and risk...?"

There is no reason to keep from juries what judges and lawyers know about the misuse of the Witness Cooperation Agreement. I believed that within the circuit, if there were a judge with courage to take on this problem of the penalty provision, it was Judge Weinstein. Judge Weinstein was a sterling member of the judiciary, and I decided I was going to test him on this provision.

One day, a woman named Cathy Burke asked for an appointment and came to see me.

"I am Jimmy Burke's daughter," she said. "Are you familiar with him?"

"Jimmy Burke...wasn't he suspected of being behind the Lufthansa heist?"

"That's him," she said.

The heist was committed on December 11, 1978, at JFK Airport in New York. It netted Burke and others five million dollars in cash (valued today at nearly twenty million dollars) and 875,000 dollars in jewelry (valued today at more than three million dollars), making it the largest air cargo theft ever.

I knew that, one by one, the persons who it was said assisted Burke had been murdered. Eventually, he was the only one involved left standing; no other witnesses were alive. The papers painted him as a person who had committed a number of murders but was not a member of the mafia because he couldn't trace his ancestors to persons of Italian decent. Later, there was an enormously successful movie directed by Martin Scorsese, entitled *Goodfellas*. Robert De Niro played the part of Burke. Ray Liotta played the part of the government witness and former confidant of Burke, Henry Hill.

Though everybody knew Burke was the main man behind the crime, the government was not able to make a case against him for the robbery because of the lack of witnesses and evidence. Therefore, the government proceeded to try to convict him in the U.S. District Court in the Eastern District of New York for engaging in point shaving to aid gamblers betting on the Boston College basketball team. One crime had nothing to do with the other, but the government was determined to get justice for the heist in any manner possible.

One of the major witnesses against Burke had been a former member of his alleged mob. The witness had been in the witness protection program, where marshals arranged to have him live under an assumed name in an undisclosed part of the country. The witness remained an informant protected by this program, but criminals at heart, and the program, could not prevent one from committing crimes and believing they were protected by the government.

"I'd like you to visit my dad. He is at the Metropolitan Correctional Center," Cathy Burke said to me.

Her father was there because of a provable lie that Henry Hill had told at Burke's point shaving trial. Burke had been sentenced to twenty years. He was hiring me for his appeal.

"I have heard a lot about you," Burke said to me when I entered a small counsel room at the prison.

"All good, I hope?"

"Of course, of course," he said.

We didn't talk about the robbery at all. Though the government no doubt used the point shaving scandal to "make up" for him not being charged in the robbery, it was the scandal that I needed to focus on.

"I know you are in an unfortunate situation," I told him. "You are being punished now because they couldn't charge you in the robbery, and it's only because of the Witness Cooperation Agreement that you are sitting here. I can't make any promises, but I need to test this agreement with this judge. It's a long shot, but it is the only chance we have."

"I understand," he said. "If my daughter had confidence in you, then so do I. What happens if we win?"

"If the judge sides with us, I will ask for a new trial based on the fact that a witness violated the Witness Cooperation Agreement. So, your problems won't necessarily be over, but you will get another chance to defend yourself."

I wish I had a dramatic conclusion to this story as I have in some others, but there isn't one. Judge Weinstein gave my motion zero consideration. Not even a hearing. The courtroom was packed from wall to wall with defense attorneys who knew I was going to put the agreement to the test and who knew I was right. They, of course, wanted nothing more than to see me win this battle, which would have changed the landscape of how they would fight for their clients. But the judge did not have the balls to do anything. It was a waste of everyone's time. I knew, and was reminded, that even if you make a very good point, it doesn't mean the judge will open his or her eyes to what you are saying. He should have taken an interest in this. It was an opportunity for him to be part of a groundbreaking case. But he quickly denied the motion, and Burke was ordered back to prison to serve the remainder of the twenty-year sentence.

"I'm sorry," I said to Burke. He just shrugged his shoulders.

"I knew I didn't have much of a chance," he said.

Burke died of cancer while serving his prison term.

The time will come, mark my words, when juries will be told the true facts with respect to the lack of bonafide witnesses who testify under Witness Cooperation Agreement, and that they are not permitted to see if the government has been able to verify the truthfulness of a witness's story. According to the government's behavior, the end justifies the means, but the Rule of Law provides otherwise.

CHAPTER 36

BEWARE OF THE UNGRATEFUL CLIENT

ANTHONY SPERO, THE FOUNDER OF a highly successful limousine business in Brooklyn, was the acting boss of the Bonanno crime family while Carmine Galante was in prison.

Spero had been charged with the murder of one Frank Russo. The assistant U.S. Attorney handling the case in the Manhattan federal court had just one witness, Mel Greenberg. Though standing thirty feet from the shooting, Greenberg was absolutely certain he had correctly identified Spero as the shooter. Relying solely on his word, the government indicted Spero for the murder of Russo.

"Mr. Goldberg, I didn't do it," Spero said to me when we met for the first time to discuss his case.

Many clients I'd represented, including mobsters, often claimed they were angels who didn't do anything to anyone, though I of course knew better. But I believed Spero when he told me he was innocent. There was just something about him, about his demeanor, that convinced me Greenberg had made a mistaken identification and the government had the wrong guy.

"Give me a little time to come up with a strategy," I told Spero. "I have a couple ideas in mind."

My first thought was to have Spero testify on his own behalf, but that thought was very short-lived. I'd have been foolish to do it, given Spero's extensive criminal record. The prosecutor would have had a field day cross-examining him, making a conviction more than probable.

My next instinct was to contact the prosecutor and say, "Hey, my client is innocent. You have the wrong guy!" And 999 times out of a thousand, that claim would be met with the response, "Yeah, whatever. That's what trials are for. See you in court."

But it couldn't hurt to try, right?

I called the assistant U.S. Attorney.

"Look, I don't necessarily think this about all of my clients, but I am certain Spero is innocent," I said.

"Well, I'm convinced our witness knows what he saw," he replied.

"From thirty feet? Seriously?"

"It's not that far, Goldberg."

"Far enough that I have my doubts."

"He knows what he saw. Our investigators concur with him."

"Then all I ask is that he convince me of that before we drag this into a trial."

"Convince you how?" he said.

"Bring your client into my office tomorrow night and let's do a lineup. I'll have Spero and a few other guys for him to look at. If he picks Spero, I'll leave you alone and see you in court."

"Are you kidding?" he asked.

"I'm not. We both want justice, right? This will plug a lot of holes one way or another. How about tomorrow night at eight?"

There was a long pause.

"I'll see you tomorrow at eight."

I hung up the phone before he could say another word. I was stunned. Never in all of my years as a defense attorney had a U.S. Attorney agreed to come to my office for any reason. Every other defense attorney could probably make the same claim. To this day, I cannot explain why he agreed to come, but he did.

Spero arrived at my office at seven. I spent the next forty-five minutes gathering four men in my law firm who were the approximate height, weight, and shape of Spero. I had them remove their ties, unbutton their shirts, and shape their hair to look as much like Spero as they could. At eight o'clock, the assistant U.S. Attorney arrived with his investigator and Greenberg.

"I have five men," I told the attorney. "Mr. Greenberg is welcome to walk right up to each of them and look them over. He can take as long as he needs."

Greenberg approached each man, looking each one in the eyes and noting their other features. He spent probably thirty seconds to a minute on each one, then went back through them all again and took even more time. He wasn't tipping his hand at all. I couldn't tell if he was leaning more toward one guy over the others. The way I saw it, if he wasn't certain from thirty feet away who pulled that trigger, the odds were well in our favor.

After considerable time, Greenberg said he was finished and ready to make his identification.

"It's number three," he said.

"Are you certain?" I asked.

"I am."

"Thank you, Mr. Greenberg," I said.

I looked at the prosecutor, who knew what had just happened.

"I expect you will move to dismiss your indictment," I said.

Spero was number five. Number three was a senior partner in the bankruptcy division of my firm.

I believe, given his past and the fact that I would not have put him on the stand to defend himself, that had this case gone to trial, Spero would have been found guilty and would have spent the rest of his life in jail. It simply would have been too difficult to convince a jury otherwise.

But, as I've stated, when the government doesn't get its man in one case, they will find another reason to indict him until they finally get him. A few months after Spero's release, I received a phone call from his daughter. He'd been arrested in another crime and was again facing a life sentence.

"He'd like you to represent him again," she said.

"I am happy to," I replied.

"But," she said, "I do not expect you will be charging a fee."

"Excuse me?"

"You already charged us a fee for the first case, and you didn't do anything."

I couldn't believe what I was hearing.

"What do you mean I didn't do anything? I made him a free man."

"Yeah, and it took what, an hour? It's not like you went through a trial."

"The goal was to make him a free man. I did just that."

"Well, we're not paying you anything this time around."

"Then you can find yourself another attorney," I said, and I hung up.

I half expected her to call back, but she didn't. They hired another attorney, and Spero was convicted. He received a life sentence and later died in prison. A friend of his asked me after the conviction if I could have done better for him.

"I don't know," I said, "but I certainly couldn't have done any worse."

Chapter 37

PISSING OFF A JUDGE HAS ITS BENEFITS

CHARLIE "THE JAP" ERRIGO, A high-ranking member of the Genovese crime family, had been charged with narcotics trafficking for a second time. He already had one conviction for this offense. He was scheduled to go to trial in Manhattan federal court before the dreadfully harsh Judge Edmund Palmieri, who detested narcotic dealers and, to be sure, lawyers who defended them. For multiple offenders, it was expected that he would impose the then-maximum sentence of forty years. Errigo had just gotten married and had two children. He was willing to do anything to avoid a trial before Judge Palmieri.

One day while in my office, Errigo showed up with a suitcase.

"Mr. Goldberg," he said, "I cannot go before Judge Palmieri."

"I understand why you don't want to," I replied, "but I don't think there is anything we can do about that."

"Well, that's why I am here, because I believe there is."

He opened the suitcase. It contained 200,000 dollars neatly wrapped, as though straight out of the movies. I didn't understand; he had already paid an advance fee to me.

"Paying me more money isn't going to change anything," I said, though the bills looked awfully nice.

"They are not for you," he said. "I would like you to make a connection with someone in the clerk's office to get the case reassigned. This is for the person who helps us. We'll call it a little incentive."

I closed the briefcase.

"That's out of the question," I said. "One, I would never do it simply because it's wrong, and two, if I were to do it, it would end my career if I were caught. You need to use that money for other purposes. We'll work with what we have to win your case."

"I think that's a mistake," he said.

"This would be an even bigger one," I replied.

And, with that, he left with his money.

I would hate to think that any attorney would have taken him up on his idea, but there was no way that I, the man who once took on corrupt New York City cops by himself, was going to let a mobster sway me.

Just prior to Errigo's case, I defended labor racketeer Benny "the Bug" Ross in front of Judge Palmieri. Benny had taken the witness stand in his own defense, and when asked a question on cross-examination, he told the prosecutor that before he answered, he would first have to get guidance from his wife. His wife had died five years before. I never told him to say that, but I did find it quite hilarious.

Anyway, my battle with Judge Palmieri in the Ross case was over whether a prosecutor in the Manhattan federal court would likely withhold evidence that would be helpful to the accused. I argued that the prosecutor had such evidence in this case, and I asked repeatedly that it be turned over pretrial. That included exculpatory evidence under *Brady v. Maryland* and *Giglio v. United States* (373 U.S. 83 and 405 U.S. 150). Judge Palmieri told me in no uncertain terms that prosecutors in this jurisdiction do not withhold *Brady* or *Giglio* material. His position was nothing short of silly. He did not even ask the prosecutor whether such evidence existed. It is not an overstatement to say that the relationship between Judge Palmieri and I was horrendous. After a two-week trial, Ross was convicted.

Following the verdict, Judge Palmieri summoned me to the robing room.

"Jay, I am a senior judge," he said.

"Yes, I know that," I said, refusing to stroke his already inflated ego.

"And, as a senior judge, I am able to select the cases that I want to try."

"So?"

"So, I never want to see your face in my courtroom again."

I certainly had no problem with that.

"Therefore, I am assigning the upcoming Errigo case to another judge."

I turned away and, like Jack Benny, I looked at ceiling with my hands folded and my lips pursed. I'd pissed him off so much over the years that I inadvertently got my next client exactly what he wanted.

Should I ask Errigo to come back with his suitcase full of cash? I pondered as Palmieri continued rambling. *After all, I just accomplished what he wanted. I got Palmieri off his case.*

When Palmieri was finished babbling, I told him to have a good day and I bolted out the door. Of course, I wasn't going to ask Errigo for the cash. But it was funny how soon after he offered it, everything worked out exactly as he'd hoped.

Errigo ended up receiving an eight-year sentence, and he had to serve only three years of it. It was a far cry from the forty Palmieri would have likely given him.

Errigo was not out more than two years when he had another encounter with law enforcement; this time he was to appear before a federal judge in Brooklyn. There was a search and seizure problem arising from the government obtaining Errigo's property at his home, and I did substantial work on a motion to suppress and to keep him free on bail. A happy man again, he agreed to meet me at the Water Club in Manhattan to pay me my fee.

We met, he paid, and we parted ways.

The next day, for reasons unbeknownst to me, he was murdered.

CHAPTER 38

A PORN/COMEDY FILM ABOUT NUNS

AS DISCUSSED EARLIER, IN THE 1970s, New York was very different in terms of law enforcement than it is today. At the top of the list, as a danger to the community, was obscenity—material thought to be in excess of contemporary standards and appealing to the prurient interest of the observer. For example, I recall a police officer once gave a summons to a store owner who allowed his plastic mannequin to be unclothed until he found a more recent fashion to put on it. Looking back, I think New York City is a better place today in terms of the priorities given by law enforcement.

I became involved in the obscenity law soon after New York City passed an ordinance that required the local licensing of motion pictures in advance of their showing. City officials thought that in some way they could exercise their judgment as to what was in the best interests of the viewer and society in general, for they believed viewers of obscene films were more likely to commit sexual offenses.

I was retained by the owners of a well-known movie theater chain which had a cinema at 42nd Street. The company asked me to challenge the ordinance after some of their equipment was seized by police due to their showing of "obscene" films. I chose to vindicate the right of free speech and expression in Manhattan federal court, for I did not have confidence that state courts were up to the task of rendering a fair and impartial judgment.

It was my good fortune that the case was assigned to a legend, Judge Edward Weinfeld. He held that his court would not abstain from exercising its jurisdiction in an action challenging the constitutionality of certain municipal ordinances. Judge Weinfeld went on to state that motion pictures were included within the free speech and free press guarantees of the First Amendment. The court wrote that in view of First Amendment protection of the distribution of motion picture films, no state or municipality may significantly interfere therewith, and that the requirement that a film be pre-licensed before it was shown was unconstitutional. This was considered to be a deathly holding to the police department and the "forces of good government," for they had believed that requiring a license would put an end to the showing of films they considered to be obscene.

Soon after that victory, Mickey Zaffarano, a well-heeled captain in the Bonanno crime family, contacted me. He asked that I defend him in his obscenity film case that was slated for federal court in Washington, D.C. Mickey owned a theater two blocks from the White House. It was there that the alleged obscene film was shown.

"I'm a little worried about having Judge (John) Pratt," Mickey said.

"Why?"

"Because I know how conservative he is," Mickey said.

"I've won tougher cases before conservative judges that people didn't expect me to win," I said.

"But his daughter is a nun," Mickey said.

"So?"

"Well..."

Mickey paused.

Uh-oh, I thought to myself. I was afraid to ask, but I knew I had to.

"Tell me about the film," I said.

He took a deep breath.

"There are some sex acts," he said.

"Yes, I figured that."

He paused some more.

"And..."

"And what?"

"Some of those acts are between...nuns."

Oh, dear lord. What had I gotten myself into?

"But it's a funny movie, too!" he was quick to state.

I laughed.

276

"So it's a comedy about nuns having sex?" I asked.

"Well, you know..."

No, I didn't know, but I agreed to take the case because I believed he had every right to show his film, and I knew it was important to stop these obscenity police from trying to take over every element of free speech the Constitution afforded us.

I agreed to try the case before a jury of twelve women. I am certain the prosecution thought I was foolish, but after viewing the film myself—which, yes, was certainly funnier than I had expected—I was confident the women would find the government's case deficient.

To prove the deficiency, I wandered outside the box by testing just how much this film offended contemporary community standards. I stopped by the theatre where the film was being shown and spoke to the cashier, explaining to her who I was and why I needed her help.

"If you could please, count the number of D.C. police officers who come into your theatre to see that movie over the next two weeks."

"I can do that," she said.

"Oh, and if you see any leave early," I said, "give me that number too."

"Sure thing," she replied.

Two weeks later I went to the theatre to get the information she had gathered. At the trial, after the jury viewed the film, I shared with them the cashier's findings.

"Over the course of the last two weeks, ten D.C. police officers entered the theatre and viewed that film," I stated to the court. "In addition, not a single one of them left early. From this, one can only conclude that they were not only interested in watching the film, but they apparently liked what was depicted and took no offense to it, for they watched it in its entirety."

The inaction of police officers and the apparent comical aspects of the film, according to several jurors interviewed after the trial, caused them to render a not guilty verdict.

After the case ended, I hightailed my way out of town. As I headed home, I can't say I felt very proud of taking a case that involved such a film, especially in the city that the Kennedys owned when they hired me, and with a friend like Congressman Charlie Rangel right down the road. But, upon further reflection, and considering how much New York and other cities have changed, I realize how important of a case it was. I acted to vindicate the Constitution. The First Amendment was at stake, and we won.

CHAPTER 39

WE WERE HOODWINKED BY THE KILLING MACHINE AND HIS BEAUTY QUEEN

MARCO CIPRIANI, A CLIENT WHO I successfully represented after being accused of the possession and sale of stolen diamonds—though, in reality he was a professional safe cracker who preyed upon the 47th Street diamond district in Manhattan—brought me Lili Dajani. She had won multiple beauty contests in Israel. Once moving to New York, she met Dr. Scholnick, and the two opened legal abortion clinics in each of the five boroughs. The business was enormously successful. When Lili arrived at my office along with Marco, she was bedecked with jewels. Her skin was porcelain colored, with jet black hair, and a beautiful figure to match. She needed a lawyer to represent her, for the Department of Health and the New York City Police Department, prejudiced as they then were against abortions, treated clinics as a den of wrongdoing. Problems arose with raids being conducted by law enforcement at her clinics throughout the boroughs. I was retained to represent her interests through securing injunctions and commencing federal court actions to restrain the police department's illegal targeting of her business.

One night I prevailed upon her to meet with her and her current boyfriend Greg—not Marco—for dinner at the Sea Fare of the Agean on West 56th Street. My wife accompanied me, and I must say, this was a rare occasion that my wife was "fooled" in a way that could have cost me my life. When Greg walked in, it was apparent to me that he was a person of class. He dressed impeccably, wore a well and expensive toupee, and had a deep suntan. We talked for a number of hours, and he was well-versed on the political happenings of the day. I sensed, of course, that he was a part of organized crime and was in the gambling business. He seemed to have ready resources at his command. When I locked my keys in the car in the restaurant parking lot, he told me to wait inside the restaurant and ten minutes later someone arrived with a key. I was impressed. Over a six-month period, my wife and I, along with Lili and Greg, had approximately fifteen dinner dates. I met with Greg virtually every week or so at the Brass Rail restaurant, then South of Grand Central Station. He talked about his gambling enterprise, and at his side was his aide, Joey Brewster. He too was later murdered.

Shortly after Greg and I met, Marco, who had introduced Lili to me, was murdered, but I didn't put two and two together. I didn't even put it together when Dr. Scholnick, who had a deep crush on Lili was murdered. We all know the story of when Clark Kent takes off his suit and becomes a force of good. Greg, apparently, when with me, wearing his toupee, was a person of class, but when he returned to Brooklyn to support a crime family boss, he removed the toupee and became a notorious killing machine—supposedly aided, shockingly, by members of the FBI. Supposedly he was told where to find potential "marks" and where to avoid going. The story reminds me, in retrospect, of the way Whitey Bulger, the notorious killing machine in Boston, had a contact with an FBI agent who was initially assigned to monitor his interests, but found himself so close to the person of interest, that he supposedly protected the person he was charged with surveilling. To law enforcement, it was a case of too close for comfort. The FBI agent and Bulger are doing enormous terms of imprisonment since the arrangement came to light.

What was the story behind Greg's influence on me? For me, Greg was so impressive that when I went to Puerto Rico, I had a statue sculpted for him of a bull, the meaning of his name, and carried it home on the plane—heavy as it was. When his mother died, my wife and I attended her funeral. Few "men of honor" were able to pull off such a split personality. I fashioned myself as a person who could pierce the facade and get at the true character of a person, but

I never did so when it came to Greg or Lili. Greg combined violence with the enormous ability to con.

One morning I received a call from Greg Scarpa, Jr. that his father had been arrested by the District Attorney's Office in Kings County for involvement in a massive gambling enterprise. I went to the detention center on Court St. in Brooklyn and I could not find Greg. When I spoke to the prosecutor, she did not know what had happened, but only that federal authorities had taken custody of Greg. Just who really was he?

I met with an agent of the FBI, much like the setting of *Deep Throat*. He told me that the FBI had actually used Greg (known on the street as "the Grim Reaper") and several of his cohorts to go to Mississippi in order to help find missing civil rights workers, Andrew Goodman, James Chaney, and Michael Schwerner. Their bodies could not be found. Normal interrogation techniques came to naught. Local FBI agents supposedly provided Scarpa with guns and money, and encouraged him to kidnap a TV salesman and pistol whip him in order to reveal the location of the civil rights worker's bodies. I have no personal knowledge of this, I am only reporting on what was told to me. The FBI supposedly paid Scarpa well over 130,000 dollars for his services. We hear nothing but grandiose comments about the purity of the FBI, but one can hardly think of a more shocking set of dirty tricks. Whenever Scarpa was arrested an FBI agent would submit a confidential memo to the judge setting forth all of Scarpa's contributions to the FBI.

But, the participation of the FBI went beyond that. According to an indictment (later dismissed), Scarpa allegedly had the assistance of the special agent assigned to lead the group surveilling him to tip him off in ways that led to an enormous number of killings. No, Scarpa did not wear his toupee when he "worked" in Brooklyn— that he saved for me. According to knowledgeable persons in law enforcement, it is said that Scarpa committed a minimum of eighty, but more likely 100 to 120 murders. He was prosecuted for none of them.

Here is where my life was jeopardized. Greg was a member of the Colombo crime family, whose boss was the imprisoned Carmine Persico. He had Greg's undying loyalty. There was an insurgent group that sought to take the reins away from Persico. Greg's mission was to eliminate members of Vic Orena's rebel Colombo faction. Greg was constantly on the prowl for Orena. One night, a week or so after my wife and I had dinner with Greg and Lili, with Greg's toupee in place, Gus Newman, a well-respected attorney, invited me to have dinner at Giordano's, an Italian Restaurant on the west side. Gus brought along a client of his, Vic Orena, and the three of us sat eating at a table. In retrospect, how possible it was that while having dinner with Gus, Greg, without his toupee, having been tipped off by the FBI as to Orena's whereabouts, could have barged in and murdered the three of us.

Following ulcer surgery, he received blood from a fellow mobster, who unbeknownst to him had aids. This was transferred to Scarpa. The illness progressed and Greg died, but not before the mobster who gave him the blood had been murdered.

It is hard to think of a blacker eye on law enforcement than the role played by the FBI and its conspiracy with "the Grim Reaper."

The New York Times said this about him after his death: "Now, through disclosures arising from recent court proceedings, another portrait has emerged of Mr. Scarpa: Almost to the end of his life, he was a mole for the Federal Bureau of Investigation, betraying Mafia secrets and his own boss for at least 20 years. 'The man was the master of the unpredictable and knew absolutely no bounds of fear,' said Joseph R. Benfanti, a lawyer for Mr. Scarpa. 'He abided by no moral codes; he made his own rules.'"

He'd hoodwinked everybody.

BOXING LEGENDS

CHAPTER 40

BOWE AND HOLYFIELD SLUG IT OUT IN COURT

A.J. LIEBLING SAID IT BEST when he described boxing as the "sweet science" in his classic work, *A Neutral Corner*. Why the "sweet science?" Because it is not a team sport, but a battle between two warriors who must presage their opponent's next move, parry a blow, and counter-punch to avoid defeat, which sometimes arrives with one strike. The sport requires technique, which is the science, and finesse, which produces the sweetness.

The golden age of boxing can be said to have begun with the victory of James J. Corbett over John L. Sullivan in 1892. Of course, there have been countless individual luminaries in more recent decades, such as Muhammad Ali, George Foreman, Evander Holyfield, Sugar Ray Leonard, Riddick Bowe, Mike Tyson, Cesar Chavez, Manny Pacquiao, and Floyd Mayweather, to name just a few.

A good way to judge the public's interest in boxing is to give an example with respect to attendance. The Barclays arena in Brooklyn reported a record turnout for a fight for the World Welterweight Title in April 2017. "The record crowd of 16,533 fans witnessed the battle between Thurman and Garcia," one news outlet reported. Compare that with the bout held at Sesquicentennial Municipal Stadium in Philadelphia in 1926, where Jack Dempsey and Gene Tunney fought for the World Heavyweight Title before a crowd of more than 120,000 people. The ring was twenty feet by twenty feet on a platform raised three feet off the ground. Can you imagine the visibility from the last row in the upper deck? But nobody cared. Just being there meant being a part of history.

One of the best boxers in the last thirty years was Evander Holyfield. He was known in the boxing world as a gentleman, but he was powerful enough to win the Heavyweight Championship of the World on October 25, 1990, when he knocked out Buster Douglas in the third round at the Mirage Casino in Las Vegas, Nevada. This was Douglas's first title defense following his upset win over Mike Tyson. The title Holyfield retained was recognized by the WBC, WBA, and IBF. On November 13, 1992, Holyfield was scheduled to defend his titles against Riddick Bowe, who was 31–0 as a heavyweight fighter. Bowe defeated Holyfield in that fight and was recognized by each of the governing bodies as Heavyweight Champion of the World. The tenth round of that fight was recognized by *Ring Magazine* as the "Round of the Year" in 1992.

Following the fight, Bowe had orally promised Holyfield a rematch. Bowe, however, had already signed a contract to first fight Michael Dokes. Holyfield initiated a lawsuit, claiming that under the rules of the governing bodies, he was entitled to a return fight before Bowe could fight Dokes. Because the fighters lived in different jurisdictions, the case went to federal court. I became involved when another lawyer referred Bowe to me and a learned colleague, Michael Berger. We arranged an appointment, and Bowe came to my office.

"Mr. Bowe, it's a pleasure to meet you," I said.

"You, too," he said, shaking my hand with an expected strong and firm grip.

He explained to me the situation he was in. During our encounter, he came across as a very ordinary guy. He wasn't taken with himself. He spoke intelligently. He seemed very happy and at ease.

"The bottom line is that I signed a contract to fight Dokes next, and that is who I want to fight," he said.

"I think this will be an easy case with that contract," I said. "I have no doubt I will win this for you."

"Thank you," he said with a huge smile.

As he was getting up to leave, I had one more question for him.

"Riddick, if you don't mind me saying, you don't seem to have any muscles. How are you so successful in the ring against these guys who look so much bigger?"

If this had been an act on the *Gong Show*, I'd have been gonged right off stage. *What the hell did I just say?* Boxers pride themselves on their physique, and I was telling him he didn't really have one compared to his foes? Fortunately, he laughed at me rather than show me his strength by smashing in my face.

"Always remember," he said, "it's not the muscles that matter, it's the speed of the hands."

That was probably true, though I'm guessing muscles do matter some, and he probably had some pretty large ones hiding under his clothes.

Our case went before a judge, where Holyfield had sought a temporary injunction barring the fight between Bowe and Dokes. While we agreed that it was often customary in boxing to give a guy a rematch, it is an unwritten custom, and we had a signed contract with Dokes. We prevailed on that argument, meaning we didn't completely win, but we also didn't lose. The fight between Bowe and Dokes was still on, but the court case with Holyfield was set for immediate trial before another judge.

In the end, the judge, in a non-jury trial, ruled in our favor due to the contract. Bowe could proceed with his scheduled fight against Dokes, and Holyfield would simply have to wait for his turn. Bowe defeated Dokes by technical knockout in the twelfth round on February 6, 1993, but he went on to lose to Holyfield nine months later. In one final match between the two on November 4, 1995, Bowe defeated Holyfield.

It is rare for me to be starstruck by any of my clients or those we go up against, but I have to admit, as someone who embraced boxing at such a young age, I was in awe sitting in court between Bowe and Holyfield. They were two of the greatest heavyweight fighters in modern times, and somehow I'd managed to be in the midst of one of their outside-the-ring disputes.

Bowe would have legal issues years later involving domestic disputes with two of his wives, incidents that he blamed in part on brain damage suffered from boxing. But when I represented him, well before those troubles, he couldn't have been a better client to represent.

Bowe retired with a record of 43–1. On June 20, 2015, he was inducted into the Boxing Hall of Fame.

CHAPTER 41

LOSING TO LENNOX LEWIS

THIS IS A SHORT TALE about how what happens in the courtroom can be emotionally separated from life outside the courtroom.

Panos Eliades, the former manager and promoter of Heavyweight Champion of the World, Lennox Lewis, asked for an appointment to see me. He owned Panix Promotions and was the defendant in a case to be tried in the U.S. District Court in Manhattan before Judge Harold Baer, Jr., sitting with a jury. He told me that despite the allegation that he had stolen monies from Lewis, he had been faithful to Lewis's interests at all times and had given his principal a fair and just accounting. Monies deducted from the receipts due to Lewis were in connection with services Eliades had supposedly performed for him, and on and on.

Quite frankly, I wasn't convinced of Eliades's honesty simply because I knew from my knowledge of boxing that fighters are often short-changed or cheated by their managers. But I felt he definitely had a case if he were telling the truth, so I went with it.

An attorney I'd known for many years with whom I'd worked on various cases was representing Lewis. I felt early on that my chances of winning increased when Lewis's brother did not show up in court. The two men were close and it was expected that his brother would be a witness, but he never appeared. Certainly, I stated to the court, if Lewis were being truthful, his brother would have been there to defend his sibling considering the money at stake. My gut told me that some of the jurors concurred, but everything for our side went downhill from there.

I cross-examined Lewis, but he was as strong on the stand as he was in the ring. I approached him with clenched fists to try to match his toughness in appearance.

"How quickly do you knock out your opponents?" I asked him.

"Sometimes pretty fast," he said calmly.

"And when you knock them out, are you ever concerned about their safety?"

What did this have to do with money? Nothing. But it was a case about character. Either he or my client was lying, and I wanted to try to rattle him the best I could. But it didn't work. He couldn't have been cooler under the pressure I was trying to levy.

After the cross-examination, our case was crushed by the numbers. The jury was presented with an accounting of monies due to Lewis and what was paid to him by Eliades. In the course of an audit conducted by forensic accountants, it was revealed that Eliades had, in fact, been stealing from Lewis. Eliades had lied about the conversion rate between British pounds and American dollars on a number of occasions, and at other times withheld purses altogether. The jury found that Eliades defrauded Lewis through a pattern of theft that amounted to racketeering. They awarded Lewis eight million dollars.

I mentioned that I knew and had worked in the past with Lewis's attorney. We were so close, in fact, that I didn't expect him to represent Lewis once he found out I was defending Eliades, but he did anyway. It annoyed me, but I didn't take it personally. Attorneys go where the money is, and the money in this case was with Lewis.

When the trial was over, that attorney approached me.

"Hey, Jay, do you have any plans right now?"

"Just heading home," I said as I packed my papers into my briefcase.

"Do you want to join Lennox and me for dinner?"

He knew my love for boxing, and he knew he didn't have to ask twice. The three of us went to Bobby Van's, a popular and elegant steakhouse in Lower Manhattan.

"You did a nice job questioning me today," Lewis said.

"Evidently not good enough," I said with a grin. "You were tough to crack up there."

I told him about my early life in boxing, and of course I asked him many questions about his career. When it came time to order, we all got steaks, though I was struck by the fact that the other attorney and I ordered portions that were larger than what Lewis ordered. When our food arrived, he commented on the disparity.

"I just can't believe how Americans are served such large portions," he said.

"Is it that much different in England?" I asked, referring to his homeland.

"Oh my gosh, yes!" he said. "The food we are served in England will usually fit into the palm of your hand. I just don't understand how Americans are able to digest such huge amounts of food in one sitting."

This, from the 270 pound heavyweight champion of the world.

As an attorney, it can be difficult sometimes just to be in the same room with your opponent because of how strongly you believe in your client's case and because of tactics your opponent may use to try to win. I'm not saying that after a case you should go out to dinner with your opponent, or that you should even speak to him or her. But do your best to leave your emotions behind when it's over. The decision belongs to the jury or judge. As long as you know you put forth the best effort possible for your client, there is nothing more you can do.

CHAPTER 42

ALI VS. SPINKS AND THE MISSING MONEY

BUTCH LEWIS ASKED ME TO represent him. He was one of the vice presidents of Top Rank, Inc., the premier boxing promotions organization where the principal was Bob Arum. Lewis was involved in the promotion of the heavyweight championship fight in New Orleans between Muhammad Ali and Leon Spinks on September 15, 1978. Ali defeated Spinks, but the scandal that followed the fight truly took the boxing world by storm.

The donnybrook began with the discovery of two questionable 400,000-dollar finder's fees (monies given to the person who "set up" the fight) paid to Louisiana political figures. A civil lawsuit was filed charging misappropriation of funds by the collector of proceeds and a ticket-duplicating scheme that may have netted more than 500,000 dollars to wrongdoers. Others filed a fifteen million dollar slander lawsuit. Everybody was suing everybody because nobody knew who was responsible.

There were a multitude of entities involved in the promotion and collection of funds. Arum fired Lewis, but it was never clear whether it was because he believed Lewis received some of the ill-gotten gains or failed to monitor the receipt and disbursement of funds to Top Rank. One thing was made crystal clear: the magnificent reputation that Arum had earned for his company through decades of honor in an otherwise grimy field stands as a monument to how one can perform in a credible way.

The U.S. Attorney's office was confronted with a number of non-cooperating witnesses, a maze of corporations, with one group complaining about the other group, but with little record keeping to support a claim of wrongdoing sufficient to reach the threshold of criminal prosecution. Lewis remained on the periphery, but thought was given to the view that he had orchestrated the misuse of the monies at all levels. The U.S. Attorney in New Orleans, aided by the FBI, opened an investigation but received little support from witnesses or an analysis of such records as there were.

The stakes were high, for Lewis had raised himself from the streets of Philadelphia to the position of vice president of the most prestigious fight promotion company in the world. Lewis and his father came to me for help. The assistant U.S. Attorney was completely forthcoming in providing me with the documents necessary for me to examine whether Lewis was truly guilty of wrongdoing. Lewis also furnished such documents. I engaged forensic accountants. I prepared a written analysis that I believed absolved Lewis of any responsibility for monies that were found to be missing. The responsibility for any shortfall could not be fastened upon Lewis, I argued. After a meeting in New Orleans, the prosecution advised that they would drop any further investigation of Lewis.

While Muhammad Ali and Leon Spinks weren't there, nor was I given the chance to "perform" in my "theatre" through a lengthy trial with fiery cross-examinations and a humor-laced closing argument, it is one of my most memorable victories because of what it meant to Lewis. His name had been cleared, and he went on to have a fabulous career in the entertainment world, creating a management company that represented top flight entertainers and celebrities of note.

The last time I saw him was at the Friars Club, a New York club that catered to entertainers. I was the youngest member of the club's board of governors. Lewis that day was happy, carefree, and gave no indication that he was ill, though he was. He died at the age of sixty-five, but proudly free of any blame fastened upon his reputation for what had happened in Louisiana.

From *The Daily News* to De Niro and More

CHAPTER 43

SAVING THE
NEW YORK DAILY NEWS

FRED DRASNER CALLED ME IN 1999 at the recommendation of Donald Trump and asked me to meet him at his home in the apartment he maintained at the Waldorf Towers. He was the co-publisher with Mort Zuckerman of *The Daily News*, and I had assisted Drasner's primary attorney years earlier in Drasner's matrimonial litigation. When I arrived at Drasner's home, he was sprawled on a lavish couch. He told me that upon graduation from law school he drove a taxi for many years, and yet, here he was a billionaire at fifty-five years of age.

Drasner called me in because he said *The Daily News* had posted closing notices due to an arbitrator's award that was upheld by a federal judge. According to *The New York Times*: "A Federal judge yesterday upheld a labor arbitrator's decision to award retroactive wages to members of the drivers' union at *The Daily News*, a move that could eventually cost the newspaper tens of millions of dollars." Not just tens of millions of dollars, but the life of the paper, which would be forced into bankruptcy. Zukerman and Drasner reluctantly decided to shut down rather than pay the enormous sums required by the arbitrator. The eighty-year-old paper was going to die, leaving New York with only Rupert Murdoch's *New York Post* and, of course, *The New York Times*.

"You may think there is no hope," I said to Drasner, "but based on what you are telling me, I think we can have this judgment dismissed, or at least reduced considerably."

"How do you figure?" he asked.

"Because the arbitrator refused to allow evidence that his award would result in the bankruptcy of the paper, which will ultimately result in the loss of countless jobs, not to mention the death of a daily institution that has been around since the end of World War I."

Drasner was intrigued and wanted me to run this idea by Zuckerman's attorney, a partner at a prestigious law firm who, when I met with him, seemed quite taken with himself.

"It's a horrible idea," he said, talking down to me as if I were some second-rate lawyer. "No way will a judge ever consider that."

"I believe he will," I said confidently.

The attorney, no doubt, thought I was just going for a money grab from a billionaire, that I knew I would lose the case but still get paid. This attorney obviously had not done his homework on me. I never took a case I didn't think I could win. It didn't mean I would always win, but I sure as hell was going to fight to the death for my client with what I felt was a sound defense.

Drasner, ignoring his partner's attorney, told me to go for it, so I did. I brought a motion to vacate the award on the grounds that the arbitrator had disregarded critical evidence as to the ability of *The Daily News* to financially survive the award that was issued. On the day set for argument, it was discovered that the union representative and their lawyer had met ex-parte (with regard to the interests of one side only) with the arbitrator regarding the ability of *The Daily News* to pay the award. The court was of the view that the ex-parte meeting was improper, as it showed a particular access to the arbitrator not shared by *The Daily News*. The court was also of the view that the arbitrator had not considered the effect his ruling would have on the paper. It was the confluence of these factors that led the court to vacate the award.

Following the decision, the parties met and agreed to a settlement, which satisfied the workers while permitting the paper to remain alive. I'd done my job, one that positively affected numerous lives.

Ah, but you haven't heard the most entertaining part of this case.

Twelve long years after the settlement, in 2011, Donald Trump told the *New York Post* during an interview that he had "saved" *The Daily News*. The comment came after *The Daily News* had published a cover that mocked Trump's desire to one day be president.

In an interview with the *Huffington Post* the day after making that claim, Trump elaborated on his statement to the *Post* by saying that Zuckerman and Drasner had called him about their predicament after the arbitrator's ruling and the federal judge's upholding of that ruling, and he suggested that they hire me.

"I recommended him, Jay Goldberg. I saved the paper," Trump said. "All I do, for years, is get negative press out of *The* Daily News. The good news is, nobody cares, obviously."

Zuckerman fired back, saying he never called Trump and had no idea who I was.

"If they think this saved the News, it's certainly news to me," Zuckerman said.

Also according to the Huffington Post article:

"In a subsequent phone call later that day, Zuckerman said he'd learned that his former business partner already knew Goldberg before The Daily News was in legal trouble and Trump could have intervened. Indeed, Goldberg had represented Drasner in his divorce.

"But Goldberg, by his account, said he only assisted another attorney in Drasner's divorce case and that it never went to trial. Therefore, Goldberg said Drasner would still have likely have needed Trump's reassurance that he was up to the task of representing the newspaper."

The article concluded with Trump and Zuckerman trading humorous final barbs:

"Zuckerman said that he likes Trump but joked that, if Trump thinks that by recommending an attorney—which remains a matter of debate—he saved The Daily News, 'I'd like him to send a lawyer to the U.S. Congress to save the budget.'

"While Trump described Drasner as a 'great guy,' he didn't have such kind words for Zuckerman.

"'Mort has a very short memory,'" Trump said. 'And Mort has always wanted to be a star and he can't be. It's not in his blood. Stardom can't be his.'"

"Drasner did not respond to a request for comment on what happened 12 years ago."

Donald Trump had somewhat of a point about *The Daily News*. I don't know any attorney anywhere who would have devised the defense I did to save the paper. Zuckerman's attorney certainly wouldn't have done it—he dismissed my idea the moment I presented it and likely would have let the paper fold. So the fact that Donald recommended me to Drasner at least got the process in motion.

No matter who is credited for "saving" the paper, what matters today is that the paper is still in business, thanks to the effort of several people who cared enough to keep it alive.

CHAPTER 44

USING A JUDGE'S ATTRACTION TO ME TO WIN A CASE

I WAS HIRED BY A gentleman to represent him in a case involving the construction of a building and millions of dollars. To not cause embarrassment to the judge who presided over the case, I am going to avoid using names or locales.

The client was seeking monies that he claimed were due to him under a contract for services that he had rendered in the building's construction. He had a different attorney when the case started, one who took it to arbitration and lost. The client was not awarded a single penny. Since non-binding arbitration allows the loser to opt for a trial, the client decided to do just that, and he hired me to help him and his current attorney get the arbitration judgment vacated.

As the trial began, I had several court conferences with the judge—and I noticed something very odd that I had not experienced since Rema had become smitten with me decades earlier when she and I first met.

The judge liked me.

Not *like*, but *like like*.

Seriously.

"We're going to win this case," I told my client and the other attorney after the first day of litigation.

"How can you be so sure?" my client asked.

"Because the judge likes me."

"I'm sure he likes a lot of people," the client said.

"No, I mean he *likes* me."

They both stared at me as if I'd lost my mind.

"Oh, c'mon!" the attorney piped in.

"I'm not kidding."

"No way," the client said.

"You're trying to tell us that this highly respected judge has a crush on you?" the attorney asked.

"That's exactly what I'm saying," I said.

"And how do you know this?" the attorney asked.

"I have a sense," I said, "not to mention that I can see it in his eyes. Trust me, it's real, and we need to take advantage of it."

They continued to scoff and laugh at me, but they agreed to follow my lead. They'd already lost once and had brought me on board for my skills to help them win the next round, so they were willing to trust me, no matter how crazy I seemed.

I told the attorney to bring a motion to vacate the award. He advised me that the proper procedure was for the other side to have the award confirmed first, and then we would move to vacate.

"Well, we're not going to do it that way," I said. "I feel so strongly about my intuition toward this judge that I want us to take the lead on this."

"Whatever you say," the attorney replied with an eye roll.

After the motion was made, the judge took the lawyers from each side into the robing room separately, which itself was odd. He asked us some questions about our motion, then spoke with the other side. While we were questioned for just minutes, he talked with the other side for roughly two and a half hours.

"Is this good or bad?" my client asked as we waited impatiently.

"I would think it has to be good," I said. "There must be some negotiating going on for them to be in there this long."

The other attorneys finally returned to the courtroom, followed soon after by the judge.

"We have come to an agreement," the judge declared. Though the other side had prevailed in arbitration, they had agreed to not only vacate the original order, but provide my client with a financial package that would net him twenty million dollars. While I always expect to win every case, even I was flabbergasted by what had transpired. Getting the initial judgment vacated was one thing. Being awarded that much money was unfathomable.

After the judgment, the other attorney and I returned to his office to celebrate our victory. While we were there, his phone rang. He answered it.

"Hello?"

"Is Jay Goldberg with you?" the voice on the other end asked. "I'd like to speak with him."

The attorney pulled the phone down from his ear and looked at me shocked.

"It's for you," he whispered. "It's the judge."

"Hello, your honor," I said cheerfully.

"Jay, how did you like the award I got the other side to agree to?" he asked.

"I thought it was wonderful," I said.

"It took a lot of convincing," he said.

"I know it must have. You were in there with them for a long time."

"Well, I'm glad you're happy," he said.

"Yes, your honor, so am I."

"Hey, Jay, I wanted to ask you, do you have plans for this weekend?"

"This weekend?"

"Yeah, you got anything going on?"

My intuition kicked in again. This was not small talk.

"Well, your honor, I'm going to probably just head home. I know my wife misses me."

He paused.

"Oh," he said, with disappointment. "Well, okay, you have a safe trip home."

"I will, your honor. And thank you, again."

I handed the phone to the attorney and smiled.

"What was that about?" he asked.

"I just turned down a judge."

"No!"

"Yes."

As attorneys, it is our job to follow procedures. It is our job to dot every "i" and cross every "t." It is our job to have a plan of attack or defense that is solid going into the trial. But, sometimes, a lawyer

301

must veer from the plan or what is considered to be the norm and simply go with his intuition. A lawyer must be alert to the body language and words and actions of judges, juries, and his opponent, and make adjustments to his plan as necessary. If he doesn't, he could miss the obvious right in front of him and blow his whole case. If he does, good things can come his way.

CHAPTER 45

THE NEON LIGHTS ARE BRIGHT ON BROADWAY

I HAD TWO CASES TIED to Broadway. I'll share the most entertaining one second. This first one was quickly resolved, but it also turned out to be one of the most lucrative for any client I have ever represented.

Barry and Fran Weissler, veteran Broadway producers, had the novel idea in the 1990s of seeking the rights to produce and stage a revival of the show *Chicago*. It had previously been produced in the 1970s as an award-winning musical featuring Bob Fosse and Gwen Verdon. Talk in the offices of National Artists Management Company (NAMCO), a production company owned by the Weisslers, was that the show could be revived with a few changes.

On the staff of NAMCO was Joan Croft. She listened to the Weisslers' idea, and she and her husband made the necessary contacts with the person owning the rights to *Chicago* to secure for herself and her husband the right to produce the show before the Weisslers did. The Weisslers, my clients, brought suit in U.S. District Court in Manhattan claiming a breach of trust. They said they should have the rights because Croft had seized a corporate opportunity which rightfully belonged to NAMCO.

Croft and her husband countered with a motion to dismiss the case on jurisdictional grounds. When that was denied in a lengthy opinion by the U.S. district judge, the parties met and we effected a settlement. The Weisslers received the rights to revive the show, while Croft and her husband received what would prove to be a pittance of money.

Barry Weissler surmised that if properly staged and by changing the lead every few months to a different celebrity, he could garner great success for the show and NAMCO. His vision was correct. The 1996 revival has won numerous Tony awards and continues to run today. It is the longest running revival on Broadway and the second-longest running musical of all-time, behind only *The Phantom of the Opera*.

After representing Barry Weissler in another case years later, he said to me, "Your summation was great; you should be an actor." Sensing the moment, I replied, "How about if I play Billy Flynn, the lawyer in *Chicago*? I know I can do a great job." Barry laughed. He said he would speak to his fellow producers.

The show has been performed more than eight thousand times.

I am still waiting to be cast.

In another Broadway play dispute involving the Weisslers, they had turned to actor Anthony Quinn to play the leading role in *A Walk in the Woods*. Quinn, however, fell ill during rehearsals, and the insurance company refused to pay the Weisslers, claiming that Quinn concealed a heart condition. The Weisslers sought millions of dollars from Quinn to compensate for their loss. They claimed Quinn knew of his condition, kept it from them, and exposed them to loss.

The matter was referred to arbitration.

Quinn claimed during the arbitration hearing that he had told the Weisslers about his heart problems and that the Weisslers took the risk. We, of course, claimed that he never told the Weisslers. When it came time for me to cross-examine Quinn, I directly impugned his integrity which, of course, angered him to no end.

How incensed was he?

He jumped up from the table we were gathered around and came at me with his arm raised. Being arbitration, there was no marshal or security officer present. I had only me to defend myself.

"Mr. Quinn," I quickly said, fearing that I was about to be assaulted, "you should know that I won the Golden Gloves."

He stopped, looked at me with fury in his eyes, and then retreated to his seat. He finished answering my questions, and the arbitrator soon after ruled in our favor that he had indeed concealed his condition. The Weisslers were entitled to a multi-million dollar award that was to be paid promptly.

Days after the ruling, Cindy Adams, the *New York Post* columnist who had been at the arbitration hearing, arranged a meeting between Quinn and me at the Stanhope Hotel.

"Why does he want to meet?" I asked Adams.

"He needs your help," she said. "He just wants to talk to you."

When I arrived at the hotel, he couldn't have been more cordial. He stood up to greet me and shook my hand with a smile. The man of fury who was ready to punch me at arbitration looked vulnerable.

"Mr. Goldberg," he said, "I need more time to pay."

"More time? I don't think so," I said, realizing I had the upper hand.

"Please, Mr. Goldberg, this is causing a lot of stress within my family. I promise I will get the money, but I just don't have it right now."

We continued our discussion; he begged and I listened.

"It will be up to my clients," I said, "but I will ask them."

I called the Weisslers, who agreed to give him more time.

I can't describe for you just how weak this man who recently was going to inflict damage to my face really was. When I told him the Weisslers had agreed, he grabbed my right hand with both of his hands and shook it.

"Oh my gosh, thank you! Thank you so much, sir!" he exclaimed. "This means everything to me and my family."

"You're welcome," I said. "Just get the money."

"Oh, I will. Don't worry, I will!"

The Quinn case is also a good lesson for young attorneys. Quinn had called a major cardiologist to attest to his recent heart condition, which allowed me to subpoena all of his medical records. For several days before the arbitration I immersed myself in the field of cardiology. Quinn's cardiologist was so impressed with my knowledge of the subject that he later called a fellow attorney, Michael Rosen, and told him that the extent of what I knew was beyond belief. The lesson is that to be a good trial lawyer takes inordinate attention to complex subjects. Don't ever be intimidated by what you have to face. Put in the effort and commitment that your client deserves and you, too, can pose as a cardiologist—if just for a day.

305

CHAPTER 46

MY LOST CHANCE AT STARRING WITH ROBERT DE NIRO

PETER PETRELLA WAS CHARGED IN federal court with offering an IRS agent a bribe. I agreed to represent him because he was referred by my good friend Hy Lieberman, but Petrella could not pay an advance fee. Petrella told me that while he was in prison previously, he had written a screenplay that was currently in production. He said Robert De Niro would be playing a leading role in the film, and that in return for representing him in his case, I could also have a "rewarding" part in the movie.

"Are you kidding?" I said to him, quite skeptical of course.

"Not at all," he insisted. "Go to the Director's Guild of America on 57th Street and you'll be interviewed by the casting director."

Why would I waste my time on such a thing? I worked for money, not alleged parts in movies written by convicted felons who had no cash. But, attracted by the possibility, and given that the guild was just blocks from my home, I decided to stop by.

When I arrived I only had to wait in the lobby for a few minutes before I was taken to a room and introduced to the casting director.

And then to Robert De Niro.

"Thank you for coming," De Niro said as he shook my hand.

"It's my pleasure," I replied, taken aback that this was actually happening.

"I know Peter has a lot of confidence in you as his attorney," he said.

"I appreciate that."

"Hey, listen," De Niro said, lowering his voice. "You really need to do your best to keep Peter out of prison. It is very important to this project that he be here for it."

"I can respect that," I said. "I can't make any promises since I am not the judge, but I can tell you that I work my tail off for all of my clients. Peter is in good hands."

He smiled as he shook my hand again.

"That's good to know," he said.

On that note, in walked Petrella along with Martin Scorsese. I was flanked by motion picture royalty, which was starting to look like pretty good compensation for defending Petrella. *What kind of movie could this felon have written that could attract such people?* I wondered. I read some lines for them the best that this inexperienced actor knew how, and then I sat alone for a while as they let the room to discuss my performance. A few minutes later, Petrella emerged.

"We have a role for you," he said.

"You do?"

"Absolutely. You did a great job. You're going to be in a Robert De Niro film. We'll be in touch."

Was this real? Or was I being conned by a guy who couldn't afford to pay his attorney? I may have been a fool, but the fact that I had met De Niro and Scorsese made me think this might be a pretty darn good payday. I decided to proceed with representing Petrella.

On the first day of shooting for the film, I was in Albany representing a member of the Hell's Angels Motorcycle Club whose nickname was "Grumpy." The charge was assault in the second degree. The publicity in this case was huge, and rumor had spread that there would be at least a hundred members of the Hell's Angels that would come to Albany and attempt to "rescue" Grumpy from the courtroom at the time of his sentence. There was much agitation in the community. An enormously large contingent of state troopers was called to provide security. Sharp shooters with automatic weapons were on the rooftops of nearby buildings.

The fears, however, never materialized. Grumpy received a sentence of ten years from Judge John Kline. Grumpy made the most of his time while incarcerated, earning a doctorate in Russian history. He is now a college professor.

In the middle of Grumpy's trial, I received a call from Petrella.

"Jay, we need you now in California," he said. "We need to shoot your part in the film."

"Peter, I'm in the midst of a trial in Albany. I can't leave now."

"It's got to be now," he insisted.

"Okay, let me see what I can do."

The next day I went into Judge Kline's courtroom, hoping he would understand.

"Your honor, I would like to ask that we take a break for a few days in this case so I can tend to personal matters in California," I said.

"What personal matters?" he asked.

Crap! I was hoping he wouldn't ask.

"Well, I've been cast in a movie with Robert De Niro, and they need to shoot my scene now."

"Really?" he asked.

"Yes, your honor."

He thought about it for a good second, maybe second-and-a-half.

"No," he said. "Now, let's move on with this case."

And that was the end of my movie career. As much as I wanted to argue, I didn't. It would have been highly inappropriate. It didn't hurt to ask, but when he said no, I had to do just as he said and "move on." My acting days on the big screen were over before they started. I called Petrella and told him I couldn't make it.

"You're still my lawyer, right?" he said.

"Yes, of course." We had made a deal, and I was the one who had to back out. I wasn't going to hold that against him.

When it came time for negotiation with the prosecutor in Petrella's case, he accepted a lesser plea of "attempting to bribe an IRS agent." The night before sentencing, De Niro called my home.

"Jay," he said, "I heard about Peter's plea. What kind of sentence do you think he will receive?"

"I don't know for sure, but I think the judge is going to be lenient," I said.

<aside>308</aside>

"Can you guess on the length? Like maybe months?"

"That is my hope," I said. "I did the best I could, now we just have to wait for the judge to decide."

Peter received a sentence of one year in jail with the possibility of parole. He served just four months, and the film barely missed a beat.

I still didn't know the name of the film or even what it was about until one day I emerged from the subway and saw a giant billboard announcing its opening.

It was *Raging Bull*.

The film about, of all things, the life of boxer Jake LaMotta, would receive numerous award nominations. De Niro won an Oscar for his portrayal of LaMotta.

Though my representation of Grumpy cost me a golden opportunity to play a role in this classic film, I was offered a nice consolation prize by Hell's Angels.

After Grumpy's sentencing, I received a call that Sonny Barger, the notorious founder of Hell's Angels, wanted to meet with me in a town north of San Francisco. After settling in at my hotel, I was met there by one of Barger's henchmen, who took me to what he called "a secret location." I arrived to find Barger presiding over a meeting of a hand-picked group of comrades and chosen women. To all present, he was treated like God. Ferocity emanated from him. He made it a point to emphasize his diction, and one never knew if a single word would enrage him.

Barger wanted to know whether I would be willing to represent the Hell's Angels nationwide. Here I had lost Grumpy's case, yet I had earned enough respect from the organization that they wanted me to be their main attorney. As lucrative as it would have been, which would have made missing my role in *Raging Bull* a little easier to swallow, I turned them down.

"As much as I appreciate it, it's just not for me," I told them after giving it some thought for a couple days. "To be traveling all over the country to work for just one organization it not what I want to do."

Fortunately, they understood.

I still think about what could have been if Judge Kline had let me go to California for a few days, but it was simply not meant to be.

Maybe it's for the best. Had my role in the film led to other acting opportunities, I might have been swayed to give up law all together for the Silver Screen.

Okay, not really.

But it would have been a hell of a lot of fun to see my name in the same credits as De Niro, Scorsese, Joe Pesci, and Cathy Moriarty.

CHAPTER 47

A SEDUCTRESS OUTSMARTS CELEBRITIES

OVER A PERIOD OF YEARS, a woman known as "Miranda Grosvenor" somehow gathered the phone numbers of such luminaries as Robert De Niro, Quincy Jones, Billy Joel, Art Garfunkel, and countless other male celebrities. A story about the unbelievable spell she had on these men was published in *Vanity Fair* entitled "The Miranda Obsession." Miranda signed a contract to share her experiences in a memoir style book with Harper Collins, where she received an advance of one million dollars, with an obligation to write a second book. The story shows the weakness of the male, where a beguiling feminine voice is the protagonist.

Miranda would call the men often and talk to them in her sexy voice for maybe twenty minutes at a time—not sex talk, but just warm, intimate, comfortable conversation. She would build relationships with them over the phone, but never actually meet with them. She eventually sent some of them photos of a gorgeous, long-legged blonde, though that wasn't really her. Becoming suspicious, record producer Richard Perry, a recipient of Miranda's calls, persuaded Miranda to meet him at a hotel in New York. According to the *Vanity Fair* article:

> "She was no model. As Perry's eyes adjusted to the darkened room, he saw a short, frumpy woman in her thirties, maybe thirty pounds overweight, with a large mole on her right cheek. She wasn't ugly. But she wasn't, he realized in a moment of self-loathing and almost unbearable sadness, a woman he could spend his life with. 'I felt I had been conned,' he says today."

Why these men were so attracted to her simply by hearing her voice is uncertain, especially given that most of them often had their choice of female companionship given who they were. And how Miranda got their unlisted numbers is also unknown.

After Miranda was outed—she told Perry her real name was Whitney Walton—she approached Regan Books about writing a story that would detail her encounters. The book was in the galley stage, meaning that the publishing company had given her a substantial advance, the text had been written, and it was in the process of being formatted and finalized for printing. It was thought to be a surefire best seller, given the personalities involved and the "trick" that she had played with only a mellifluous voice and a gift of gab.

I was called one day prior to publication by a well-known lawyer who specialized in entertainment affairs. Seated behind a dimmed light was an extremely popular and internationally-loved entertainer, his client, who was regarded not just for his work but also as a good human being—one who had had many conversations with Miranda. He was not named in the galleys. I believed Miranda kept his name out for the moment intending to extort him by stating that she would prepare a supplement to the book. He looked nervous, concerned that his tie to her would be made public.

"We need you to kill this book," the lawyer said after telling me the story.

"She has already received an advance?" I asked.

"Yes, it is my understanding that she has."

"And the book has been written?"

"Yes."

"Well, since the publisher has already paid her and it just needs to be printed, it's not likely that I or anyone else will be able to stop it at his stage," I said.

"We really need you to try," he pleaded. "I don't know anyone else who could possibly help us."

I agreed to take the case, though I felt I took on an impossible mission. As for fees, the lawyer told me that if I succeeded, he would "fill a city garbage can with monies." I violated my rule that some of the money must be paid in advance for legal work that I do. I mistakenly trusted the lawyer and his high-profile client.

I consulted with numerous lawyers in the publishing field and they told me what I had expected to hear: they had never heard of a book already in galleys that wouldn't be published once the advance had been paid. So, from my perspective, that left me just one option.

"Hello, Miranda?"

"Who is this?"

"Jay Goldberg. I'm an attorney here in New York."

I told her who I was representing and why I was calling: to see if we could discuss the possibility of leaving my client out of her book. Well, that's what I told her anyway. Actually, since I knew she likely wouldn't agree to that, what I really wanted was to develop enough in the conversation with her for her publisher to realize that extortion was her goal. I was recording every word.

"For the right price," she said, "I can leave your client out. Otherwise, he will be in this book or my next one."

Armed with the tape-recorded conversation, I contacted officials with Regan Books, but they didn't care.

"We're not killing the book," a representative said.

So I went a step higher, to Harper Collins. Regan was a subsidiary of Harper, and Harper's chairman was Rupert Murdoch. I attended a meeting with fifteen of their representatives gathered around a large conference room. I played the tape recordings for them.

"If you publish this book," I said with thirty eyes glaring at me, "one could argue that Harper Collins was encouraging someone to seek profits from acts of extortion."

Soon after that meeting, I received a telephone call from an official at Harper Collins.

"We are not going to publish the book," he said. Despite having paid a large sum of money to Miranda as an advance, my client's nightmare was over.

My client, of course, was thrilled beyond measure. After giving him the good news, I mailed an invoice to him and his manager for my "city garbage can" of money.

But I didn't hear from either of them. Maybe they didn't receive it. So I mailed it again.

Nothing.

And again...nothing.

I called.

They didn't call back.

Nine times over several weeks I tried to make contact with them and was rebuffed each time. Obviously, this highly-acclaimed and extremely wealthy entertainer, for reasons unknown to me, had no intention of ever paying me. A few clients, no matter how wealthy they are, will simply do anything to avoid paying. Sometimes I think that's why they are so wealthy.

Fed up with his lack of response, I drew up a summons for "money not received." I named "Jay Goldberg" as the plaintiff and "John Doe" as the defendant. I sent it to him and his manager. Within a couple days, my phone rang. It was the manager.

"What is the purpose of this?" he asked.

"The purpose? You owe me money for doing exactly what your client hired me to do," I said. "Right now, he's John Doe. But there will come a time, if he doesn't pay me, when I will have to divulge his name."

I received my payment in full the next day.

And that is why, to this day, the name of that entertainer has never been revealed.

CHAPTER 48

WHEN "MULES"
ARE MODELS

SOMETIMES THE LEGAL SYSTEM IS not as black and white as it should be. Sometimes a case that seems open and shut becomes anything but. Why? Because the system relies on the judgment of human beings, who often think they know what they see, when in fact they may be entirely wrong.

This is a short but entertaining story about a trial before Judge Weinstein in the Brooklyn federal court, where I was defending my client on narcotics charges. The case was prosecuted by an extraordinary assistant U.S. Attorney, and it was thought to be a "lock" for the government. It is very difficult to ever stop the train marked "U.S. Government" when narcotics are involved.

In this case, the government claimed that narcotics were brought into the country by "mules"—people who smuggle drugs across a border—and then distributed by other persons. My client was allegedly a major player in working with these mules on the U.S. side of the border. Getting an acquittal for him, we both knew, was going to be a near-impossible task given the mounting evidence. He faced up to twenty years in prison. My hope was to reduce that potential sentence as much as I possibly could.

For the government, everything about their case was easily falling into place. I could only sit and watch as they continued to pile on the evidence against my client. I have to admit, a twenty-year sentence was looking like a strong possibility...but I knew I still had a chance once the "mules" entered the courtroom.

There were fifteen of them. They entered in a single file line, the next one more beautiful than the previous. No, these weren't your typical sinister, shady-looking, scum-of-the-earth men who would do anything for a dollar, including smuggling drugs. They were fifteen stunning blonde, brunette, and red-headed women, tall and leggy in skin-tight dresses and with breathtaking physical features. These so-called "mules" were models from an elite agency in Boston. They, the government claimed, were the ones responsible for smuggling and distributing the drugs in question.

I knew before they walked in that they were going to turn heads and, hopefully, get into the heads of the jurors. When they were in the corridor before the trial began, I observed the many male attorneys (and, in a couple instances, female attorneys) gawking at them, unable to keep their eyes off them. As I stated, our legal system is driven by humans, and humans have emotions. These women were eliciting emotions that daily regulars in a courthouse don't normally experience at work.

My question to the jury, which I stated more than once, was the obvious one: "Are we supposed to believe that these attractive women with successful modeling careers would risk losing everything to smuggle drugs?"

Some said yes. But some also said no. We didn't secure an acquittal, but we did get a deadlocked jury. When asked after the trial, those who could not vote to convict my client said there was no way they could ever believe such gorgeous women would ever engage in the conduct the government claimed they engaged in.

When the government decided to retry the case, the judge knew that the chance of a new jury convicting my client after the fifteen women returned for an encore appearance was slim. Why go through all of the time and money and effort for nothing? He suggested we lock ourselves in a room to try to hammer out an agreement, so we did. We agreed that instead of twenty years in prison, my client would receive three.

Justice is supposed to be blind. It is supposed to be applied "without regard to wealth, power, or other status." But when that "other status" is the beauty that entered the courtroom that day, it can be pretty difficult for some jurors to ignore.

CHAPTER 49

AN ACQUITTAL SECONDS AFTER A CONVICTION

THIS IS ANOTHER SHORT STORY, but with a good lesson on the importance of professionalism.

The trial was before Judge Leonard Wexler in Brooklyn federal court. It was alleged that the defendant, my client, was at the apex of Chinese heroin distribution in the U.S. On the second day of the trial, the government agent testified to conversations he had had with persons whom the government conceded were not co-conspirators. I immediately moved for a mistrial.

"I am going to reserve decision on that motion," the judge said.

You may recall Judge Neaher doing this with regard to my client, Alphonse Esposito, in Chapter 33. It was a rare occurrence. The judge would make a decision on my motion, but he'd do it later. Maybe the next day, maybe the next week. Whenever he felt like it.

As the trial proceeded, and as the chances of my client coming out of this without a conviction looked bleaker each day, I grew angrier and angrier about the judge reserving his decision. Inside the courtroom I remained professional, optimistic, and did my job to the best of my ability. Outside the courtroom I often voiced my anger to friends and colleagues at the judge's indecision.

The trial lasted two long months and, as I expected, the jury voted to convict my client. The government lawyers, including the late and great assistant U.S. Attorney Charles Rose, were all but dancing with joy. They were happy that they not only had secured a conviction, but that the conviction might force my client to make a deal with them concerning his sentence. If he would provide them information about the Chinese importation and distribution ring, they would soften his prison term.

But their celebration was short-lived. And I mean *short-lived*. It lasted just seconds.

"Regarding the matter of the defendant's motion on the second day of trial to dismiss the case, I hereby grant that motion due to the wrongful and prejudicial testimony of the government agent."

The entire courtroom went silent. Nobody, including I, could believe what we'd just heard. When it sunk in, I smiled and explained to my client what had just happened. The government attorneys, meanwhile, verbally lashed out at the judge. I had never seen such anger in a courtroom.

Why did the judge wait nearly two months to render his decision of my motion? He told me he wanted to put the case in the hands of the jury first to see if they would acquit my client. In other words, he knew, like I did, that my motion was a solid one. But he wanted to let the trial play out before revealing his decision. Whether you agree or disagree with how the judge handled it, the correct decision was made in the end, and the government's lawyers had to have known that. They were, in my opinion, sore losers.

As a postscript to this case, the defendant was tried again and lost, but I was not his attorney that second time around. He told me he could not pay me to defend him again, so he hired new counsel.

So what is the lesson in this? Some may assume it's that if your attorney wins your case, you must find a way to use that same attorney in your next one. Well, yeah, I guess, though if he couldn't pay, he couldn't pay. There was nothing he could have done about that.

No, the real lesson is to always remain professional in the courtroom no matter what. I was so angry that the judge refused to immediately make a decision on my motion, but I never let him know how angry I was. I saved my frustration for outside the courtroom walls and I focused on what I could control, which was the trial at hand. I had to assume the motion would not be granted and that the only hope we had was for me to win the trial. I wonder—if I would have lashed out at the judge or if I had said or done anything during the trial to let him know that I was not pleased with him—

would he have granted my motion? He should have, based on the law, but again, we are only human. I believe that maintaining my professionalism for two months, as difficult as it was, may have been the reason the judge dismissed the case.

CHAPTER 50

THE ONE I LET GET AWAY

SOON AFTER THE BESS MYERSON case, and likely due to all of the publicity that case had brought me, a woman named Ruth Kligman came to my office and told me that she had had an intimate relationship for a number of years with the world famous abstract artist Jackson Pollock. She was in the car with him and another friend on August 11, 1956, when, while drunk, they crashed into a tree. He died along with Kligman's friend. Despite the intimate relationship Pollock had with Kligman, he was married to another well-regarded artist, Lee Krasner.

Kligman showed me a picture of a painting which she said was given to her by Pollock. With Pollock dead, there was a panel controlled by Mrs. Krasner that had been set up to decide whether to accredit any painting, drawing, or other such matter to Pollock. The panel decided Kligman's work, despite the facts, was not done by Pollock. Ms. Kligman was devastated. She begged me to represent her against the decision of the panel, but there was one problem: she didn't have any money to hire me.

"I am sorry," I said, still on a high from the Myerson victory. "I don't take cases where the fee is contingent."

"But this painting is worth millions," she said. "I will easily be able to pay you handsomely afterward."

"You mean it *could be* worth millions," I replied. "And that's not only contingent on it being one of his paintings, but on a jury believing it is one of his paintings."

I rejected her case, and she left my office in dismay.

I thought nothing more of it until several years later when *The New York Times* reported that through developed forensic tests, a panel of experts had authenticated that Kligman's piece was the work of Pollock's. The *New York Post* stated that a similar-size Pollock painting had once sold for 58.3 million dollars at a Sotheby's auction.

I mentioned in the seductress story that I had violated my own rule by not insisting my client, the wealthy entertainer, pay up front, and it would have burned me if I hadn't filed the summons to make him pay. So, was I wrong to turn Ms. Kligman away for not being able to pay in advance? In hindsight, of course. How about in that moment? Again, I would say of course, only because it was my inflated ego that resulted from my well-publicized win in the Myerson case that clouded my judgment.

I still follow my long-held rule that I should be paid up front, and every attorney should follow that rule unless he or she enjoys working pro bono. However, when presented with potential exceptions, weigh the pros and cons as impartially as you can. Had I given Ms. Kligman's case proper consideration, it would have been obvious that the possible payoff, not to mention the expected media publicity, would have been enormous. And considering how close she was to Jackson, there was a pretty good chance that not only what she was telling me about the painting was true, but that I could have convinced a jury of the same.

I was wrong to not take that case. Don't let your ego from any previous victories cloud your judgment of future potential cases.

CHAPTER 51

A GIFT FROM HEAVEN

I WAS SITTING IN DONALD Trump's office one day when he summoned a young lady to come into his office.

"Do you know who this is?" he asked me.

"I'm sorry, I do not," I said.

"She is Miss Universe," he said.

"How do you do," I said politely. She smiled and said hello.

"What do you think of her?" Donald said.

I looked him straight in the eyes.

"Donald," I said, "I cannot look at her given my duty and devotion to my wife."

It was just this young woman and us two guys in the office. I could have said anything and "gotten away" with it. But that's not who I am and it's not who I've ever been.

At my response, Donald called one of his chief assistants.

"Find out if *The Apprentice* crew is still here," he said, referring to the crew of the reality television show he hosted. They were there and immediately came into his office. He told them to roll the cameras.

"Jay, repeat what you just said to me about your thoughts on Miss Universe," he said.

I repeated my statement and, sure enough, during an episode of the show, my interaction—or lack thereof—with Miss Universe was shown.

I don't say this seeking compliments, for this is always how loyal a man should be to his wife. I share it to publicly express my love for Rema, without whom I would be nobody.

Long ago, while in my twenties, there were "singles weekends" at the Concord Hotel, a Catskill gem that has since been demolished. During one of those weekends my mother, father, sister, and I stayed in a small hotel near the one my aunt owned. I went to the mixer on that Saturday afternoon; there had to be five hundred people maneuvering to meet one another. Minutes after I walked in, my eyes fastened upon this girl with long black hair; she was truly beautiful. I sat at a distance for some three hours, lacking the courage to approach her since she was at a table engaged in conversations with a number of people, but my eyes continued to stay focused on her. When the afternoon mixer ended, I returned to my aunt's hotel.

My aunt had planned a wonderful evening for our family, but I could not shake the fact that I had not made a move to meet this girl. The mixer was to resume that night, and I was determined to be there. Skipping the outing with my family, I returned to the Concord that night. Standing there in the lobby, by herself, was that girl. I had no choice, right? I went over to her, spoke with her, and eventually obtained her phone number and address. We arranged for a date even though she lived in the Bronx, I lived in Brooklyn, and my driving skills were minimal.

But we were destined to be.

From the time we first met and dated, we were an inseparable couple. We were married by the end of the year in a wedding at Tavern on the Green in Central Park. Frank S. Hogan and Chief Justice Murtagh were both in attendance. As you have hopefully ascertained, our relationship has been an extraordinary one.

The Daily News once wrote an article entitled, "When It Comes To Cracking High Stakes Criminal Cases, Nick And Nora Have Nothing On Jay And Rema." The *News* went on to write: "From '*The Thin Man*,' to '*Adam's Rib*,' to '*Hart to Hart*,' movies and TV have thrived on criminologist couples. Over at the Park Avenue law offices of Jay Goldberg, life imitates art. Most every day, Goldberg and wife Rema, consulting psychologist, strategize on some of the City's highest profile criminal defenses."

I recall one humorous moment when I was defending Matty in a case. We were in the process of selecting the jury when a large-breasted woman was seated as a juror. She caught Matty's attention right away, and he leaned over to Rema.

"Hey, Rema, I think that juror likes Jay," he said.

She glared at him but said nothing.

"Hey," he continued, "maybe if she has sex with Jay it will guarantee that we will win."

Rema leaned in close to Matty, meeting him eye to eye.

"If she has sex with Jay," Rema said, "I can guarantee you will be convicted."

Matty laughed.

Rema did not.

All of my clients knew that when they got me, Rema was part of the package, and it benefitted them more than many of them will ever know.

From waking up in the middle of the frigid night with me in Gary to race to the courthouse to seal our long-standing case, to correctly predicting that juror 6 would be the key to winning our case in the Bess Myerson trial, Rema and I have always been a team, and we have far more often than not come out victorious. Outside the courtroom we have raised two children, supported numerous charitable organizations such as the Chemotherapy Foundation, and have carried each other through personal medical issues from spinal meningitis to cancer.

I don't know, nor do I want to think about, my life without her.

I have been asked what the key is to such a successful marriage. There are many, but the one that stands out above all others dates back many years.

Rema and I had gone to a marriage counselor. There wasn't anything seriously wrong; our marriage was not in any danger. We were simply looking for ways to strengthen what we already had. After talking with us for a while, the counselor gave each of us a piece of paper.

"I want you each to go into separate rooms and write down ten things the other person can do to make the marriage better," she said.

We each went into our rooms, emerged a few minutes later, and shared our papers.

I had written down ten things.

Rema had written down nothing.

And that was when I realized, looking at Rema's blank piece of paper, the key to a successful marriage, and what has the two of us still going so strong today:

Unconditional love.

EPILOGUE

FATE CAN OFTEN WORK MIRACLES, how else to explain this? I was set to sum up in a federal securities fraud case before the honorable Dudley B. Bonsal in the Southern District of New York. During the night, "it" started – a migraine headache that felt like it would burst my skull. I never seek to put off a case because of illness. It is critical to show strength. I passed up breakfast and took the train from Tarrytown to Grand Central, carrying the materials needed for summation, all the while with my head terribly throbbing. As we know, a trip on the subway was then necessary, and up the stairs to the courtroom. I wondered how I could ever sum up in a case that was complicated and lengthy. The prosecutor, Bobby Lawyer, rose to make an application to the court. I watched him intently. As soon as he rose, he keeled over at a ninety-degree angle, his head hitting the prosecution table in front of him. We awaited the ambulance. The attendants came and carried him away. I thought to myself, not that I wished him ill, but how fortunate the turn of events was and how lucky I was. I went home to nurse the migraine as best as I could. Who or what had intervened to save me?

The law was my salvation from the turmoil of my formative years. I looked forward to going to court and watching the extraordinary lawyers of the day, and I soon became a fixture in the courtroom myself. I attribute this to a reading of *Courtroom: The Life and Times of Samuel S. Leibowitz* (Garden City Books 1950), by Quinton Reynolds. Leibowitz was the Clarence Darrow of his day. He was such a thorn in the side of the prosecution that truly he was elevated as a justice of the Supreme Court just so prosecutors could get rid of him. Despite a lifetime of defense work, he was vicious towards those accused of crime who came before him when he sat on the court.

A judge may say that a trial is a search for the truth. That is a ground for a mistrial, for the issue is in a civil and criminal case, whether the plaintiff or the prosecutor has met its burden of proof, and the defendant need do no more. As to the role of the defendant, keep in mind the following:

As Justice Powell has noted:

"In our system, a defense lawyer characteristically opposes the designated representative of the state. The system assumes that adversarial testimony will ultimately advance the public interest in truth and fairness. But it posits that a defense lawyer best serves the public not by acting on behalf of the state, or in concert with it, but rather advancing 'the undivided interest of the client.'" *Polk County v. Dodson*, 454 U.S. at 318-319 (1981).

"Defense counsel has no comparable obligation to ascertain or present the truth. Our system assigns him a different mission. Defense counsel need present nothing, even if he knows what the truth is. He need not furnish any witnesses to the police or reveal any confidence to help the state. If he can confuse a witness, even a truthful one, or make him appear at a disadvantage, unsure or indecisive, that will be his normal course. Our interest in not convicting the innocent permits counsel to put the State to its proof, to put the State's case in the worse possible light, regardless of what he thinks or knows to be the truth...In this respect, as part of our adversary system and as part of the duty imposed on the most honorable defense counsel, we countenance...conduct which in many instances has little, if any, relation to the search for truth." *United States v Wade*, 388 U.S. at 256-258 (1967) (Justice White, dissenting in part and concurring in part).

These points are essential to have in your armamentarium whenever the judge "scolds" you for doing nothing more than the law commands.

Aside from what you have already read, here is some of what I have learned:

- One must never engage in conduct that overstates or ignores what the law requires. If, for example, there is a conviction in a criminal case, often the defendant, aside from discharging you, will seek to win lenient treatment by informing against you. The appeals lawyer can be counted on in virtually every case to claim you "missed" a material point. Generally, there is little loyalty, but of course, it does exist from those clients I have included in this book.

- You can lose a case and still have the court embrace you as a true warrior. I remember trying a case before a judge in the Brooklyn federal court, and he invited my wife and me to celebrate the Seder with his family at his home one Friday night. Other times, I have gone away with judges for weekend judicial conventions. None of this was done by me to win favor, but by them because they respected my work. You must always carry yourself as a warrior. As Judge Cardozo said, "Let the timid stay home."

- Everything must be in writing. If your adversary verbally agrees to "put the case off," send a confirmatory letter.

- As I have said, be careful of the lawyer you bring into the case to act as an aide to you and second seat you at trial. It is possible he will talk to the client privately and criticize your performance.

- Often, nothing is as represented. Apply that maxim when promises are made, assurances are given, and the like.

- Use similes, metaphors, and especially charts in court. You are not speaking, most likely, to a group of PhDs. Take the proof, organize it, and chart it. Judge Weinstein permitted charts to be distributed to each juror once the charts were vetted. Judge Keenan did the same. No amount of words can emphasize enough that the use of charts is the makeweight to a successful summation. Of all lawyers, only Fred Hafetz can give a summation for three hours without any notes—remarkable.

- If there is a multiple-month trial, or one of great complexity, don't be afraid to write out your summation. This will ensure that you don't sit down and say that you missed something. You must never read the summation, but if you treat the summation you have written much like medicine, three times a day after meals, it will be so ingrained in you that you will never have to look at it at the time of its giving. You will have such confidence that you will often veer into new, productive areas.

- If a client is acquitted and you foolishly await the verdict to collect money owed, he will sometimes renege on his promise, saying, "You didn't do anything for me, I was innocent all along." In one case, the client did not pay the agreed upon fee because the jury was out too long. Never let a client get ahead of you. Say to the client, "If I don't get the money agreed upon, my mind plays tricks." You will get your money. Money sticks.

- If a potential client comes to you and says, "Have ever tried a case involving this subject?" reply with "There are no new cases, only new faces. The law is the law. If you know it, you know it, and I know it."

- Don't think that because you won a client's case, as difficult as the case may have been, that the client will come to you when he is indicted, or the subject of an investigation, or when there is need for the prosecution or defense of a civil case. There are a host of people who will get the ear of the client and say, "I've got a better lawyer for you." They will say this whether it is true or not. It is not out of the question that the new lawyer will give a share of the fee to the person who brings them the client.

- Always save your money, for no matter how big you are today, there will come a time when a new lawyer comes on the block and says, "That lawyer is too old, you need a young person, not Jay Goldberg." Fortunately, that time has not come yet for me.

LINKS TO ARTICLES ON JAY GOLDBERG

THE FOLLOWING ARE JUST SOME of the many links to articles on Jay Goldberg. Many more links can be found at www.jaygoldberg.com.

https://en.wikipedia.org/wiki/Jay_Goldberg

http://jaygoldberg.com/

https://www.lawyercentral.com/jay-goldberg-interactive-profile--20-466898.html

https://www.nytimes.com/2017/07/05/magazine/all-the-presidents-lawyers.html

https://www.law.com/newyorklawjournal/almID/12027326 93806/?slreturn=20180027120742

http://fischettilaw.com/NYLJ_2003.pdf

http://images.nymag.com/images/2/daily/2017/06/ LeadersPDF.pdf

http://www.24-7pressrelease.com/press-release/jay-goldberg-honored-for-excellence-in-civil-and-criminal-law-429371.php

https://www.gettyimages.com/detail/news-photo/bess-myerson-chats-with-attorney-jay-goldberg-on-65th-news-photo/97258705#bess-myerson-chats-with-attorney-jay-goldberg-on-65th-street-and-3rd-picture-id97258705

https://www.washingtonpost.com/archive/
lifestyle/1988/10/06/bess-defense-hits-ex-wife/b23e6cdb-
9cf5-4726-b7bd-1f719e4f634c/?utm_term=.ca1f03cede7f

http://www.nytimes.com/1988/10/28/nyregion/sukhreet-
gabel-admits-her-deep-resentment.html

http://articles.latimes.com/1988-12-07/news/mn-1015_1_
myerson-s-boyfriend

https://www.washingtonpost.com/archive/
opinions/1994/10/17/the-quiz-show-scandals/38f42ab1-
7128-4a14-aff5-3773360a7e98/?utm_term=.3e358862b473

https://books.google.com/books?id=0MeH1Z-Dd-QC&pg
=PA163&lpg=PA163&dq=%22jay+goldberg%22+%22rob
ert+kennedy%22&source=bl&ots=Mtu1pfxNSl&sig=CUv-
L2ywVLJqhqfVejqN2J2Rne0&hl=en&sa=X&ved=0ahUKEwiczI
qp1PjYAhXO6lMKHY4HDAwQ6AEIPzAJ#v=onepage&q=%22j
ay%20goldberg%22%20%22robert%20kennedy%22&f=false

http://nodepression.com/article/waylon-jennings-sex-drugs-
rockabilly-part-6the-end

https://books.google.com/books?id=smqH_h6UAmUC&pg=PT
175&lpg=PT175&dq=%22jay+goldberg%22+%22robert+ken
nedy%22&source=bl&ots=Jv0AXSAvUN&sig=SxWm1UpYO1k
w3UJNgORsiV9jUxc&hl=en&sa=X&ved=0ahUKEwiczIqp1PjYA
hXO6lMKHY4HDAwQ6AEISDAM#v=onepage&q=%22jay%20
goldberg%22%20%22robert%20kennedy%22&f=false

https://archive1.jfklibrary.org/JFKOH/Oberdorfer,%20
Louis%20F/JFKOH-LFO-01/JFKOH-LFO-01-TR.pdf

https://sivertelegram.com/donald-trump-is-a-devotee-of-
ex-lawyer-and-human-rights-defender-released-a-book-a-
revelation-about-the-president-of-the-united-states/26083

http://www.nytimes.com/1990/07/15/us/wife-s-heir-sues-armand-hammer.html

http://www.newsweek.com/whose-art-it-anyway-206480

http://articles.chicagotribune.com/1990-11-28/entertainment/9004080762_1_ivana-jay-goldberg-donald-trump

https://www.lawyers.com/new-york/new-york/jay-goldberg-p-c-471527-f/

http://www.nytimes.com/2012/06/02/nyregion/rangel-challenges-proceedings-that-led-to-his-censure.html

http://www.nytimes.com/2001/04/12/nyregion/judge-deals-blow-to-plans-for-casinos.html

http://www.nytimes.com/1990/08/03/us/law-bar-highwaymen-come-singing-singing-much-chagrin-originals.html

http://people.com/archive/the-taxman-is-taking-almost-all-willie-nelson-owns-now-its-his-turn-for-some-farm-aid-vol-35-no-8/

https://law.justia.com/cases/federal/district-courts/FSupp/690/200/2359266/

http://www.nydailynews.com/archives/news/puffy-settles-beaten-exec-article-1.835760

http://www.mtv.com/news/514342/record-executive-says-puffy-combs-aimed-to-kill-him/

https://nypost.com/1999/05/21/beaten-record-exec-ill-see-puffy-behind-bars/

http://www.nytimes.com/1985/12/31/nyregion/9-of-10-found-guilty-in-skimming-trial.html

https://www.upi.com/Archives/1986/05/13/Reputed-Mafia-boss-Matthew-Matty-the-Horse-Ianniello-and/6120516340800/

http://www.nytimes.com/1992/03/26/nyregion/defending-mob-user-s-guide-for-defense-lawyers-favored-strategy-attack-attack.html

https://law.justia.com/cases/federal/appellate-courts/F2/439/751/337364/

https://www.huffingtonpost.com/2011/04/15/donald-trump-refutes-mort-zuckerman_n_849754.html

BIBLIOGRAPHY

"'Brady' and the Unfulfilled Promise of an Even Playing Field," *New York Law Journal*, December 3, 2013.

"Method of Proving Prior Charging Decision by Government," *New York Law Journal*, January 8, 2013.

"Further Reflections On The RFK I Knew: His Conduct During The Cuban Missile Crisis - 13 Days in October 1962," *Monograph*, Winter 2013.

"Allowing Jurors to Take the Indictment Home: Could It Happen In State Court?" *New York Law Journal*, November 6, 2012.

"The Civil War: A Bitter Disappointment," *Lincoln University Press*, Fall 2012.

"Unequal Justice: Distinctions Between Federal and State Trial Practice," *Atticus*, Fall 2012.

"Defendants' 'Informational Disadvantage' Continues in Federal Criminal Cases," *New York Law Journal*, August 20, 2012.

"Underutilized Methods of Dealing With Government Witnesses," *New York Law Journal*, June 26, 2012.

"The Doctrine Of Other Crimes Evidence Admissible Under Federal Rules of Evidence, i.e., Rule 404(B): The Bane Of Every Criminal Defense Trial Lawyer," *New York Law Journal*, March 15, 2012.

"Abraham Lincoln: Which Branch of Government Seriously Diminished His Legacy?" *The International Lincoln Center for American Studies*, March/April 2012 edition.

"The Second Circuit Offers a Primer for Criminal Law Practitioners," *New York Law Journal*, October 19, 2011.

"The Administration's Problems with RFK as the Attorney General," *Federal Bar Council Quarterly*, May 2011.

"The Use of Humor as a Trial Technique," *New York Law Journal*, May 18, 2011.

"Do We Have The Best And The Brightest New York State Supreme Court Justices?" *Monograph*, April 2011.

"The Appropriateness of Military Trials for Terrorists," *White Collar Crime Reporter*, June 1, 2010.

"Military Tribunals Versus Civilian Trials During War And Peace," *New York Law Journal*, May 17, 2010.

"Allow Jurors to Arrive at a Third Verdict: 'Not Proven,'" *New York Law Journal*, December 10, 2009.

"How to Get a Hearing Under FRE 104(A) To Test The Bona Fides of the Government's Witness Cooperation Agreement," *New York Law Journal*, November 20, 2009.

"Miranda Redux," *White Collar Crime Reporter*, July 25, 2009.

"Interrogations and the Law: Does 'Miranda' Work?" *New York Law Journal*, June 10, 2009.

"A Call to Action: The Need To Ensure Protection of New York's Privacy Law - Civil Rights Law 50 and 51," *New York Law Journal*, February 5, 2008.

"Reflections: The Robert F. Kennedy I knew," *The Champion, National Association of Criminal Defense Lawyers*, November 2007.

"Testimony of Government Informers and Jury Knowledge of the Risks They Pose," *New York Law Journal*, August 11, 2006.

"When an Attorney Forfeits the Right to Fees," *New York Law Journal*, May 15, 2006.

"The Power of the Jury: Is it Diminished by Court Rulings?" *New York Law Journal*, March 9, 2005.

"The Adversarial System in Criminal Cases," *New York Law Journal*, November 17, 2005.

"Multi-defendant Trials: Sixth Amendment Rights Get Little Protection," *New York Law Journal*, September 12, 2005.

"RICO Conspiracy: The Need for Appropriate Jury Instruction," *New York Law Journal*, July 7, 2005.

"Caution to the Bar: The Reach of Federal Rule of Evidence 612," *New York Law Journal*, July 12, 2004.

"The Need to Assure That Justice is Done," *White Collar Crime Reporter*, June, 2004.

"Government Witness Cooperation Agreements: A Defense Perspective," *New York Law Journal*, November, 2003.

"The Need for Consistency When Dealing With the Right to Obtain Constitutionally Mandated Discovery," *New York City Association of Criminal Defense Lawyers*, October 2003.

"Why the Southern and Eastern Districts of New York Should Adopt a Brady Rule," *New York Law Journal*, June, 2003.

"Counsel Beware: It Is Not Enough to Have One-Party Consent Before Recording a Conversation," *New York City Criminal Bar Journal*, January/February 2001.

"A Little Known Hidden Problem Within the Federal Wiretap Statute," *White Collar Crime Reporter*, October 2000.

"A Seldom Used But Often Effective Rule of Evidence," *New York City Association of Criminal Defense Lawyers*, September/October 2000.

"Nuances in Federal Law that Must Be Known by State Practitioners Trying Federal Cases," CLE Lecture, August 25, 2000.

"Humor: Does It Have a Place in the Trial of a Criminal Case," *American Bar Association*, July, 2000.

"The Best Kept Secret in the Trial of a Federal Criminal Case," *White Collar Crime Reporter*, May 2000.

"Tape Recorded Evidence: A Little Known Impediment to Use of Electronic Devices To Gather Evidence, Even in a One-Party Consent State," *The Champion, National Association of Criminal Defense Lawyers*, April 2000.

"Brady/Giglio and the Defendant's Right to Such Material," *The Champion, National Association of Criminal Defense Lawyers*, August 1998.

"Truth in Government Summations: The Need for Judicial Intervention," *White Collar Crime Reporter*, July/August 1998.

"The Need for Enforcement of Brady/Giglio Rights," *New York City Association of Criminal Defense Lawyers*, March/April 1998.

"Awaken Defense Bar: Your Client's Rights Are Not Protected," *New York Law Journal*, March 12, 1998.

"When Will They Understand the Role of the Criminal Defense Attorney?" *The Champion, National Association of Criminal Defense Lawyers*, September 1997.

"Criminal Defense Is Often a One Night Stand," *National Law Journal*, July 21, 1997.

"Megatrials: The More, the Messier," *White Collar Crime Reporter*, November 1991.

"Problems in the Trial of a Multiple Defendant Case," *New York State Bar Association*, 1989.

"Essentials of Cross-Examination," *New York State Bar Association*, 1987.

"Multiple Representation of White Collar Targets and Witnesses During the Grand Jury Investigation," *Practicing Law Institute*, 1985.

"Remedies for Private Plaintiffs Under the Civil RICO Statute," *Practicing Law Institute*, 1984.

Congress, House, Committee on Interstate and Foreign Commerce, *Investigation of Television Quiz Shows*, 86th Cong., 1st Sess., October 6–10, 12, 1959 (Washington, D.C.: U.S. Government Printing Office, 1960).

"The Perils of a Motion Seeking a Judge's Recusal," New York Law Journal, October 4, 2018.

ACKNOWLEDGMENTS

THIS BOOK HAS ALWAYS BEEN in my mind and heart, but it couldn't have reached your hands without help along the way.

Thank you to William Croyle, who helped me organize my thoughts and get them down on paper in a compelling and eloquent way.

Thank you to Ronald Goldfarb, my good friend since the Kennedy administration, and to the publisher, Post Hill, for believing in my story.

And thank you to all my clients over the years who put their trust in me. There is no greater responsibility than defending someone's livelihood or liberty. I am grateful for your faith in my abilities.

ABOUT THE AUTHOR

"There has never been a lawyer more important to me than you. *It is very important to me that you know that.*"
(emphasis his)
—THE PRESIDENT OF THE UNITED STATES

"Deeply grateful for your loyalty to the President. He has abiding respect for you and great affection. You are a prince! Deeply grateful my friend! Honored to know you!
—TY COBB, Counselor to the White House, Office of the President, April 13, 2018

JAY IS A GRADUATE OF Harvard Law School and has taught trial advocacy there.

He was appointed by Attorney General Robert F. Kennedy as acting United States Attorney for the Northwest District of Indiana. He served as Special Attorney and counselor to the United States Department of Justice, Washington D.C. He was legal assistant to James B. Donovan at the time of the transfer of a convicted Russian Spy, Rudolph Abel, for American U-2 pilot Francis Gary Powers (*Bridge of Spies*). He served as an assistant District Attorney, New York County.